Rethinking the Just War Tradition

SUNY series, Ethics and the Military Profession

George R. Lucas Jr., editor

Rethinking the Just War Tradition

Edited by

Michael W. Brough
John W. Lango
Harry van der Linden

State University
of New York
Press

Published by
State University of New York Press, Albany

© 2007 State University of New York

For information, address State University of New York Press,
194 Washington Avenue, Suite 305, Albany, NY 12210-2384

Production by Susan Geraghty
Marketing by Michael Campochiaro

Library of Congress Cataloging-in-Publication Data

Rethinking the just war tradition / [edited by] Michael W. Brough, John W. Lango,
Harry van der Linden.
     p. cm. — (SUNY series, Ethics and the military profession)
   Includes bibliographical references and index.
   ISBN-13: 978-0-7914-7155-5 (hardcover : alk. paper)
   ISBN-13: 978-0-7914-7156-2 (pbk. : alk. paper)
    1. Just war doctrine. I. Brough, Michael W., 1970– II. Lango, John W.
III. Van der Linden, Harry, 1950–

U22.R45 2007
172'.42—dc22
                                                            2006027727

10 9 8 7 6 5 4 3 2 1

To our children,
in the hope that their world
will be more peaceful

CONTENTS

PREFACE

The purpose of this volume, adumbrated in its title, is to rethink the just war tradition. As the table of contents indicates, the authors seek to rethink that tradition in a variety of ways. In addition to such familiar topics as noncombatant immunity, supreme emergency, and terrorism, some unusual topics are explored—for example, child soldiers, *jus post bellum* principles, and environmental justice. The editors want to stress that this volume is not intended to advocate or promote a unified conception of just war theory, for the authors write from diverse viewpoints. The volume contains essays representative of a number of disciplines, and a number of conceptual methodologies and perspectives. Although most are philosophers, our contributors also include scholars of political science and literature, as well as a number with relevant military or nongovernmental organization experience. As editors, we elected not to assign projects but instead asked our writers to choose their own directions. The issues they have chosen to explore are not, of course, comprehensive—no volume this size that seeks to "rethink the just war tradition" could be. But the variety of our authors' backgrounds and their chosen topics has resulted in a germane, variegated collection, one that examines the just war tradition through a number of important lenses.

Our intent has been to collect timely, stimulating papers for an audience that is willing to engage our subject. We include in this audience scholars in the field of war and morality, but other readers, as well. The book has been written with an eye to making it valuable to those who lack an in-depth understanding of the tradition: it is designed to be accessible to students, as well as interested general readers. Accordingly, we have included an appendix containing an introduction to just war principles and some suggestions for further reading. Moreover, we hope the book will be of value to practitioners—to political and military leaders. Of course, in democratic societies, we are in a sense all practitioners. Whenever war is declared by one's state, it is declared in one's name, and one should struggle to make sure that the wars one's state fights are just.

Intellectual activity requires periods of stimulation and repose. Careful consideration of a topic requires quiet, concentrated time to read and contemplate. Most thinkers will admit, though, that their best ideas shine only when burnished by discourse with others. In the summer of 2004, the editors and authors of this volume engaged in a month-long experience of thinking, writing, and talking about war and morality at the United States Naval Academy at Annapolis, Maryland—an Institute sponsored by the National Endowment for the Humanities entitled "War and Morality: Re-thinking the Just War Tradition for the 21st Century." The idea for the present volume emerged during the final days of the NEH Institute. Interested participants proposed paper topics and editors were chosen. The editors refereed the papers submitted for consideration for inclusion in this volume.

The editors and authors would like to collectively thank the Naval Academy and the NEH for the remarkable opportunity and express their gratitude to the Naval Academy's George Lucas and Albert Pierce for their arduous personal efforts in making the institute a success. Their institute has planted potent seeds; this book is only a small part of the fruit.

Michael W. Brough
John W. Lango
Harry van der Linden

ACKNOWLEDGMENTS

The editors wish to thank the National Endowment for the Humanities for the support provided for the publication of this book. Michael Brough wants to thank the U.S. Army for encouraging him while on active duty to participate in the editing of this volume. John W. Lango wishes to thank the City University of New York PSC-CUNY Research Award Program for a grant in support of his work on the ethics of war. Harry van der Linden would like to thank Butler University for awarding him a Summer Fellowship in support of working on this book.

Introduction

Michael W. Brough, John W. Lango, and Harry van der Linden

I. THE JUST WAR TRADITION TODAY

In studying the history of the ethics of war, the just war tradition may be interpreted as a historically evolving body of tenets about just war principles. (See the appendix for an introduction to these principles.) Instead of a single just war theory, there have been many just war theories—for example, those of Augustine, Aquinas, Vitoria, and Grotius—theories that have various commonalities and differences. A comprehensive history of the evolving just war tradition should feature a thorough study of how these just war theories were rethought. For example, in his landmark work *Just and Unjust Wars*, written during the Cold War, Michael Walzer exclaimed: "Nuclear weapons explode the theory of just war."[1] In his rethinking of the just war tradition in light of the superpower practice of nuclear deterrence, he contributed his influential conception of supreme emergency exceptions. Now that the Cold War is over, the authors of the articles in this book are primarily concerned with the question of how the just war tradition—which is understood somewhat differently by the different authors—should be rethought today. Echoing Walzer's exclamation, among the particular post–Cold War questions that can be raised are these: Is just war theory exploded by terrorism? Is it annihilated by genocide? In their various rethinkings of the just war tradition, our authors state their own particular post–Cold War questions, and answer them from their diverse viewpoints.

In order to rethink the just war tradition cogently, it is important to answer the question: What is the place and standing of the just war tradition today? Recently, in his provocatively titled article "The Triumph of Just War Theory (and the Dangers of Success)," Walzer wrote: "Perhaps naively, I am inclined to say that justice has become, in all Western countries, one of the tests that any proposed military strategy or tactic has to meet—only one of the tests and not the most important one, but this still gives just war theory a place and standing it never had before."[2] In light of moral controversy about the Iraq War, it cannot be said that all Western countries always concur about the justice or injustice of the use of armed force. Arguably, however, it can be said that just war theory has triumphed in most Western countries, insofar as just war principles are frequently presupposed in debates about the justice or injustice of the use of armed force.[3]

Even if just war theory has triumphed as a moral framework for debate in most Western countries, it still may be doubted whether it will eventually triumph in all countries. Presently, 192 countries are members of the United Nations. Two of the aims stated in the Preamble to the UN Charter are "to save succeeding generations from the scourge of war" and "to reaffirm faith in fundamental human rights." And a third aim is "to ensure, by the acceptance of principles and the institution of methods, that armed force shall not be used, save in the common interest." With the aim of ensuring that armed force is used only in the common interest, should all 192 countries accept just war principles?

An answer to this question can be found in a recent report to the United Nations, which was commissioned by Secretary-General Kofi Annan, and released in December 2004—namely, the Report of the High-level Panel on Threats, Challenges and Change.[4] A purpose of the High-level Panel Report is to encourage a rethinking of the ideal of collective security in the UN Charter. In particular, the report proposes that whenever the Security Council deliberates about "whether to authorize or endorse the use of military force," it should utilize "five basic criteria of legitimacy":

(a) *Seriousness of threat.* Is the threatened harm to State or human security of a kind, and sufficiently clear and serious, to justify *prima facie* the use of military force? In the case of internal threats, does it involve genocide and other large-scale killing, ethnic cleansing or serious violations of international humanitarian law, actual or imminently apprehended?

(b) *Proper purpose.* Is it clear that the primary purpose of the proposed military action is to halt or avert the threat in question, whatever other purposes or motives may be involved?

(c) *Last resort.* Has every non-military option for meeting the threat in question been explored, with reasonable grounds for believing that other measures will not succeed?

(d) *Proportional means.* Are the scale, duration and intensity of the proposed military action the minimum necessary to meet the threat in question?

(e) *Balance of consequences.* Is there a reasonable chance of the military action being successful in meeting the threat in question, with the consequences of action not likely to be worse than the consequences of inaction?[5]

These five criteria of legitimacy resemble traditional just war principles. The criterion of seriousness of threat resembles the just war principle of just cause, the criterion of proper purpose resembles the just war principle of right intention, the criterion of last resort resembles the just war principle of last resort, and the two criteria of proportional means and balance of consequences together resemble the combined just war principles of proportionality and reasonable chance of success. In anticipation of the moral-relativist objection that just war principles embody Western ethical concepts, and must not be imposed on non-Western cultures, it should be recognized that the sixteen members of the High-level Panel are distinguished citizens of Australia, Brazil, China, Egypt, France, Ghana, India, Japan, Norway, Pakistan, Russia, Tanzania, Thailand, United Kingdom, the United States, and Uruguay.[6] If such criteria of legitimacy were accepted by a substantial majority of member states of the United Nations as principles governing Security Council deliberations about threats to or breaches of the peace, just war theory would indeed have triumphed globally as a moral framework for debate about the justice or injustice of wars.

In rethinking the just war tradition, it is important to rethink the just war principles individually. Using the wording of the five criteria of legitimacy, some examples of questions that can be raised about individual just war principles are as follows. Is genocide (or other large-scale killing or ethnic cleansing or a serious violation of international humanitarian law) a just cause for the use of military force? If the primary purpose of a proposed military action is to halt or avert genocide, may a secondary purpose be regime change? If all nonmilitary options for meeting a future threat have to be explored, with reasonable grounds for believing that they will not succeed, can a preventive war ever be a last resort? Note that these questions also indicate that the five criteria of legitimacy need to be rethought. For instance, recognizing that those criteria do not implicitly contain anything like the just war principle of legitimate authority (presumably because the UN Charter makes the Security Council the supreme authority), we can ask: to satisfy that principle, must a war be authorized by the Security Council? Of course, these questions are only intended to be representative. The authors of the articles in this book rethink the just war tradition in their own terms.

Although a comprehensive survey of questions germane to the project of rethinking the just war tradition is beyond the scope of this introduction, it is worthwhile to mention several additional examples. What is the ethical import of new military technologies (e.g., robot aircraft)? For instance, is it morally permissible to develop bunker-busting precision-guided nuclear weapons? What moral issues are raised specifically by asymmetrical warfare? When terrorists hide among civilian populations, whom or what may counterterrorists target? What moral limits should be placed on the interrogation of captured terrorists? Are the actions of private military contractors (e.g., private security forces) also subject to just war principles? For the sake of deterring an attack with chemical or biological weapons, is it morally permissible to threaten nuclear retaliation? When armed humanitarian intervention has resulted in considerable civilian casualties in a target state, is there a moral obligation of restitution?

In light of these examples, it should be clear that, even if the five criteria of legitimacy were accepted by a substantial majority of UN member states, they would still need to be rethought. Unfortunately, to evidence why they might not be accepted, some recent events have to be recounted.[7] In support of the goal of reforming the United Nations in a summit meeting of "the largest assemblage of world leaders ever brought together in a single location"[8]—the 2005 World Summit— Kofi Annan made his own report (21 March 2005) to the General Assembly.[9] In particular, drawing upon the High-level Panel Report, he summarized the five criteria of legitimacy, and recommended "that the Security Council adopt a resolution setting out these principles and expressing its intention to be guided by them when deciding whether to authorize or mandate the use of force."[10] Responding to this Report of the Secretary-General, an "Outcome Document"—dated 15

September 2005—for the 2005 World Summit was adopted by "Heads of State and Government."

In an earlier draft of the Outcome Document—dated 10 August 2005—there are significant, albeit truncated, references to the five criteria of legitimacy:

> 55. We also reaffirm that the provisions of the Charter regarding the use of force are sufficient to address the full range of security threats and agree that the use of force should be considered an instrument of last resort. We further reaffirm the authority of the Security Council to take action to maintain and restore international peace and security, in accordance with the provisions of the Charter.
>
> 56. We recognize the need to continue discussing principles for the use of force, including those identified by the Secretary-General.[11]

This draft of the Outcome Document expressed a "delicately balanced agreement" among member states of the United Nations about a variety of contentious issues (e.g., the Millennium Development Goals).[12] However, extreme pressure exerted by some member states (notably, the United States) "blew apart the hard-won compromise."[13] As a consequence, these two paragraphs were removed from the draft Outcome Document. Concerning the five criteria of legitimacy—and even the principle that the use of force should be an instrument of last resort—the Outcome Document adopted by world leaders is silent.[14]

In conclusion, the High-level Panel Report demonstrates that the just war tradition is part of global political culture, but the 2005 World Summit demonstrates that the tradition has not yet been realized sufficiently in practice. It is our belief that academics can contribute to the acceptance and efficacy of the just war tradition today by engaging in the project of rethinking it.

II. OVERVIEW

The authors of the twelve chapters in this book raise their own particular questions about the just war tradition, and answer them from their own diverse viewpoints. Is there a single frame of reference by which their various questions should be organized? In the just war tradition, such a query might be answered through a typology of interstate wars (i.e., wars of conquest, border wars, and so forth). However, to rethink the tradition sufficiently, there is need to reevaluate any answer of this sort. Indeed, even though the Cold War has ended, the threat of interstate wars remains. But other threats to the security of states have emerged. In the High-level Panel Report, a broad range of threats to international security is scrutinized, under the rubrics of poverty, infectious disease, environmental degradation, conflict between states, conflict within states, weapons of mass destruction, terrorism, and transnational organized crime. These rubrics comprise, we submit, a thought-provoking frame of reference by which questions about the just war tradition—not only questions raised by our authors but also questions raised by other authors—can be fruitfully organized. The project of rethinking just war theory is interrelated with the project of rethinking the theory of international security.

Moral questions about the use of armed force can be organized in terms of this frame of reference. For each type of security threat, we may ask: how might armed force be used to counter the threat? And then, in response to each answer, we may ask: how might that use of armed force be assessed by means of just war principles? Such questions about the threat of conflict between states are standard in the just war tradition. And such questions about conflicts within states arise familiarly while investigating how just war principles might pertain to armed humanitarian interventions. Concerning the threat of terrorism, a ladder of kinds of armed force might seem appropriate, from targeted assassination to military invasion, thereby provoking a correlative ladder of moral questions. Moral questions about the use of weapons of mass destruction were raised during the Cold War, especially questions about nuclear deterrence; but other questions are featured more today, especially questions about the preemptive or preventive use of armed force to counter the threat of weapons of mass destruction. In accordance with the last resort principle, we should also ask, concerning each type of security threat: how might the threat be countered by nonmilitary measures? And then, in response to each answer, we may ask: how might that nonmilitary measure be morally assessed? Such questions about nonmilitary measures are customarily raised about the threats of transnational organized crime, poverty, infectious disease, and environmental degradation. Nevertheless, sometimes threats of these four types might have to be countered by the use of armed force. For, as the High-level Panel Report asserts, "Today, more than ever before, threats are interrelated."[15] Consider, for instance, the threats interwoven in the following hypothetical scenario: worldwide infectious disease resulting from a bioweapon purchased from a transnational criminal organization by a terrorist group. Some examples of moral questions about threats of these four types are as follows. May armed force be used to assassinate a criminal chief, to protect humanitarian relief workers, to implement a quarantine, or to stop poachers from killing animals on the verge of extinction (e.g., the mountain gorillas of Rwanda)?

The chapters in this book are distributed in three parts: "Theory," "Noncombatants and Combatants," and "Intervention and Law." The first chapter is pertinent to the threat of environmental degradation: Mark Woods's "The Nature of War and Peace: Just War Thinking, Environmental Ethics, and Environmental Justice." The harm war does to the environment and the inadequate protections in place to prevent that harm are recounted, as well as prior work about how the disparate goals of war and environmental endeavor might be reconciled. An environmental ethics of war and peace is introduced, which demands that *jus ad bellum*, *in bello*, and *post bellum* pay significant regard to environmental considerations. In order to be comprehensive, it is advocated that new just war criteria be developed that would govern preparations for war (including training and testing): *jus potentia ad bellum.*

The second chapter is concerned primarily with the threat of conflict between states, but it is also relevant to the threat of conflict within states: Eric Patterson's "*Jus Post Bellum* and International Conflict: Order, Justice, and Reconciliation." Patterson contends that *jus post bellum* is a neglected part of just war theory and offers pragmatic and moral reasons for including it. In striving for the just cessation of a war, there should be three successive goals. The minimal just peace is achieved with the attainment of order, which is defined as a condition of security between states. Better than mere order, though, is the combination of order with justice (holding the guilty responsible). The best, but most elusive, ending to a war adds conditions of order and justice to a conciliation (or reconciliation) between peoples. States should aim for the highest reasonable goal to guide terms of justice at war's end.

The third chapter focuses on the threat of conflict between states, but it has relevance to the threats of terrorism and weapons of mass destruction. Since the Soviet Union's collapse, the United States has tried to cement its position as military hegemon by investing heavily in military technology. In "Just War Theory and U.S. Military Hegemony," Harry van der Linden explores the moral repercussions of our unipolar military world, which seems unanticipated by thinkers from the just war tradition. If weaker countries are precluded (by the *jus ad bellum* principles of reasonable chance of success and proportionality) from declaring (an otherwise just) war against the U.S., does the tradition unfairly favor the hegemon? This question is answered affirmatively, and a new direction for the tradition is advocated that takes into account that hegemonic military force contributes to terrorism and the proliferation of weapons of mass destruction. Van der Linden concludes that as long as the United States seeks to sustain its status as hegemon, the bar for just resort to war is raised considerably.

The fourth chapter is concerned primarily with the threats of conflict between states, conflict within states, and terrorism; but it has relevance for the other types of security threats. In "Generalizing and Temporalizing Just War Principles: Illustrated by the Principle of Just Cause," John W. Lango proposes that just war principles should be generalized and temporalized, so that they are applicable to military actions of every sort (e.g., military actions in UN peacekeeping operations). He suggests that, when the principles are appropriately revised, so as to be applicable to every form of armed conflict—not only wars but also forms of armed conflict that are not wars—they should be renamed "just armed-conflict principles." To illustrate the proposal, he discusses especially the just cause principle.

The fifth chapter (which begins the second part of the book, "Noncombatants and Combatants") concentrates primarily on the threats of conflict between states and terrorism. In "Just War Theory and Killing the Innocent," Frederik Kaufman explores the morality of killing civilians, finding that the acceptance among just war theorists of unintentional civilian deaths in the pursuit of military objectives means that noncombatants' rights can be infringed (resulting in justifiable, though regrettable, deaths) without being violated. He then applies this finding to the idea of supreme emergency and argues that Walzer mistakenly views the idea as a concession to utilitarianism and a move away from the constraints of rights. The chapter ends with a challenge: is there any reason that exempting *jus in bello* norms for the sake of averting catastrophe would not be equally justified when pursuing a very great good?

The sixth chapter is concerned primarily with the threats of conflict between states, conflict within states, and terrorism. Many contemporary forms of armed conflict—for example, ones involving suicide bombers dressed like civilians, irregular forces, and belligerent populaces—show the problematized state of the distinction between combatants and noncombatants. Pauline Kaurin considers this issue in "When Less Is *Not* More: Expanding the Combatant/Noncombatant Distinction" and calls for an amplification of the traditional combatant/noncombatant distinction that not only assesses the parties to a conflict more precisely, but also provides a commonsense guide for soldiers on the ground. Within a theater of operations, troops can initially identify those they encounter with the help of two categories of noncombatant and three categories of combatant; as the troops discover more about the strangers, they can continually update their categorizations and continue to treat them (with special attention to battlefield context) in accordance with their level within the multipart distinction.

The seventh chapter focuses primarily on the threat of conflict within states. In "Just War Theory and Child Soldiers," Reuben Brigety and Rachel Stohl encounter a different challenge to the just war tradition's standard principle of discrimination. They argue that a combination of causes (including the availability of guns and some groups' requirement for more troops) have given rise to a class of soldiers who are also children. Deciding whether to categorize the child soldier as a combatant or a noncombatant is a conundrum, because a soldier is generally considered a combatant (and, therefore, targetable), whereas a child is usually considered a noncombatant (and, therefore, protected). In the end, it is allowed that child soldiers may be justly targeted, but only when the considerations of self-defense and proportionality are accounted for sufficiently.

The eighth chapter is relevant primarily to the threats of conflict between states, conflict within states, and terrorism. Michael W. Brough's "Dehumanization of the Enemy and the Moral Equality of Soldiers" seeks to make a statement about the entire class of combatants: that they ought not to be dehumanized by their enemies. Three basic reasons are given: First, dehumanizing the enemy risks wartime atrocities, which are both morally repugnant and (often) strategically injurious. Second, a policy of dehumanization endangers a state's own soldiers, since good evidence indicates that soldiers' post-combat psychological well-being depends to some degree on respecting, rather than reviling, the enemy. Third, dehumanization propagates a perspective of the enemy that is not only practically and morally harmful, but also inaccurate: wartime foes generally have a great deal in common and should at least recognize each other's common humanity.

The ninth chapter (which begins the third part of the book, "Intervention and Law") is concerned primarily with the threats of conflict between states and terrorism: Whitley R. P. Kaufman's "Rethinking the Ban on Assassination: Just War Principles in the Age of Terror." In doing so, Kaufman considers recent appeals to assassination, which he characterizes as largely consequentialist and, therefore, incompatible with the just war tradition. But he also takes up the question of what makes a person a combatant. His answer, that combatancy is a function of the direct threat one poses to other combatants, directs him to assign most political leaders to the ranks of noncombatants. He tenders other reasons to consider a policy of assassination immoral and inadvisable, but finally admits that the just war tradition could justify particular assassinations.

The tenth chapter is pertinent to the threats of conflict between states and weapons of mass destruction. Jordy Rocheleau's "Preventive War and Lawful Constraints on the Use of Force: An Argument Against International Vigilantism" stakes out a position that compares unilateral preventive war to vigilante justice: like vigilantes, individual states in pursuit of punitive actions are bound to be biased, and they threaten to undermine the rule of international law. Only preventive wars endorsed by the international community in response to illegal possession or development of weapons of mass destruction are justified. These wars must also satisfy such *jus ad bellum* principles as last resort and proportionality. Rocheleau concludes with the claim that international vigilantism may not be exonerated as a form of civil disobedience.

The eleventh chapter is concerned primarily with the threat of conflict between states. Legitimate (or right) authority has often been listed in the just war tradition's *jus ad bellum* principles, but the criterion has encountered trouble in recent years, causing many to ask what, exactly, is its measure. In "Faith, Force, or Fellowship: The Future of Right Authority," Hartley Spatt traces the history of right authority from its origins, when it was bequeathed by religious faith, through a middle period, when right authority is seized by those who can punish dissent. Spatt offers what he considers a better grounding for right authority: a nonhierarchical ethical commonwealth that is inadequately embodied by the United Nations.

The twelfth and last chapter focuses primarily on the threat of conflict within states. Robert W. Hoag's "Violent Civil Disobedience: Defending Human Rights, Rethinking Just War" considers how current international law limits armed interventions to prevent state violations of basic human rights. Employing a "domestic analogy" with civil disobedience, he argues that preventing such violations may require military actions that although illegal could serve as a means of reforming current international law. A *jus ad bellum* assessment of such interventions involves considering both the immediate humanitarian aspects and the eventual contribution to improving international law's defense of basic human rights. His assessment of legal reform through armed humanitarian interventions calls upon recently neglected aspects of the just war tradition's attention to principles of right authority, long-term purposes or intentions, and just cause beyond state self-defense.

It is our hope that the chapters in this volume will challenge readers to rethink the just war tradition as scholars, as thinkers, as practitioners, and as citizens. Through reasoned debate and the airing of ideas, we might come closer to solving some of the difficult issues of our times. And there are few issues more worth solving than those that arise in this book.

NOTES

1. New York: Basic Books, 1977, 282.
2. Michael Walzer, *Arguing About War* (New Haven: Yale University Press, 2004), 12. As his words "perhaps naively" indicate, his recent views about just war theory are not fully stated in this quotation.
3. One example is Gareth Evans and Mohamed Sahnoun, "The Responsibility to Protect," *Foreign Affairs* 81:6 (November/December 2002): 99–110. Also, in the academic journal of the U.S. Army War College, there is an article that criticizes the Iraq War in terms of just war principles: Franklin Eric Wester, "Preemption and Just War: Considering the Case of Iraq," *Parameters: US Army War College Quarterly* 34 (2004–05): 4–20. Available at http://carlisle-www.army.mil/usawc/Parameters/04winter/wester.htm.
4. *A More Secure World: Our Shared Responsibility*, Report of the High-level Panel on Threats, Challenges and Change (New York: United Nations, 2004), par. 25. Available as a book or at http://www. un.org/secureworld.
5. Ibid., par. 207.
6. The members of the panel are as follows: Anand Panyarachun (chairman), former prime minister of Thailand; Robert Badinter (France), member of the French Senate and former minister of justice of France; Joao Clemente Baena Soares (Brazil), former secretary-general of the Organization of American States; Gro Harlem Brundtland (Norway), former prime minister of Norway and former director-general of the World Health Organization;

Mary Chinery-Hesse (Ghana), vice-chairman, National Development Planning Commission of Ghana and former deputy director-general, International Labour Organization; Gareth Evans (Australia), president of the International Crisis Group and former minister for foreign affairs of Australia; David Hannay (United Kingdom), former permanent representative of the United Kingdom to the United Nations and United Kingdom special envoy to Cyprus; Enrique Iglesias (Uruguay), president of the Inter-American Development Bank; Amre Moussa (Egypt), secretary-general of the League of Arab States; Satish Nambiar (India), former lieutenant general in the Indian Army and Force Commander of UNPROFOR; Sadako Ogata (Japan), former United Nations high commissioner for refugees; Yevgenii Primakov (Russia), former prime minister of the Russian Federation; Qian Qichen (China), former vice prime minister and minister for foreign affairs of the People's Republic of China; Nafis Sadik (Pakistan), former executive director of the United Nations Population Fund; Salim Ahmed Salim (United Republic of Tanzania), former secretary-general of the Organization of African Unity; and Brent Scowcroft (United States), former lieutenant general in the United States Air Force and United States National Security Adviser. These brief biographies were obtained from http://www.un-globalsecurity.org/panel.asp.

7. An abridgement of this paragraph and the next paragraph is contained in an article by one of the editors of this book: John W. Lango, "The Just War Principle of Last Resort: The Question of Reasonableness Standards," *Asteriskos: Journal of International and Peace Studies* 1:1–2 (2006): 7–23.

8. "The Lost U.N. Summit Meeting," editorial, *New York Times*, 14 September 2005.

9. Report of the Secretary-General, *In Larger Freedom: Towards Development, Security, and Human Rights for All* (21 March 2005). Available at http: //www.un.org/largerfreedom.

10. Ibid., par. 126 (boldface removed).

11. "Revised draft outcome document of the high-level plenary meeting of the General Assembly of September 2005 submitted by the President of the General Assembly" (10 August 2005), A/59/HLPM/CRP.1/Rev.2. Various drafts of and sets of proposed amendments to the Outcome Document—including those cited in this introduction—are available at the website of the Global Policy Forum: http://globalpolicy.igc.org/msummit/millenni/m5outcomedocindex.htm.

12. Peter H. Gantz and Michelle Brown, "The UN Summit: U.S. Spoiler Role Weakens Draft Outcome Document," *Refugees International* (09/14/2005), 1. Available at http://www.refugeesinternational.org/content/article/detail/6777.

13. Ibid., 1. See also "The Lost U.N. Summit Meeting."

14. United Nations General Assembly, 2005 World Summit Outcome (15 September 2005), A/60/L.1. It would be a mistake to assume that the

United States alone was responsible for the removal of these paragraphs. Indeed, the reference to the last resort criterion in paragraph 55 and the entirety of paragraph 56 are missing in the document called (at the Global Policy Forum website) "US Amendments to the Revised Draft Outcome Document from August 10th (August 25, 2005)." But paragraph 56 also is rejected in the document entitled "Proposed Amendments by the Non-Aligned Movement to the Draft Outcome Document of the High-level Plenary Meeting of the General Assembly (A/59/HLPM/CRP.1/Rev.2)."

15. *A More Secure World*, par. 17.

PART 1

Theory

CHAPTER 1

The Nature of War and Peace: Just War Thinking, Environmental Ethics, and Environmental Justice

Mark Woods

> When in your war against a city you have to besiege it a long time in order to capture it, you must not destroy its trees, wielding the ax against them. You may eat of them, but you must not cut them down. Are trees of the field human to withdraw before you into the besieged city? Only trees which you know do not yield food may be destroyed; you may cut them down for constructing siegeworks against the city that is waging war on you, until it has been reduced.
>
> —Deuteronomy 20:19–20[1]

> Why vent anger on inanimate things, which are themselves kindly, and bring forth kindly fruit? Do trees, like the men who are your enemies, display signs of hostility, so that for the things they do or threaten to do they must be uprooted?
>
> —Philo Judaeus, as quoted by Hugo Grotius[2]

In *The Just War: An American Reflection on the Morality of War in Our Time*, Peter Temes argues that we need to rethink the platform for just war thinking. As part of this, he claims that "we must reaffirm the idea of safe passage and duty to the environment."[3] This suggests bringing environmental justice and environmental ethics considerations into the just war tradition (JWT). How might this be done?

Consider the following scenario. An environmentalist asks a military commander to avoid harming nature. Nature can be likened to a noncombatant, and following from the criterion of discrimination, it should not be directly targeted. The military commander agrees with the environmentalist that because nature has some kind of value, damage to it should be minimized. Military necessity in war, however, overrides environmental concerns. Following orders, winning battles, and protecting one's own troops are a military commander's primary responsibilities, and much of combat will require killing (at least indirectly) animals and plants, disrupting community and ecosystem structures, and causing land, water, and air pollution. The military commander does not intend to do such things, and the environmentalist is told that environmental collateral damage will be minimized and proportional in relation to military necessity, as long as people's lives are not put in jeopardy. The environmentalist, however, remains uneasy. How far do collateral damage considerations go toward protecting nature? Can we do better than this?

Before I begin to answer these questions, two points of clarification are in order. First, in terms of practical ethics, the issues I discuss in this chapter collectively have no proper name. They are sometimes called the *ecology of war and peace*. This is a bit misleading. Ecology is a natural science, and ecologists study the relationships between organisms and their environments. The ecology of war and peace thus is the scientific study of such relationships in light of additional factors created by people waging war or seeking peace. Discussions about what *should* be done because of these additional factors, however, go beyond the descriptive science of ecology and enter the prescriptive realm of ethics. Accordingly, I will restrict use of the term "ecology of war and peace" to describing the effects of war and peace activities on the environment and will use the term *environmental ethics of war and peace* to define the normative range of issues that are the focus of this chapter. A second point of clarification pertains to this latter term. It connotes the intersection of three types of concerns: the ethics of war and peace, environmental ethics, and environmental justice. Environmental ethics and environmental justice obviously are related insofar as they both address environmental issues, but, as stipulated by academics and activists, there are somewhat different types of concerns involved. Environmental ethics consists of the ethical relationships between people and nonhuman nature, while environmental justice consists of the ethical and political relationships between people as mediated through nonhuman nature.[4] Collectively they constitute environmental philosophy within academia and environmentalism and social justice within the world at large. My term *environmental ethics of war and peace* is meant to be inclusive of *both* environmental ethics and environmental justice, and I will use it for the sake of brevity—instead of the more awkward term *environmental ethics and environmental justice of war and peace*.

There are a number of *ecology of war and peace* monographs that outline the environmental damage and destruction caused by militaries at peace and at war.[5] Many of these environmental concerns stem from advances in military technology that have amplified environmental hazards since the rise of the modern environmental movement. There has been, for example, focused discussion about the nuclear winter effects of a thermonuclear war between the Union of Soviet Socialist Republics and the United States during the Cold War,[6] widespread use of defoliants—notably Agent Orange—by the United States in the Second Indochina War,[7] the ecocide effects of armed conflicts against peoples and landscapes in Central America in the 1980s,[8] and the oil fires and oil pollution of the 1991 Persian Gulf War.[9] In more conventional terms, warfare and military activities have many negative environmental consequences. A partial list of these consequences includes the following: (1) the compaction, erosion, and contamination of soils by bombs and missiles and their hazardous and toxic residues and by the passage of military vehicles, (2) other forms of land pollution ranging from latrines and garbage dumps to landmines, unexploded ordnance, and radioactive dust, (3) defoliation, deforestation, and land degradation, (4) contamination of surface waters and groundwater, (5) atmospheric emissions and resulting air pollution from military equipment and vehicles, (6) direct and collateral killing of animals and plants and loss of habitat, (7) degradation and destruction of protected natural areas, and (8) noise pollution. Further environmental harms for people include the damage and destruction of water storage and distribution systems, waste and wastewater treatment facilities, sewer systems, croplands, pasturage, marine fisheries, and other human structures ranging from buildings to power grid systems and entire towns. These environmental harms in turn can disrupt or destroy the social and economic infrastructures of human communities, dislocate human populations and result in displaced peoples and refugees, and create new opportunities for pathogenic microbes and the spread of infectious diseases among human populations. Many environmental impacts linger long after a war ends, and the resulting peace can lead to further negative impacts as demographic and economic frontiers expand into remaining natural areas and fragile land- and waterscapes.[10] Wars, of course, do not operate in isolation; they necessitate and are preceded by war systems to prepare for war. Although clear data do not exist—largely because of national security secrecy practiced by many nation-states—collectively the world's militaries are estimated to be the largest single polluter on Earth, accounting for as much as 20 percent of all global environmental degradation.[11] It needs to be said that not all of the environmental consequences of war are necessarily negative. Wars, for example, can create no-go zones for people that relieve human impacts; perhaps the most dramatic modern example of this is the demilitarized zone (DMZ) on the Korean Peninsula and the adjacent Civilian Control Zones in North and South Korea that collectively constitute a biodiversity hot spot.[12]

All of the aforementioned concerns raise acute issues of environmental ethics, but surprisingly there is virtually no discussion of military activities and war within the academic field of environmental ethics. There is, in contrast, considerable discussion of the relationship between the environment and armed conflict within the social sciences, notably political science and international relations. Rather than viewing environmental damage and destruction as an undesirable consequence of military activities and armed conflicts, environmental degradation and resource use are seen as contributing (and sometimes major) causes of violent conflicts and wars. Environmental protection and the conservation of resources thus become an important or even necessary step for "environmental security."[13] Thomas Homer-Dixon marshals empirical research to support his thesis that environmental scarcity of renewable resources can contribute to civil violence and armed conflicts, and Michael Klare argues that the global distribution of resources, especially oil and freshwater, will play a key role in shaping the military policies of nation-states and other political actors in the twenty-first century.[14]

Monographs in environmental security importantly focus attention on how the environment is linked to violence and armed conflict. Some of this work, however, can be problematic in terms of both the ecology of war and peace and the environmental ethics of war and peace. As Matthias Finger has argued, environmental security has largely been understood in terms of a military model whereby threats to political governance and national security become synonymous with environmental insecurity.[15] Rather than examining the environmental impacts of militaries and wars—the ecology of war and peace—this military model focuses on environmental degradation per se that can be a security risk and lead to armed conflicts. Environmental security discourse thus can be directed toward new environmental reasons why militaries are needed to prevent and wage wars and inverts the point of ecology of war and peace discourse that examines the (usually deleterious) environmental consequences of war and preparation for war. In terms of the environmental ethics of war and peace, the environment needs military protection to prevent wars and solve environmental security problems rather than the environment needing protection from wars and military activities. To be sure, some environmental security writers—such as Klare—are decidedly antiwar and argue that a military solution to environmental insecurity can lead to further problems. People looking to protect the environment from military impacts might need to go beyond the military model of environmental security discourse or seek more enduring ways to regulate and eliminate war and the seeming need for war.

One possible source of environmental protection can be found in international laws that regulate war.[16] There are three environment-specific international treaties. Concerns about the U.S. use of herbicides in the Second Indochina War motivated the United Nations Convention on the Prohibition of Military or Any Other Hostile Use of Environmental Modification Techniques of 1976—known as the ENMOD Convention. The parties to this convention are prohibited from engaging in "military or any other hostile use of environmental modification techniques having widespread, long-lasting or severe effects as the means of destruction, damage or injury to any other State Party" (Article I). Article II of the ENMOD Convention defines environmental modification as the deliberate manipulation of natural processes (including the Earth's biota, lithosphere, hydrosphere, or atmosphere) such that they are used as weapons of war. Many legal commentators point out that the ENMOD Convention deals with using forces of the environment as weapons rather than preventing military forces from damaging the environment. The second environment-specific international treaty is the Protocol Additional to the Geneva Conventions of 12 August 1949 and relating to the Protection of Victims of International Armed Conflicts—known as Protocol I (1977). Article 35(3) of Protocol I employs similar language from Article I of the ENMOD Convention, but rather than prohibiting environmental modification techniques the former prohibits any methods or means of warfare intended or expected "to cause widespread, long-term and severe damage to the natural environment."

Article 55(1) of Protocol I repeats this and adds a further prohibition against damages to the natural environment that "prejudice the health or survival of the [human] population." The third environment-specific international treaty is the Rome Statute of the International Criminal Court, July 17, 1998. Repeating some of the same language from Protocol I, Article 8.2(b)(iv) of the Rome Statute defines causing "widespread, long-term and severe damage to the natural environment" as a war crime.[17]

There are a number of problems with these international treaties. First, when analyzed, they seem to have little legal bite.[18] Second, it is telling that they have never been invoked to protect the environment before, during, or after a war. Third, as legal mechanisms they are an attempt to regulate the conduct of war through outside enforcement, and the drafting of these laws stems from outsiders looking into matters of war and peace.

The environment might be more effectively protected by building environmental considerations into how Western militaries view war and peace from the inside out—via the just war tradition (JWT). As the quotes from Deuteronomy and Philo Judaeus that opened this chapter suggest, there is some precedent for this. Both the author of Deuteronomy and Philo show that the ancient Israelites built some direct concern for trees into their conception of a just war. Throughout history, in fact, one can find examples of various restrictions placed upon the permissible damage and destruction of buildings, towns, cities, and the economic base of civilian life. James Turner Johnson suggests that the *jus in bello* criterion of discrimination implies that there should be "no Carthaginian peace" or "devastation that leaves a land uninhabitable after the war is over."[19]

Before environmental considerations can be brought directly into the JWT, however, there are environmental ethics questions that need to be identified. What precisely is the environment, in what does its value consist, and what duties do people have to protect it? An environment is one's surroundings or larger milieu and literally can designate any spatial location ranging from the inside of an M1 Abrams Main Battle Tank to the entire universe. For the purposes of this chapter, the term "environment" denotes the nonhuman world (environmental ethics) and human relationships as mediated by this nonhuman world (environmental justice). The nonhuman environment might consist of a variety of different entities such as individual organisms, species (including evolutionary processes), populations of organisms that belong to the same species, animal and plant communities, ecosystems (including ecological relationships), landscapes, the biosphere, the entire Earth, or outer space.[20] Moral value might be directly attributed to any one or combination of these different entities or to only people. One standard divide in environmental ethics has been between anthropocentrism and nonanthropocentrism. People in the former camp believe that the environment or nonhuman nature has only instrumental value for human use or contemplation, while people in the latter camp believe that some, many, or all environmental entities have some kind of noninstrumental or intrinsic moral value. This is a rather simplistic division because there are a wide variety of different positions within environmental ethics, some that do not fall into a clean anthropocentric/nonanthropocentric divide. For example, in Holmes Rolston's nonanthropocentric theory of environmental ethics, individual *Homo sapiens* have maximum intrinsic value over nonhuman individuals, and in Bruce Morito's anthropocentric theory of environmental ethics, a premium is put on allowing for nonhuman creatures to flourish.[21] There are also a variety of different ways to specify why people might have duties toward the environment, what these duties are, and how these duties should be discharged. The story one tells about duties to the environment will be interconnected to one's beliefs about environmental values and about what the environment is.[22] All of this can complicate attempts to bring the environment into the JWT.

Three philosophers have attempted to develop environmental ethics of war and peace within the rubric of the JWT. Merrit Drucker argues that the environment itself should be considered a noncombatant and wants to classify direct attacks against it as violations of noncombatant immunity.[23] He claims that the environment should be treated as a noncombatant because (1) it is not a fighting combatant and poses no direct threat to combatants, (2) it is like other noncombatants that did not choose to be involved with combat fighting, and (3) it is similar to noncombatant chaplains and medical personnel that do not participate in killing but instead heal and nurture people.[24] Although Drucker seems to define the environment in a number of ways, his central argument is that the environment has inherent worth because species—particularly endangered species—have inherent worth. He thus offers a decidedly nonanthropocentric environmental ethic of war and peace.

Gregory Reichberg and Henrik Syse argue that environmental destruction might violate the *jus in bello* criteria of proportionality and discrimination:

The point is that the just war tradition urges us to *combine* the criteria of proportionality and discrimination. Viewed in this way, destruction with severe and/or long-term consequences may in some cases (albeit not in all) be deemed both *proportionally* wrong in connection with the projected military gains (not least since the environmental consequences most likely outlast the military campaign) and *indiscriminate*, since the destruction threatens to eliminate vital natural resources upon which civilian life depends. In addition, such destruction may be condemnable insofar as it irreparably destabilizes ecosystems for which man can rightly be seen to be a sort of custodian.[25]

Reichberg and Syse define the environment as natural resources (for human use), ecosystems, and natural objects, which include humanity itself. With respect to value, they refuse to classify their environmental ethic as either anthropocentric or nonanthropocentric—recognizing that a forced choice between these two types of value is a false dichotomy—and instead claim that it is grounded in the notion that humans have duties toward nature, as developed in the stewardship tradition of St. Thomas Aquinas.[26]

The agnostic manner in which Reichberg and Syse address environmental values effectively appeals to a wide audience who might value the environment for a variety of different moral reasons. Rather than getting bogged down in debates over anthropocentric versus nonanthropocentric, instrumental versus noninstrumental, and extrinsic versus intrinsic environmental values, I suggest that the environmental ethics of war and peace follow Reichberg's and Syse's value agnosticism.

If the *jus in bello* criteria of discrimination and proportionality can be used to regulate military force against civilian targets, it seems possible to regulate the use of military force against environmental targets. Drucker's classification of the environment as a noncombatant puts more bite into this regulation, as attacks against environmental targets might be indiscriminate, disproportional, and a violation of noncombatant immunity. In order to operationalize these *jus in bello* proposals, military professionals need to more clearly know *what* it is that they're not supposed to harm and destroy through their battlefield actions. Admonishments to "protect the environment" are far too abstract to be of much help.

Although I lack the adequate space to discuss this here, I argue elsewhere that environmental protection is probably most effective—in terms of maximizing protection of nonhuman nature and human dependency on it—if it is directed toward protecting localized, spatially distinct populations of organisms and ecosystem processes.[27] In terms of feeding and breeding, most individual organisms belong to particular, local (species) populations for most of their lives; populations of these populations—or metapopulations—are linked by dispersal; and the spatial locations of populations and metapopulations delineate a geographic range. Protecting populations and metapopulations will lead to larger efforts to protect geographic ranges, all of which protects individual organisms. An ecosystem consists of physical, chemical, and biological processes, expressed at different trophic (nutrition or feeding) levels, which cycle materials in such a way that exhibits identity as an interacting system. Effective protection of an ecosystem is best directed toward protecting these processes that collectively constitute this identity or ecological integrity. Thus, protection of ecosystem processes complements and synergizes the protection of localized, spatially distinct populations of organisms. One can do this for the sake of ecosystems and populations themselves, or for the sake of people who depend on these ecosystems and populations. This, I believe, is the most effective way to "protect the environment."

All of this might not sound particularly helpful for a military commander who is asked to factor in the environment as a noncombatant to adhere to *jus in bello* criteria. Michael Diederich suggests educational requirements in the science of ecology for military commanders and service personnel and the creation of scientific advisors to accompany troops into combat.[28] This might be a good idea. Recall, however, the scenario with which I opened this chapter. In the heat of battle military necessity will probably override environmental protection, no matter how well aimed and informed this protection is. Time runs short to make decisions and deliberate over the possible ecological consequences of one's actions, and one might not think twice about blowing up a rock formation that possibly contains a metapopulation of endangered species of *Parnassius charltonius* butterflies in order to protect one's own troops. Military necessity potentially seems to always stand in the way of environmental protection.

How can the environment get out of this military necessity trap? We should note that *jus in bello* criteria are not meant to prevent war but are instead meant to limit the damage and destruction by the dogs of war once they are unleashed. *Jus ad bellum* criteria, in contrast, are used to decide whether or not to unleash the dogs of war in the first place. How exactly are these two subsets of JWT criteria related? The standard picture seems to be that political leaders first deliberate over whether or not a possible war can satisfy the *jus ad bellum* criteria of legitimate authority, just cause, right intention, macro-proportionality, last resort, and likelihood of success. If these criteria can be satisfied, then it is a just war. The *jus in bello* criteria of discrimination and micro-proportionality then enter the battlefield to regulate the conduct of war; if these criteria are satisfied, then the war is fought justly. Four combinations are possible: a just war fought justly, a just war fought unjustly, an unjust war fought justly, and an unjust war fought unjustly. Only politicians are supposedly responsible for *jus ad bellum* criteria, and military professionals are not responsible for the crime of war; it is military professionals who fight wars and who are held responsible for *jus in bello* battlefield conduct.

Jus ad bellum and *jus in bello* criteria, however, might be more tightly tethered together than this. Many antiwar pacifists condemn war because they find it problematic to use immoral means to achieve a moral end. Duane Cady argues that however much *jus ad bellum* criteria are satisfied, "if the war cannot be conducted within the *jus in bello* guidelines it is not a just war."[29] A number of JWT proponents seem to agree. William O'Brien argues that *jus in bello* violations can be so significant that they critically affect *jus ad bellum* criteria and render a war unjust.[30] John Finnis argues that it must be right to choose to engage in a war in order for it to be just, and if one's chosen means are vicious, then the whole choice of going to war is wrong.[31] Henry Shue argues that justified conduct is a "strictly necessary condition of a justified war," and regardless of how justified one might be to go to war, if war cannot be conducted within firm limits, it is not morally permissible to fight the war.[32] The point I wish to draw here is that a good case can be made for not considering *jus in bello* criteria in isolation from *jus ad bellum* criteria, and when deliberating about whether or not to go to war, political use of the latter should also include the former. If an upcoming war might involve significant attacks against environmental targets and adherence to the *jus in bello* criteria of discrimination and proportionality is not likely to be forthcoming, it will be an unjust war (and fought unjustly) as per the environmental standards I am proposing here.[33]

Of course trying to accurately predict the possible targets in a future war is difficult, if not downright impossible. A myriad of decisions ranging from political and strategic leadership to the tactical moves of individual battlefield commanders—all combined with chance, luck, and the fog of war—typically will create much uncertainty about what the environmental impacts of any given war are likely to be, as well as how widespread, long lasting, and severe they might become. Future uncertainty, however, should be tempered by past history. Most twentieth-century wars have had detrimental environmental consequences for people and for nonhuman nature, and there is a strong probability that this trend will continue. Preventing environmental damage demands heightened caution and an injunction against military activities likely to lead to this damage. This is an application of the precautionary principle. Invoking it when deliberating about whether or not to go to war can, in turn, be seen as an application of the *jus ad bellum* criterion of proportionality. This brings environmental benefits and burdens for people—environmental justice—and concern for nonhuman nature—environmental ethics—directly into the macro measure calculation of overall harms and benefits that must be satisfied in order to prosecute a just war. Environment considerations thus can be more than mere collateral damage constraints and instead could be more fully built into *jus ad bellum* deliberations.

Beyond macro-proportionality, the environmental ethics of war and peace also might involve other *jus ad bellum* criteria. Proportionality importantly is related to the likelihood of success criterion, and damage and destruction of the environment might count against the success of winning a war. Reichberg and Syse question whether a truly competent authority should be able to legitimately destroy natural resources.[34] This suggests that legitimate authorities have duties to protect both their human political constituents and their natural environments. This plays into the just cause criterion. The most commonly accepted rationale for having a just cause to go to war today is self or national defense (which can include one nation-state assisting another). If we are to take seriously the notion of protecting the environment—for people and/or for the sake of nonhuman nature itself—sacrificing the environment for political and/or military goals might be a questionable practice. That is, a patriotic defense of one's home*land* should not involve military activities that denude or destroy the land in order to supposedly protect the home.[35]

In addition to self or national defense, the criterion of just cause can be invoked to justify so-called humanitarian interventions in cases of "weak states" that lack a sufficiently strong government to protect people from internal violent conflicts or that have a government waging violent conflicts against its own people. Intervention can come from other nation-states, security alliances, or the United Nations. Armed humanitarian interventions are of central importance within the JWT today given their increasing occurrence and due to the fact that the vast majority of armed conflicts in the world are intrastate as opposed to interstate wars between separate nation-states. If humanitarian interventions can be justified on grounds of ending human rights abuses, rescuing people threatened with massacre, and/or stopping acts that shock our moral conscience, can such interventions constitute a just cause to protect the environment?[36] Might armed environmental interventions be justified to protect, for example, environmental entities such as the Amazon rainforest or the endangered mountain gorillas of central Africa?

Although military force or the threatened use of such force could possibly be a means to protect rainforests and mountain gorillas, we should be careful here so that we do not recreate a military model of environmental security as discussed earlier in this chapter. The main concern of the environmental ethics of war and peace is to regulate military activities to minimize or prevent environmental harms, and it seems problematic to justify further military activities—and the mostly negative environmental impacts that come packaged with such activities—to protect the environment. As people such as Klare argue, it is unsustainable and unjust economic activities that are usually the real culprits at work when environmental harms such as rainforest destruction and mountain gorilla extinction occur.[37] Providing people with just, economic assistance and/or controlling so-called free markets so that they do not harm people might be the correct thing to do to protect the environment. Because direct military intervention can harm the very people it purports to protect, such intervention can violate the *jus in bello* criteria of discrimination and proportionality. And if military intervention to protect the environment were to occur without first attempting to rectify unfair and unsustainable economic practices, such intervention might fail the *jus ad bellum* criterion of last resort. Under the guise of humanitarian or environmental interventions, the criterion of just cause thus can wield a double-edged sword that can cut down those who would destroy the environment *and* the environment itself. Petitioning military necessity to protect the environment might be barking up the wrong tree.

The problem of military necessity points to a larger problem with the JWT. Because military necessity can so easily override environmental protection during wars, that is, merely avoid environmental collateral damage when convenient, I have argued that environmental *jus in bello* criteria should come into play when deliberating about whether or not to go to war, and environmental considerations should be brought directly into *jus ad bellum* criteria. Backing up a step further from *jus ad bellum*, environmental protection might be more effectively brought into the JWT by extending the JWT backward. The political deliberation about whether or not to go to war occupies but a very small fraction of any given nation-state's existence. Beyond militaristic regimes constantly at war, most nation-states are at peace most of the time. But for many of these nation-states, there is constant peacetime military readiness, training, and preparation for possible future wars. The JWT is unhelpfully silent about peacetime. Or is it? U.S. military forces argue for and sometimes win exemption from environmental laws so that they can train and conduct what they believe are essential peacetime operations. Their argument is that national security overrides environmental protection. This sounds like military necessity overriding environmental protection during wartime. Drucker acknowledges this, argues that military commanders have stronger obligations to protect the environment during peacetime than they do during wartime, and suggests practical ways to meet these obligations.[38] He concedes that a weak form of military necessity might come into play when military training operations seem to necessitate environmental damage. If military necessity is at work during peacetime, JWT criteria seem to apply not merely during war and when deliberating about whether to go to war but also during peacetime military activities. In keeping with Latin parlance, I suggest that we call this prior subdivision of the JWT *jus potentia ad bellum*, which translates into something like the "justice of the potential of going to war."[39] Some variety of JWT criteria might apply to this in regard to the environment: the treatment of environmental entities such as species populations and ecosystems as noncombatants, proportionality constraints on environmental damage and destruction, and the likelihood of maintaining a successful peace by maintaining a healthy environment. If environmental *jus ad bellum* and *jus in bello* criteria could render a war unjust, it seems possible that environmental *jus potentia ad bellum* criteria could render military defense and preparations for war unjust because of military activities that are incompatible with environmental protection. The environmental justice literature is ripe with case studies toward which this new subdivision of the JWT could be applied. Examples include the U.S. Navy training use of Vieques, Puerto Rico, from 1941 to 2003 and the U.S. Department of Defense and Department of Energy use of Yucca Mountain, Nevada, for nuclear weapons testing and resulting radioactive waste disposal since the advent of the Cold War.[40] I lack the space here to say more about this new backward subdivision of the JWT and note that a sufficient account of *jus potentia ad bellum* criteria is the subject of another essay.[41]

As evidenced by Eric Patterson's chapter in this volume, there is increasing recognition being given to extending the JWT forward to *jus post bellum*. Michael Walzer argues that the end of war should be justice in settlements that create a better state of peace than existed before a war.[42] Expanding on this, Brian Orend argues that just settlements should include rectification of unjust gains, rights vindication, compensation owed to victims, punishment of guilty parties, rehabilitation to bring aggressor states back into the international community, and deterrence to prevent future aggression.[43] It seems that in many if not most cases, restorative *jus post bellum* efforts will need to incorporate environmental justice. The ecology of war peace literature is filled with examples of how negative environmental impacts linger long after wars end, and considerable ecological restoration and rehabilitation might be needed to address these impacts to repair human and ecological communities. Walzer's call for a better state of *post bellum* peace might require a better state of environmental health to help make this possible. Restitution and future deterrence of the crime of aggression is now incorporated into the current International Criminal Court with its authorization to prosecute "widespread, long-term and severe damage to the natural environment" as a war crime. The legal efficacy of this has yet to be seen. Environmental damage and destruction, however, might be more effectively prevented prior to military actions rather than mitigated during an actual war or undone after the prosecution of a war. A likelihood of success criterion for environmental *jus post bellum* importantly will be related to success at the levels of environmental protection *in bello*, *ad bellum*, and *potentia ad bellum*.

My goal in this chapter has been to lay some groundwork for future discussions of how the environmental ethics of war and peace should play a greater role across the entire spectrum of military activities before, during, and after wars. As I have argued here, environmental considerations can be built in the JWT, especially when just war criteria are viewed in a unified manner across *jus potentia ad bellum*, *jus ad bellum*, *jus in bello*, and *jus post bellum*. This might go a considerable distance toward beginning to rectify the shortcomings of environment-specific international law in regard to protecting people and the environment, and those who articulate environmental security norms have much to gain by bringing environmental ethics of war and peace into their discourse. One can hope that further articulations of the environmental ethics of war and peace might help direct us toward a more peaceful, just, and green world.[44]

NOTES

1. *The Torah: A Modern Commentary*, vol. V (New York: Union of American Hebrew Congregations, 1983).

2. Hugo Grotius, *The Law of War and Peace* (*De Jure Belli ac Pacis*), trans. Louise R. Loomis (Roslyn, NY: Walter J. Black, 1949), 361.

3. Chicago: Ivan R. Dee, 2003, 170–171.

4. This does not mean, however, that environmental justice is necessarily human centered or anthropocentric, and environmental ethics is necessarily nonanthropocentric. Both environmental ethics and environmental justice are concerned with nonhuman nature, and anthropocentric and nonanthropocentric theories and positions are held by people in both fields.

5. Stockholm International Peace Research Institute (SIPRI), *Warfare in a Fragile World: Military Impact on the Human Environment* (London: Taylor and Francis, 1980); Arthur H. Westing, ed., *Explosive Remnants of War: Mitigating the Environmental Effects* (London: Taylor and Francis, 1985); Susan D. Lanier-Graham, *The Ecology of War: Environmental Impacts of Weaponry and Warfare* (New York: Walker and Company, 1993); Mohamed Suliman, ed., *Ecology, Politics and Violent Conflict* (London: Zed Books, 1999); Jay E. Austin and Carl E. Bruch, eds., *The Environmental Consequences of War: Legal, Economic, and Scientific Perspectives* (Cambridge: Cambridge University Press, 2000); and Rosalie Bertell, *Planet Earth: The Latest Weapon of War* (London: The Women's Press, 2000).

6. Mark A. Harwell, *Nuclear Winter: The Human and Environmental Consequences of Nuclear War* (New York: Springer-Verlag, 1984) and Lydia Dotto, *Planet Earth in Jeopardy: Environmental Consequences of Nuclear War* (Chichester, NY: John Wiley & Sons, 1986).

7. SIPRI, *Ecological Consequences of the Second Indochina War* (Stockholm: Almquist and Wiksell International, 1976) and Arthur H. Westing, ed., *Herbicides in War: The Long-Term Ecological and Human Consequences* (London: Taylor & Francis, 1984).

8. Bill Hall and Daniel Faber, *El Salvador: Ecology of Conflict* (San Francisco: Environmental Project on Central America—EPOCA, 1989); Bernard Nietschmann, "Conservation by Conflict in Nicaragua," *Natural*

History 11 (1990): 42–49; and Bill Weinberg, *War on the Land: Ecology and Politics in Central America* (London: Zed Books, 1991).

9. Muhammad Sadiq and John C. McCain, eds., *The Gulf War Aftermath: An Environmental Tragedy* (Dordrecht: Kluwer Academic Publishers, 1993) and Farouk El-Baz and R. M. Makharita, eds., *The Gulf War and the Environment* (New York: Gordon and Breach Science Publishers, 1994). The use of depleted uranium might be the next historical moment in the ecology of war and peace literature; see Bernard Rostker, *Depleted Uranium: A Case Study of Good and Evil* (Santa Monica: RAND, 2002).

10. John Hart and Terese Hart, "Rules of Engagement for Conservation," *Conservation in Practice* 4 (2003): 14–22.

11. Michael Renner, "Assessing the Military's War on the Environment," in *State of the World 1991: A Worldwatch Institute Report on Progress Toward a Sustainable Society*, ed. Lester R. Brown et al. (Washington, DC: W. W. Norton & Company, 1991).

12. Ke Chung Kim, "Preserving Biodiversity in Korea's Demilitarized Zone," *Science* 278 (1997): 242–243. See also Jeffrey A. McNeely, "War and Biodiversity," in *The Environmental Consequences of War*, for more discussion of the positive environmental consequences of war.

13. For an overview of some of the environmental security debates, see Worldwatch Institute, *State of the World: Redefining Global Security* (Washington, DC: W. W. Norton and Company, 2005).

14. Thomas F. Homer-Dixon, *Environment, Scarcity, and Violence* (Princeton: Princeton University Press, 1999). Michael T. Klare, *Resource Wars: The New Landscape of Global Conflict*, second ed. (New York: Henry Holt and Company, 2002).

15. Matthias Finger, "The Military, the Nation-State and the Environment," *The Ecologist* 21 (1991): 220–225.

16. For a survey of the legal literature on international law, war, and the environment, see Michael Diederich, "'Law of War' and Ecology—A Proposal for a Workable Approach to Protecting the Environment Through the Law of War," *Military Law Review* 136 (1992): 137–160; Glen Plant, ed., *Environmental Protection and the Law of War: A "Fifth Geneva" Convention on the Protection of the Environment in Time of Armed Conflict* (London: Belhaven Press, 1992); Richard J. Grunawalt, John E. King, and Ronald S. McClain, eds., *International Law Studies, Volume 69: Protection of the Environment During Armed Conflict* (Newport, RI: Naval War College, 1996); and Peter J. Richards and Michael N. Schmitt, "Mars Meets Mother Nature: Protecting the Environment During Armed Conflict," *Stetson Law Review* 28 (1999): 1047–1090. See also the essays by Falk, Roberts, and Schmitt in *The Environmental Consequences of War*.

17. In addition to these three environment-specific international treaties, a number of legal commentators argue that there are a variety of nonenviron-

ment-specific international treaties that plausibly could be used to regulate the conduct of war with respect to the environment. See *The Environmental Consequences of War*.

18. Michael N. Schmitt, "War and the Environment," in *The Environmental Consequences of War*.

19. James Turner Johnson, *Morality and Contemporary Warfare* (New Haven: Yale University Press, 1999), 126.

20. For a discussion of how nature might be organized at some of these different levels, see Timothy F. H. Allen and Thomas W. Hoekstra, *Toward a Unified Ecology* (New York: Columbia University Press, 1992).

21. Holmes Rolston, III, *Environmental Ethics: Duties to and Values in the Natural World* (Philadelphia: Temple University Press, 1988). Bruce Morito, *Thinking Ecologically: Environmental Thought, Values and Policy* (Halifax: Fernwood Publishing, 2002). For a theory of environmental ethics that resists the anthropocentric/nonanthropocentric divide, see Joseph Grange, *Nature: An Environmental Cosmology* (Albany: State University of New York Press, 1997).

22. Robin Attfield, *Environmental Ethics: An Overview for the Twenty-First Century* (Cambridge: Polity, 2003).

23. Merrit Drucker, "The Military Commander's Responsibility for the Environment," *Environmental Ethics* 11 (1989): 135–152.

24. Ibid., 146–147.

25. Gregory Reichberg and Henrik Syse, "Protecting the Natural Environment in Wartime: Ethical Considerations from the Just War Tradition," *Journal of Peace Research* 37 (2000): 449–468, 464–465 (italics in the original).

26. Ibid., 455–458.

27. Mark Woods, *Rethinking Wilderness* (Peterborough, Ontario: Broadview Press, forthcoming).

28. Diederich, "'Law of War' and Ecology," 157. Incorporating environmental constraints more fully into military manuals might also be helpful; see Arthur H. Westing, "In Furtherance of Environmental Guidelines for Armed Forces During Peace and War," in *The Environmental Consequences of War*.

29. Robert L. Phillips and Duane L. Cady, *Humanitarian Intervention: Just War vs. Pacifism* (Lanham, MD: Rowman & Littlefield Publishers, 1996), 38.

30. William V. O'Brien, *The Conduct of a Just and Limited War* (New York: Praeger Publishers, 1981), 78.

31. John Finnis, "The Ethics of War and Peace in the Catholic Natural Law Tradition," in *The Ethics of War and Peace: Religious and Secular Perspectives*, ed. Terry Nardin (Princeton: Princeton University Press, 1996), 18.

32. Henry Shue, "War," in *The Oxford Handbook of Practical Ethics*, ed. Hugh LaFollette (Oxford: Oxford University Press, 2003), 737.

33. There are deeper ramifications for the JWT when significant attacks against human noncombatants are also considered in this manner. Many more wars will be both unjustly fought and, consequently, unjust wars.

34. Reichberg and Syse, "Protecting the Natural Environment in Wartime," 462. They also argue that damage and destruction of the environment might violate the *jus ad bellum* criteria of right intention and just cause when one intends to and aims at destroying the natural environment (460–461). Somewhat confusingly, Reichberg and Syse here are invoking right intention and just cause as *jus in bello* criteria.

35. For literary discussions of this, see Richard Nelson, Barry Lopez, and Terry Tempest Williams, *Patriotism and the American Land* (Great Barringon, MA: Orion Society, 2002).

36. Michael Walzer classically justifies a humanitarian intervention in cases that "shock the moral conscience of mankind." See *Just and Unjust Wars: A Moral Argument with Historical Illustration*, third ed. (New York: Basic Books, 2000), 107.

37. Klare, *Resource Wars*.

38. Drucker, "The Military Commander's Responsibility for the Environment," 140–143.

39. I thank Linda Peterson, Patrick Hurley, and Harry van der Linden for helping me coin this term.

40. Katherine T. McCaffrey, *Military Power and Popular Protest: The U.S. Navy in Vieques, Puerto Rico* (New Brunswick, NJ: Rutgers University Press, 2002). Valerie L. Kuletz, *The Tainted Desert: Environmental and Social Ruin in the American West* (New York: Routledge, 1998).

41. See my "Expanding the Just War Tradition: *Jus Potentia Ad Bellum*," work in progress.

42. Walzer, *Just and Unjust Wars*, 121–122.

43. Brian Orend, "Justice after War," *Ethics and International Affairs* 16 (2002): 43–56. See also Orend, "Jus Post Bellum," in *War and Border Crossings: When Cultures Clash*, ed. Peter A. French and Jason A. Short (Lanham, MD: Rowman and Littlefield, 2005).

44. An earlier draft of this chapter was presented at the Concerned Philosophers for Peace Group Session of the 2005 American Philosophical Association Central Division Meeting in Chicago. I would like to thank the participants at this session, especially Duane Cady, for helpful feedback. I also thank my wife Naomi R Goldsmith and the three wonderful editors of this book—Michael W. Brough, John W. Lango, and Harry van der Linden—for helpful comments and criticism.

CHAPTER 2

Jus Post Bellum *and International Conflict: Order, Justice, and Reconciliation*

Eric Patterson

> The object in war is a better state of peace.
> —Liddell Hart

I. INTRODUCTION

Just war theory is the bedrock of Western ethics and law regarding the resort to force. In an imperfect world, just war doctrine balances the ideal of peace with the reality that violence and bloodshed occurs. At its heart, the concept of a just war is a paradigm that privileges international security and values individual human life. Strangely, traditional just war theorists largely ignored *jus post bellum*, or the just end to war.

We should consider justice at war's end. This chapter analyzes the practical and moral arguments for and against adopting a "justice in endings"[1] framework for the cessation of conflict. The conception of *jus post bellum* presented here is multidimensional or layered, emphasizing *order* first (stopping the killing), and then principles of *justice*, including punishment, when appropriate. The essay concludes with a consideration of *reconciliation* in intra- and interstate conflicts.

II. THE NEGLECT OF *JUS POST BELLUM*

What is *jus post bellum*? Literally, it is the "just end of war." *Jus post bellum* takes the past, present, and future into account: (1) What caused this war and can the causes be ameliorated, satisfied, and/or redressed? (2) How was this war fought, and are there legitimate claims for justice due to the conduct of the war? (3) How will the settlement create a just and lasting peace?

Just war theorists have largely ignored *jus post bellum*. Augustine suggested that wars should end in ways that promote a "secure peace," but he was far more preoccupied with questions about the just resort to violence and whether the Christian, as an individual, could morally participate in war. Similarly, Aquinas focused on criteria for justly going to war, although he points out that punishment of evildoers is commensurate with just war.[2]

Spanish just war theorists in the natural law tradition like Vitoria and Suarez agonized over the morality of Spain's imperial wars in the New World. Their focus was primarily on *jus ad bellum* and *jus in bello*, but they also called for restraint on the victors in the aftermath of war. For example, Vitoria argued that systematic rape, pillage, and torture were unjust policies toward the defeated.[3] Suarez famously pointed out that "three periods must be distinguished with respect to every war: its inception; its prosecution before victory is gained; and the period after victory."[4] Unfortunately, they merely addressed the morality of specific policies rather than stipulating a theory of *jus post bellum*.

Even the most influential contemporary just war scholarship lacks a theory of *jus post bellum*. Michael Walzer's influential *Just and Unjust Wars* says little on the topic.[5] James Turner Johnson's multiple histories of the just war tradition are largely mute on *jus post bellum*, although he has recently suggested that part of the just resort to war (*jus ad bellum*) is the goal of a just post-conflict environment.[6]

Perhaps the reason that *jus post bellum* has been neglected is that there are serious arguments against adding it to the canon. The first has been heard since 9/11: some will say that an America (or "the West") trumpeting *jus post bellum* is really a thinly disguised realpolitik. The critique goes something like this: declaring principles of justice and reconciliation is simply a clever way of obscuring American power and interests via a kangaroo court. America will demand excessive security arrangements, inordinate military guarantees, and the like in its play for a "just" peace.

Of course, it may be true that victors will use the language of just war to legitimize revisionist policies. However, such machinations do not weaken the ethical power of the just war tradition; rather, they pay tribute to the power of normative issues in war and at war's end. The very fact that most realists give lip service to ethics is a testament to the value of ethics. And in the real world of conflict settlement, it is likely that politics and ethics will usually restrain the United States and other victors from imposing onerous settlements on their opponents.

A second, though polar, critique is that *jus post bellum* authorizes idealistic crusades. In other words, a doctrine of *jus post bellum* might justify radical policies against the political and military leaders of opponents, such as forced regime change, long occupation by foreign troops, the imposition of friendly governments, war guilt and massive reparations, and even (re)colonization—all in the name of justice.

This critique of *jus post bellum* is also not compelling. A thoughtful *jus post bellum* begins where all of just war doctrine begins—by emphasizing restraint. *Jus post bellum* is not a carte blanche for remaking the world in one's own image; it is the imperative to create conditions for state and human security in the aftermath of conflict.

The third critique is that of the moral relativists: *jus post bellum*, at least in its "justice" and "reconciliation" forms, employs a language of right and wrong that is inappropriate in the twenty-first century. This postmodern understanding of conflict asserts that "justice" is a problematic concept that is employed by the powerful at the expense of the weak. For most relativists all sides in a conflict, as contributors to the conflict, are equally guilty. Thus, at worst *jus post bellum* is hypocrisy and power politics, at best *jus post bellum* should apply to both winners and losers as equals or not at all.

The relativist position is unsatisfying on many grounds. At the fundamental level, it is not true that politics is the absence of values. International politics prioritizes the security of states; domestic politics (should) privilege the security of individuals. Thus, there is a hierarchy of values beginning with *order*. In addition, it is simply not true that all sides engaged in a conflict are equally guilty. For instance, it is ridiculous and morally irresponsible to suggest that the Poles were as guilty as Hitler for the conflict in September 1939.[7] Furthermore, even if we cannot employ universal values of justice in every situation, we can apply contextual notions of security, ethics, and even reconciliation on a case by case basis.

III. ARGUMENTS FOR *JUS POST BELLUM*

For numerous reasons the twenty-first century demands a dialogue about ending wars well. The loss of Cold War bipolarity means that there is no longer superpower oversight over peripheral conflicts in order to keep them from erupting across borders. The rise in racial and religious violence means that warfare is no longer merely about land and prestige, if it ever was, but also about ethnic and moral "cleansing." The War on Terror pits the greatest military power of all time against shadowy transnational terrorist networks that utilize unconventional methods. Moreover, the international community is routinely called upon to intervene in humanitarian crises and sometimes answers. None of these scenarios are likely to end with principals representing sovereign states sitting down in Paris or Vienna to sign a peace treaty. Thus, scholars and policy makers need to consider the conditions and values that establish a just post-conflict scenario in this new environment. A twenty-first-century just war theory must include a doctrine of *jus post bellum* based on both pragmatic and moral foundations.

The Pragmatic Grounds for Jus Post Bellum

For *jus post bellum* to have utility in the real world, it must deal with the past, present, and future issues surrounding the conflict. Walzer writes that one characteristic of "justice in endings" is closure: Is the cessation of hostilities part of a larger multidimensional termination of conflict?[8] A good end to conflict is one where the politics and economics that caused the war come to resolution, where the social and emotional energies of the conflict are dealt with or satisfied (through victory, compromise, or exhaustion), and where the military and geographical conditions that led to war are explicitly dealt with. In short, a pragmatic approach to war's end seeks a durable peace based on resolving the causes of the war.

Another practical reason for ending war well is that it avoids stand-offs that perpetuate the conditions of insecurity. The end of some wars is simply stalemate: the stasis of two exhausted yet surviving parties in a gladiatorial exchange. Stalemate results in long-term Hobbesian dispositions of military readiness and the potential for renewed hostilities, which is generally in no one's immediate or future interest. The Kashmir situation is a case in point. No doubt cold war is better than hot war, but a negotiated settlement would be even better. *Jus post bellum* seeks a secure peace, not an intermission.

Jus post bellum is practical because it calls for the restraint or removal of leaders who initiate conflict. In some wars there are obvious aggressor states whose policies are clearly identified with specific leaders. Slobodan Milosevic fits the bill. Milosevic was a warmonger—his policies initiated a decade of warfare, and he was explicitly responsible for not just disrupting international peace but authorizing gross violations of *jus in bello*. Imagine how different the unstable Balkans of the late 1990s would have been had Milosevic not remained in power in 1995. At times disposing of bad leaders, via systems of international justice or even buying them off into exile, sets the stage for a present and future peace.[9]

Finally, a really useful peace settlement based on *jus post bellum* may move beyond the initial causes of war to chart a "fresh start" between the combatants. This was the basis for U.S.-Japanese rapprochement at the end of World War II. It is unlikely that raw U.S. force alone, nor the Soviet threat, could have created the environment of partnership that developed between these two countries in the 1950s and beyond. The United States imposed a victor's peace on Japan, but did so in a way that nurtured opportunity for many segments of Japanese society. In retrospect, what was more in the United States' interests in 1945: to obliterate or rehabilitate Japan? The United States chose the latter course and it has proven to be spectacularly successful.[10]

The Ethical Grounds for Jus Post Bellum

Thus far I have suggested that a just and secure peace is eminently practical. In other words, it is in the interest of governments to practice restraint, seek security, and strive for closure at war's end. More importantly, what is ethical about *jus post bellum*? At the outset, we should return to the purpose of just war theory itself: restraining violence to promote international security and preserve human life. Traditional just war doctrine is a framework calling for restraint: restraint in the decision to go to war and restraint in the prosecution of war. A twenty-first-century *jus post bellum* extends this notion of restraint to war's end: post-conflict settlements should exhibit moderation in their terms and in the pursuit of justice, punishment, and reconciliation.

Jus post bellum is normative in that it is concerned with both *jus ad bellum* and *jus in bello. Jus post bellum* requires moral accountability for past actions, including the decisions by leaders that led to war. One scholar who addresses this is Brian Orend, who asserts that a just settlement vindicates "the fundamental rights of political communities, ultimately on behalf of the human rights of their individual citizens."[11] Orend suggests three "propositions" for the vindication of rights at the

end of a just war: the "roll-back" of aggression (restoration), compensation
to victims and punishment of aggressors, and deterrence of future aggression through demilitarization and the political rehabilitation of the
aggressors.[12] Orend provides a formula for *jus post bellum* that is essentially
the usual just war checklist applied to conflict. For Orend, "a just state,
seeking to successfully terminate its just war, ought to be guided by" the
following principles: just cause for conflict termination, right intention,
discrimination, and proportionality. To these, Orend adds an innovative
view of legitimate authority—"the terms of peace must be publicly proclaimed by a legitimate authority" on the world stage.[13]

Orend's model is an important start to conceptualizing a *jus post
bellum*, but it does have its limits. First, Orend himself acknowledges
that his framework only applies to interstate war. This is problematic
when so many contemporary conflicts are either intrastate wars or military humanitarian interventions. A second problem for Orend's model
is the assumption that just victors at the end of a just war will choose
to act with restraint. Most wars end in something closer to stalemate
than a clear "vindication of our rights," and even well-intentioned
democracies find it difficult to not respond to domestic public opinion
by punishing the loser.

Jus post bellum is concerned with violations of the prewar peace.
The breakdown of international peace is a complex set of circumstances, but in many cases war is directly attributable to the aggressive
policies of a specific regime or cabal within the regime. Leaders are
responsible for peace and security, and when they abrogate that obligation they should be held accountable in post-conflict settlements.

The same is true for *jus in bello* violations. Soldiers and their leaders on both sides are responsible for their conduct during the fighting.
To this end Davida Kellogg argues for a specific *jus post bellum* technique for punishing those who willfully violated the war convention:
war crimes tribunals.[14]

Another ethical principle of *jus post bellum* is restitution. Walzer
claims that since World War II, and particularly in an era of military
humanitarian intervention, it may be appropriate to consider a "more
extensive understanding of restoration."[15] Of course, the destructive
nature of war means that a complete restoration to the status quo is
impossible and may not be desirable in cases of secession or civil war.
Jus post bellum takes the cost of war, particularly the cost in lives and
material, into account and asserts that when possible, aggressors should
provide restitution to the victims.

A related moral concern that *jus post bellum* addresses is that of punishment. Punishment is punitive action against a wrongdoer. It may mean loss of rank or position, fines, imprisonment, exile, or death. Thus, punishment is the twin principle of accountability and an important feature of post-conflict justice. Punishment is ethical in that it moves beyond an abstract conception of accountability by employing sanctions against those responsible for initiating violence or transgressing the war convention. As this chapter will later argue, punishment is a lost strand of just war theory.

Finally, adding *jus post bellum* is ethical in that its full realization will work toward reconciliation. The early just war tradition was founded on the idea of "love thy neighbor," even in war. A doctrine of *jus post bellum* makes a moral commitment to viewing others as partners in a future peace. Such reconciliation is the ultimate step toward building a durable framework for domestic and international peace.

IV. THE PRINCIPLES OF *JUS POST BELLUM*: ORDER, JUSTICE, RECONCILIATION

Jus post bellum means ending wars well and should be conceptualized as multidimensional, involving the goals of *order*, *justice*, and *reconciliation*. Order is the fundamental goal of the just end of war. Some settlements will only feature order, whereas others will add to order features of justice. On rare occasions, comprehensive, deeper settlements will add reconciliation to the principles of order and justice. Order is the necessary condition for *jus post bellum*, but in the twenty-first century we should look for opportunities to create peace settlements that utilize the deeper principles of justice and reconciliation.

Order

The first and fundamental principle of *jus post bellum* is order. Order is a modest goal for it says little about justice, much less about reconciliation. However, my primary assumption is that ending the war is usually more important than continued bloodshed in pursuit of better terms. This does not mean that one side should surrender simply to end the war, rather, that a negotiated settlement that ends the fighting and creates a stable post-conflict environment but that is short on justice and reconciliation is nonetheless a moral conclusion to conflict. In other words, we should think about *jus post bellum* on a case by case basis.

Political order in the form of security for all parties is a moral good, for it is impossible for domestic politics to provide the conditions necessary for "the good life" without international security. Consequently, wars should be ended in ways that rehabilitate or create a political order that is durable. Such order, at the minimum, is a security among states and thereby a security from outside attacks on their populations. The Korean Conflict provides such an example.

Order and the Korean Conflict. In June 1950, seventy-five thousand North Korean troops attacked South Korea across the thirty-eighth parallel, the postwar boundary agreed to by the United States and Soviet Union. The blitzkrieg blasted across much of the Republic of Korea, catching the South Koreans and their U.S. allies completely off guard. The ensuing war lasted for three years and brought the United Nations and the United States and its allies into conflict with Communist China and the Soviet Union. At war's end more than four million people had died, including an estimated three million civilians.[16]

The armistice that arrested the conflict ended the fighting, demarcated a new boundary near the old border, and created a demilitarized zone between the Koreas. The agreement also led to a policy of allowing POWs a choice of remaining where they were or repatriation.[17]

Does this armistice meet any sort of *jus post bellum* standards? If we take Orend's long list of requirements (just cause for ending, proportionality in the peace agreement, and so forth), the answer is no. The killing halted at an impasse, no wrongs were righted, and violations of *jus ad bellum* and *jus in bello* were not pursued internationally. Although there was a clear aggressor, that regime remained in power without apology and without making reparations. Was this a just peace?

The Korean armistice falls short if our notion of *jus post bellum* is perfect justice. However, international politics is far from ideal. In the real world *jus post bellum* should privilege state security and protect individual human life. The armistice of 1953 did just that. It pulled major world powers, including the Chinese and nuclear-armed United States and Soviet Union, back from the brink of World War III. It de-escalated tensions not only in Korea, but in the greater Pacific and European theaters. It created a demilitarized zone and security guarantees, on both sides, that were superior to the situation in 1949.

Furthermore, the armistice preserved individual human life. On average, a million civilians died each of the three years of the conflict, as well as 250,000 troops of various nationalities. Many of those troops, both from the United States and Communist countries, were draftees. In 1954, however, no troops were killed in open combat. No civilians died as "collateral damage." Moreover, the peace held from 1954 through the present.

Was it a "just" end? Yes. The Korean armistice was a just ending because order is a moral as well as political imperative.[18] Of course, conceptualizing *jus post bellum* as order will have its critics. But consider the alternative. Should we continue prosecuting every war against aggressors until we can throw someone into prison (World War II) or force a defeated government to admit wrongdoing (World War I)? How long would that have taken and how costly would it have been in the Korean context?[19] Furthermore, should we refrain from entering into post-conflict settlements with aggressors because we refuse to recognize their existence (e.g., "Red" China)? This is hubris. In short, international politics is messy and perfect justice is rarely attainable. Therefore, we should work toward post-conflict agreements that enact a minimal *jus post bellum*: the promotion of international order and the preservation of human life.

A Richer Jus Post Bellum*: Justice*

Order is a necessary condition for *jus post bellum*. Nonetheless, at the end of some conflicts, particularly since World War II, we have employed a richer dimension of *jus post bellum*—settlements with provisions for justice. By *justice* I mean that in addition to creating a situation of security, aggressors are held accountable in some way for their actions. Accountability is an ethical principle based on the notion of responsibility—political and military leaders have a responsibility to their citizens and their neighbors to promote security. We expect this in domestic society, and when possible, should employ the notion of justice at the end of inter- and intrastate war. The same also applies for warriors and military leaders who, during the fighting, violate the war convention: they should be held, when possible, responsible.

Most wars conclude with security, not Justice Indeed, Justice is not available at the end of every war. The reality of warfare is that ending the carnage soon is often preferable to prolonging the conflict in hopes an "ending with justice." Nevertheless, in those cases where Justice is possible, it should be pursued. Justice usually takes one of two forms: compensation or punishment. Justice may take the form of compensation, a payment of some sort to the aggrieved or the victim(s). Justice may also take the form of punishment—a penalty for employing violence in the first place or for how violence was perpetrated. This essay focuses on the latter.[20] Justice is desirable and may lead to a better peace that both sides can find acceptable.

Justice in Theory: The Reviled Doctrine of Punishment. Punishment is an unpopular topic in international relations, as we have seen in debates following the U.S. response to 9/11. In contrast, early just war thinkers saw punishment of aggression as just. For instance, Augustine and Aquinas argued that just wars punish evildoers and right wrongs, because as churchmen, they recognized that politics could be the agent of restraint and moral judgment against lawbreakers.[21] A contemporary *jus post bellum* suggests that modern sovereigns have the moral authority (Right Authority) to punish violators of the peace as well as evil regimes.

Whereas *jus post bellum* is a neglected notion, the idea of punishment is largely reviled in international politics. This is probably the case because, as James Turner Johnson has written, the international legal paradigm distanced itself early on from the normative foundations of just war theory. International jurists such as Grotius and Vattel imagined international politics as a game played by sovereign equals governed by rules and custom rather than as a system of moral agents characterized by right and wrong.[22] The global norms of sovereignty and nonintervention made punishment, at least until Nuremberg, nearly impossible. Consequently, until well into the twentieth century the settlement of conflict, if not the rare occasion of absolute victory and unconditional surrender, was generally characterized as a settlement restoring some form of the status quo *ante bellum*.

Today when we consider *jus post bellum*, we should ask ourselves, "How do we want to end this war? Is our goal a return to the prewar order or do we want to see a new political order established and justice meted out to the aggressor?" Justice demands that there be consequences for unethical behavior. The consequences may be sanctions, occupation, loss of sovereignty, commitment to large-scale disarmament, and so forth. Such accountability to the moral law, as well as domestic and international conventions, is personal and individual— we hold people accountable for their evil acts.

By punishing wrongdoers, we do a number of things. First, we limit the wrongdoer. Punishment in effect says, "You transgressed the boundaries of morality, therefore we are going to confine you within strict boundaries (e.g., imprisonment or even death). At the same time punishment reinforces the moral order and the durability of law by "calling a spade a spade" and acting against injustice.

Furthermore, punishment may be a deterrent to other potential lawbreakers. Deterrence works for some crimes and restrains some criminals. The fear of getting caught, usually reinforced by a strong police reputation and various preventive mechanisms like surveillance cameras in obvious locations, will deter some criminal activity. Ergo, although deterrence is not a sufficient argument for punishment in *jus post bellum*, it may work in some cases. It is possible that the fear of punishment may restrain the behavior of combatants in battle (*jus in bello*), and that a track record of punishment in international relations may in the future help deter genocide and crimes against humanity in some contexts.

Finally, punishment avenges the suffering of victims. It is unlikely that retaliating against the aggressor will bring total, long-term peace of mind to victims, but, justice is often the first step toward healing. However, when no requital is possible or offered, the memory of wrong done by the aggressor will likely fester over time, often resulting in renewed hostilities. It is perfectly reasonable to expect the aggressors to pay some price for the misdeed. We want that price to be discriminating (the right people paying) and proportionate (to the damage caused).[23] Punition is a principle of justice.

Justice in Action: The Nuremberg Trials. The London Agreement of August 8, 1945 chartered the International Military Tribunal (IMT) to prosecute leaders of the German war effort. Made up of four judges from each of the four victorious Allied powers, the tribunal at Nuremberg and later Allied judgments ultimately passed twenty-five death sentences, twenty life sentences, ninety-seven lesser prison terms, and acquitted an additional thirty-five individuals.[24]

The defendants were charged on one or more of four counts: conspiracy to commit crimes, crimes against the peace (initiating aggressive war), war crimes (violating the laws of war), and crimes against humanity (genocide). For our purposes, two points are important. First, Nuremberg symbolized the rule of law and morality, however imperfectly applied, at war's end. The IMT argued that war is not ethical anarchy, and that the laws of civilization and morality apply even in wartime. Robert Jackson, the lead Allied prosecutor and a member of the U.S. Supreme Court asserted, "The wrongs which we seek to condemn and punish have been so calculated, so malignant and so devastating that civilization cannot tolerate their being ignored because it cannot survive their being repeated."[25]

Second, Nuremberg assigned individual responsibility for immoral and/or illegal behavior. Unlike the Versailles Treaty, which condemned the entire German nation, the Nuremberg principle was that individuals were personally responsible for their behavior. This principle was applied to senior leaders who had responsibility for the war effort and the Holocaust and was applied to a lesser degree to lower-ranking members of the military and government who committed crimes while "under orders." The rationale was to avoid the collective guilt associated with Versailles and thereby reconcile the German nation to Europe.[26]

In the end, 1945 approached justice—a comprehensive *jus post bellum*—in a way that went much further than the armistice of 1953. The terms not only ended the fighting, but also called to account the leadership responsible for initial aggression (*jus ad bellum*) as well as prosecuted *jus in bello* violations.[27] Nonetheless, even approximate justice of the Nuremberg and Tokyo variety fails to implement a richer notion of justice at war's end that can transcend past conflict and develop a partnership for peace among former belligerents—reconciliation.

A Just Future: Conciliation/Reconciliation

If order is the attainable and justice the possible, then conciliation is both improbable and desirable. Conciliation is future focused in that it sees former enemies as partners in a shared future. Sometimes, particularly in intrastate conflict, it is *reconciliation*—building bridges between parties that have some shared past. In international conflict it is more likely that the goal is *conciliation*, the mutual effort of both sides to overcome past hostility and reframe the relationship as one of partnership. If the fundamental goals of just war theory are to promote international security and to protect human life, then conciliation does this by ameliorating the conditions that can lead to new or renewed violence.

Christian just war theory has a theological basis for reconciliation: love. *Caritas*, or love (charity), is the notion of brotherly regard. Love calls on individuals to protect their neighbors and may result in self-defensive war. Love may motivate just punishment, the righting of wrongs, and restitution for the victim. Love calls into question our motives, restrains our behavior, and foresees a better peace approximating the ideal: the City of God.[28]

Although I believe that reconciliation based on *caritas* is important in individual human relationships and can be called on in intrastate conflicts, it is a tricky notion for international affairs.[29] The international system is based primarily on national interests, and unless interests are engaged, conciliation is unlikely at war's end. In other words, *among states common interests are the basis for conciliation.* In most conflicts, enemies have a history of tension and competition and have probably fought openly at numerous times in the past. In this scenario, a change in interests is the usual mechanism for conciliation to be possible.

Conciliation based on evolving interests is not a new idea. Rousseau and Kant both argued for a perpetual peace based, in part, on sovereigns realizing that war was not in their long-term interest.[30] However, in the real world, such relational changes usually take a long period of time (e.g., United States and Canada) and/or may require a shared threat to provide a context for shared interests (e.g., Cold War France and Germany).

The Scandinavian countries provide a case in point. Formerly a region of competition and violence, today it is difficult to imagine a more pacific set of relationships than those among the Nordic countries. What caused the conciliation of these governments? The answer is not culture, language, religion, or some formal acts of forgiveness. Rather, the balance of power struggles of the nineteenth century, first the Napoleonic wars and later the Franco-Prussian wars, created a situation of shared interests based on increasingly similar security concerns. Moreover, this process of conciliation has weathered the tests of the World Wars, the Cold War (including Finnish alignment with the Soviet Union and Swedish neutrality), and the rise of the "New Europe" (European Union).

Of course, in international life, justice might be a mechanism that helps change the sociopolitical context in such a way as to allow for a positive change in relationship. Certainly one outcome of Nuremberg was the effect the punishment of Third Reich leaders had on thawing relations between Germany and its neighbors. Acts of justice can provide vindication to the victims and provide the conditions wherein a change in the quality of relationship is possible.

However, it is more likely that the looming Soviet threat played a large role in Germany and its former adversaries coming to a shared set of strategic interests. The development of Western European institutions, including the Coal and Steel Community, atomic cooperation, NATO, and the EEC all are rooted in mutual interests and shared threats, not forgiveness and reconciliation.

Idealists argue that forgiveness and mercy is the fulcrum for conciliation in international affairs. I am skeptical that this is the case. We have almost no examples in international life of heads of state asking for forgiveness from their neighbors, and resulting acts of conciliation among states. The reasons for this are numerous, but primary among them is the multicausal nature of conflict and the recognition that states go to war because they feel that it is in their interest to do so. States are complex organisms—driven by self-interest but not without normative concerns. Consequently, we rarely observe states, except under the most unique of circumstances, to plea, "We were wrong, won't you please forgive us?"[31] Consequently, the mercy/forgiveness path to conciliation among states is improbable at best, however, conciliation is possible based on the evolution or reinterpretation of national interests.

V. CONCLUSION

In the past wars have simply ended, usually in stalemate or in a victor's peace. Although Augustine said that war was just if it was waged for self-defense, to right a wrong, or to punish evil, medieval and contemporary just war theorists have largely focused on *jus ad bellum* and *jus in bello*, excluding consideration of the post-conflict environment.

Therefore, a natural area of consideration for contemporary scholarship is *jus post bellum*—justice at war's end. Such a discussion is timely in light of the types of conflict we have seen in the past decade: ethnic and religious nationalisms, civil war, genocide enhanced by modern tools of warfare, international terrorism, and the proliferation of weapons of mass destruction.

Jus post bellum begins with the concept of order. Order is a moral principle in that it is the foundation for domestic and international security. Just war theory has historically privileged order as the practical and necessary condition for more robust scenarios of justice. *Jus post bellum* is built on the notion that order and security come first. Therefore, a war is said to end justly if it establishes a secure framework for peace between the belligerents even if deeper issues of justice and reconciliation are not resolved. Such a peace promotes international security and preserves human life, which should be the fundamental goals of a twenty-first-century just war theory.

That being said, the objectives at war's end should be richer than mere order. When possible, the parties involved should seek post-conflict justice. Such justice should hold accountable both the leaders who incited the war as well as individuals who violated the war convention in the prosecution of war. Of course, a settlement that does not provide a secure framework (order) for the peace will not be able to employ processes of justice except against its own personnel who violated the laws of armed conflict. Nevertheless, intra- and interstate post-conflict settlements are more likely to endure if they seek justice.

Finally, it is possible that in some cases conciliation is possible between those involved in the conflict. In international relations, conciliation proceeds from an environment of security and is based on shared interests. In some rare cases, justice provides a change in relationship that makes conciliation possible. Reconciliation is more likely in cases of civil war or past strife where there is a shared past that can be built upon, and a future that must be shared. (Re)conciliation should be the ultimate goal of *jus post bellum* because it changes the relationship of those involved in conflict from belligerents to partners in peace.

In sum, *jus post bellum* is essential to a comprehensive just war theory. Durable postwar settlements that promote order, justice, and when possible, reconciliation, restrain future conflicts from breaking out over unresolved disputes and old grievances. Moreover, *jus post bellum* provides a new venue for scholarship by philosophers and practitioners of politics in elucidating specific mechanisms and structures for a just and lasting peace.

NOTES

1. Michael Walzer, "The Triumph of Just War Theory," in *Arguing About War* (New Haven: Yale University Press, 2004), 18.

2. St. Thomas Aquinas, *The Summa Theologica* (New York: Benziger Bros., 1947), part II-II, question 40.

3. Vitoria, "On the American Indians," in *Vitoria: Political Writings*, ed. Anthony Pagden and Jeremy Lawrance (Cambridge: Cambridge University Press, 1991), 282–284.

4. Quoted in Davida E. Kellogg, "*Jus Post Bellum*: The Importance of War Crimes Trials," *Parameters* (Autumn 2002): 87.

5. Walzer does not claim that *Just and Unjust Wars*, third edition (New York: Basic Books, 2000), elucidates a Christian or traditional just war per-

spective. Although he references the tradition, his work is largely based on his own working out of justice-in-war claims within a Western worldview. He does not articulate a *jus post bellum*, but part 5 of his book does deal with the issues of responsibility, war crimes, and military necessity. In his discussion of the Korean Conflict, he speaks of "justice in settlements."

6. James Turner Johnson, *Morality and Contemporary Warfare* (New Haven: Yale University Press, 1999), 33. This book does devote a section (see chapter 6) to some of the intractable problems of war's end, but fails to theorize a *jus post bellum*.

7. Perhaps the best statement of this is Reinhold Niebuhr's "To Prevent the Triumph of an Intolerable Tyranny" in the *Christian Century* (December 18, 1940), reprinted in *Love and Justice: Selections from the Writings of Reinhold Niebuhr*, ed. D. B. Robertson (Louisville: Westminster John Knox Press, 1957), 28–29.

8. Walzer, *Arguing About War*, 18.

9. See Louis Sell, *Slobodan Milosevic and the Destruction of Yugoslavia* (Durham: Duke University Press, 2002) and Laura Silber and Allan Little, *Yugoslavia: Death of a Nation* (New York: Penguin, 1997); on Kosovo, see Leonard J. Cohen, *Serpent in the Bosom: The Rise and Fall of Slobodan Milosevic* (Boulder: Westview Press, 2002).

10. A recent Pulitzer prize–winning account of this is John Dower's *Embracing Defeat: Japan in the Wake of World War II* (New York: W. W. Norton, 1999).

11. Brian Orend, "Justice after War," *Ethics and International Affairs* 16/1 (Spring 2002): 45.

12. Brian Orend, *War and International Justice: A Kantian Perspective* (Waterloo, Ontario, Canada: Wilfrid Laurier University Press, 2000), 226.

13. Ibid, 232.

14. Kellogg, "*Jus Post Bellum*: The Importance of War Crimes Trials."

15. Walzer, Arguing About War, 18.

16. Walter Paterson, Thomas Clifford, and Robert Hagan also report 500,000 North Korean, 47,000 South Korean, 54,246 American, and 148,000 Chinese troops, as well as other UN forces died in the Korean Conflict. See *American Foreign Relations Since 1895: A History* (Boston: Houghton Mifflin, 2000), 272.

17. See William Stueck, *Rethinking the Korean War: A New Diplomatic and Strategic History* (Princeton: Princeton University Press, 2004); Spencer C. Tucker et al., *Encyclopedia of the Korean War: A Political, Social, and Military History* (New York: Facts on File, 2002).

18. Michael Walzer has an interesting account of the Korean War. His purpose is to discuss the "inflation of ends" (the goal of the war, at least for MacArthur, went from defending South Korea to punishing and liberating North Korea). His conclusion is that "just wars are conservative in character"

and should generally seek "a better peace," not a revised international system. Michael Walzer, *Just and Unjust Wars*, 121.

19. In addition, most just war theorists are extremely uncomfortable with the "unconditional surrender" policies that make war crimes tribunals and international judgments possible. Brian Orend argues that proportionality and discrimination make unconditional surrender impossible. Orend, *War and International Justice*, 228–230.

20. The distinction between compensation and punishment is an important one. Compensation is restitution provided to victims. The logic of restitution is that the aggressor "pays" damages to those it harmed. However, in many recent cases the war results in regime change or the destruction of the primary belligerent. For instance, after the Rwandan Patriotic Front (RPF) took over Rwanda after the 1994 genocide, the "state" was in the hands of those it had tried to exterminate just months prior. Did the state "owe" restitution to its victims? This is a major dilemma for international politics that I deal with in an unpublished essay. Also see Andrew Rigby, *Justice and Reconciliation* (Boulder: Lynne Rienner, 2001), chapters 2–3.

Contemporary compensation is usually about states (collectives) paying individuals (victims). In contrast, postwar punishment is usually focused on personal responsibility and bringing individuals to justice. In the Rwanda case, individual perpetrators stood trial for their actions. The same was true in the former Yugoslavia. This chapter focuses on such cases.

21. This point is made more than once in James Turner Johnson, "Just War, As It Was and Is," *First Things* (January 2005): 14–24.

22. James Turner Johnson, *Ideology, Reason, and the Limitation of War: Religious and Secular Concepts* (Princeton: Princeton University Press, 1974), especially chapters 3–4.

23. Orend, *War and International Justice*, 227.

24. See Eugene Davidson, *The Trial of the Germans: An Account of the Twenty-Two Defendants before the International Military Tribunal at Nuremberg* (Columbia: University of Missouri Press, 1997); Joseph E. Persico, *Nuremberg: Infamy on Trial* (New York: Penguin, 1995); Drexel A. Sprecher, *Inside the Nuremberg Trial* (Lanham: University of America Press, 1999). It should be noted that in addition to the trial of the twenty-two top Nazi leaders at Nuremberg, the Allies continued to try Nazis through 1949 under the Control Council 10 law; these numbers account for both.

25. Quoted in Sprecher, *Inside the Nuremberg Trial*, 103.

26. Andrew Rigby lists many arguments against Nuremberg: it was implemented by force at the hands of the victors, it was selective in prosecuting only the defeated, it pursued only a small percentage of those who could have reasonably been indicted, it was not a trial by one's peers, and it held individuals responsible for acts normally attributed to governments. The argument for punishment against these claims is essentially identical to the argu-

ment for *jus post bellum* advanced early in this chapter. See Andrew Rigby, *Justice and Reconciliation*, 4–5.

27. It should be noted that at least in the case of the United States, *jus in bello* considerations applied not only to the aggressor state, but also to the victim. Although it is unlikely that most violations of the war convention were brought to trial, it is telling that some American GIs were prosecuted for breaking the laws of war, mainly the killing or rape of civilians, in the European theater. See J. Robert Lilly and J. Michael Thompson "Death Penalty Cases in World War II Military Courts: Lessons Learned from North Africa and Italy," paper presented at the forty-first meeting of the Academy of Criminal Justice Sciences, March 10–13, 2004, Las Vegas, Nevada. Online at http://www.nku.edu/~thomson/ACJS04.pdf.

28. Paul Ramsey, *War and the Christian Conscience*, second edition (Durham: Duke University Press, 1985), chapter 27, especially page 203; Augustine, *The City of God* (Cambridge: Cambridge University Press, 1994).

29. There is a growing literature on domestic reconciliation, forgiveness, and intrastate change. For examples see A. Boraine et al., *Dealing with the Past: Truth and Reconciliation in South Africa* (Cape Town: IDASA, 1994); Brian Frost, *The Politics of Peace* (London: Darton, Longman, and Todd, 1991); Neil J. Kritz, ed., *Transitional Justice: How Emerging Democracies Reckon with Former Regimes*, vol. 2 (Washington, DC: U.S. Institute of Peace, 1995); Martha Minow, *Between Vengeance and Forgiveness* (Boston: Beacon Press, 1998).

30. Immanuel Kant, *Perpetual Peace and Other Essays*, trans. T. Humphrey (Indianapolis: Hackett, 1983); Jean Jacques Rousseau, *"The Social Contract" and Other Later Political Writings*, ed. Victor Gourevitch (Cambridge: Cambridge University Press, 1997).

31. Interestingly, we can observe countries that experience significant regime change (e.g., Latin America and Eastern Europe in the early 1990s) make public statements breaking with the past, but we do not see these countries ask for forgiveness or offer restitution to neighbors they have threatened or harmed.

CHAPTER 3

Just War Theory and U.S. Military Hegemony

Harry van der Linden

The military strength of the United States is unmatched and its political leadership is committed to maintaining this position of military dominance or hegemony. The purpose of U.S. military hegemony is deeply contested. My own view is that economic interests significantly motivate it, but the issue need not be settled in order to explore— and discuss the significance of—this chapter's main question: Does just war theory (JWT) offer adequate guidelines for adversaries of the United States when confronted with its overwhelming military might, especially in cases where its exercise of force is morally questionable?[1]

I. THE PROBLEM OF FACING MILITARY HEGEMONY

In *Hegemony or Survival: America's Quest for Global Dominance,* Noam Chomsky argues that JWT has recently "enjoyed a revival" and that it can readily be seen that the revival lacks moral credibility because the theorists behind it commit the error of ignoring and violating the principle of universality as a basic requirement of moral reasoning.[2] On his account, the error is typical of defenders of America's hegemonic ambitions and involves the failure to "apply to ourselves the same standards we apply to others."[3] Chomsky sees the error illustrated in how just war theorists defended the bombing of Afghanistan in response to 9/11. The bombing was almost unanimously viewed as a self-defensive act on the ground that the Taliban regime protected Al Qaeda, but no just war theorist raised the issue that by the same token Nicaragua, for example, would have been justified in the 1980s to bomb Washington and New York (say, in the manner that Kabul or Kandahar were bombed by the United States in 2001) since the United States mined its harbors and supported the terrorist Contras. Chomsky provides a few other similar examples involving Cuba, Haiti, and Sudan, and concludes that, since scenarios of initiating armed force against the United States on the same JWT terms that the United States uses to justify its acts of war are not even contemplated by just war thinkers, "just war pronouncements cannot be taken seriously."[4]

Chomsky portrays JWT basically as a tool of legitimizing the pursuit of American political and economic hegemony through military means, neglecting that at least some just war theorists raised critical questions concerning the necessity and, especially, the execution of the Gulf War, the intervention in Kosovo, and the Afghanistan War. Certainly, many just war theorists were opposed to the Iraq War of 2003, underlining that JWT functions less as a theory supportive of the status quo than Chomsky suggests. Still, his insistence that just war theorists must apply the principle of universality is a valuable directive for preventing facile justifications of the use of American military force. His analysis also has the merit of bringing into focus that just war theorists have paid very little attention to the significance of JWT for assessing and guiding the conduct of the countries in the South in response to American military actions. JWT should be able to guide in a meaningful fashion the deliberations and choices of action of all parties in an emerging conflict, assuming that each party is open to rational discourse. It is not clear, however, that JWT is satisfactory in this regard for most countries in the South when they are confronted with a possible military conflict with the United States alone or with an attack of military forces under its leadership.

Consider again the mining of Nicaragua's harbors in 1984 as part of the Reagan administration's attempt to overthrow the Sandinista government. It was an act of aggression, providing Nicaragua with a good ground for holding that it had a just cause to respond militarily. Nicaragua tried to solve its dispute with the United States through the International Court of Justice, but the United States ignored the court's decision that it had wrongly used force against another sovereign state and interfered in its internal affairs. A military attack by Nicaragua on the United States, then, would have plausibly satisfied the JWT principle of last resort, but, obviously, would have been foolish, for it would have led the United States to inflict even greater devastation on Nicaragua than the considerable harm that it already had inflicted. War would have violated the *jus ad bellum* principle of macro-proportionality. The principle demands that the anticipated goods of war are proportionate to its expected evils. How this principle is to be further explicated is a matter of controversy, but it seems to demand at the very least that the political leadership of a country should not initiate a war when the expected harms of the war to its own people far outweigh its anticipated benefits.[5] In the Nicaraguan case, the benefits of war, such as responding to aggression and seeking to maintain international law, would have been small and rather intangible as compared to its very concrete and huge harms of death, injury, suffering, and destruction of property. War against the United States also would have violated the principle of reasonable chance of success, for the probability of military victory and a restoration of justice by force was nil. In short, JWT shows it would have been wrong for Nicaragua to take self-defensive military action against the United States.

We can generalize this result toward most countries in the South because of America's global military dominance, as reflected in its unparalleled advantages in warfare technologies, its military budget approximating the military expenditures of the rest of the world, and its network of military bases across the globe.[6] What adds to U.S. military hegemony is that its "virtual warfare" capabilities enable it to fight wars with relatively low numbers of casualties, while as the largest economy in the world it can fight wars and pursue military buildup without imposing a great material burden on the majority of its citizens—even with the ongoing wars in Afghanistan and Iraq the American military budget is still below 5 percent of the GDP. Accordingly, JWT implies that it would be wrong for most countries in the South to respond militarily to the aggressive actions of the United States or of a coalition of forces led by the United States. Even if the United States were to seek to occupy a militarily much weaker state without a sufficient just cause, as by many JWT accounts happened in Iraq, the conclusion that JWT would disapprove of a military response by the attacked nation would still follow. This is so because the principles of macro-proportionality and reasonable chance of success count against the weaker army fighting if defeat is clearly inevitable, the human and material costs are very high, and war has basically only the benefit of standing up for justice and rights.

The conclusion that most countries of the South should not wage wars with the United States follows irrespective of whether their cause is largely just or unjust, but it is only when JWT prohibits these countries from responding militarily to U.S. (led) aggression that the conclusion is counterintuitive. Let me call the conclusion in this form the no military action (NMA) thesis. The nuclear powers in the South constitute a special case and I am not assuming that they fall under the thesis. In theory, a similar thesis can be articulated concerning many (nonnuclear) countries in the North, but it has no real practical relevance considering current political alliances. (The case of Kosovo was an exception.)

My aim here is to examine the tenability and significance of the NMA thesis. In the next two sections, I will rebut two possible attempts to show that JWT in fact permits weak countries in the South to fight wars against the United States if justice is on their side. In the fourth section, I will address the argument that the NMA thesis lacks practical significance because American military hegemony is a benign force aiming only at the good of humanity. In the final two sections, I will argue that the NMA thesis shows that JWT is in need of revision and I will offer some suggestions in this direction.

II. FIGHTING AGAINST ALL ODDS

Not all just war theorists give great weight to the principles of macro-proportionality and reasonable chance of success. The reason is that these principles require calculations of outcomes that are difficult to make since wars often take surprising turns and have unanticipated consequences. The NMA thesis is based on the contested principles, and so, by denying their importance, the thesis itself is put into question. Furthermore, James Turner Johnson has argued that macro-proportionality and reasonable chance of success are only "prudential criteria" with a lower moral priority than the "deontological norms" of just cause, legitimate authority, and right intention. On his account, one may fight a war in violation of the prudential norms if one's deontological case is compelling. He writes: "Extreme cases may exist in which the only moral course is to take action that is imprudent; examples of such action include the resistance to the invading German forces by the Poles, the Dutch, and the Belgians at the start of World War II."[7]

In my view, it is correct that resort to armed force may be morally right in the face of certain defeat and no hope of a good outcome, but this does not mean that "prudential" norms may be violated. The Warsaw Ghetto Uprising in 1943 provides a good example of a morally courageous struggle doomed to failure, a predicament that was captured movingly by Arie Wilner, one of the founders of the Jewish Fighting Organization, at the onset of the uprising: "Not one of us will leave here alive. We are fighting not to save our lives but for human dignity."[8] Similarly, the organizers of the uprising concluded their initial call to resist any further deportations by the Nazis with the slogan, "Let everyone be ready to die like a man!"[9] But the uprising was not "imprudent." In their situation there was no question left of how to best protect the community and the lives of Polish Jews in the long run: it was clear to the ghetto fighters that the Germans were intent on exterminating the Jewish people and that they had no real way of stopping this. Fighting to death appeared as an option of dignity, as a way of refusing to be further degraded, and, ultimately, each individual had to make the choice for him or herself. Politicians, on the contrary, have no right to authorize war and demand conscripted soldiers to risk their lives in large numbers when it is apparent that armed resistance cannot save political independence, would lead to many more civilian deaths and much greater property destruction than would surrender, while it also would contribute little or nothing to the ultimate defeat of the enemy. The costs of war and the chance of success are not matters of "prudence," as Johnson suggests, but rather important moral concerns for politicians in light of their duty to protect the community and the rights of all its members. Even if soldiers would be prepared to sacrifice their lives with no real prospect of victory and opt for this in a reflective manner rather than, say, in a state of induced patriotic fervor, this choice would still be wrong if it would lead to great avoidable harm to those they must seek to protect.

No doubt, calculations of costs and chance of success are indeed difficult to make, and it would be an error to condemn small countries such as Holland for opting to fight the Germans and argue that the only right course of action was to surrender without significant military resistance in the first place, as was done by Denmark. What made the calculations especially difficult was that Nazi Germany was fighting on many fronts and that surrender by one country had an impact on the fate of Allied countries and the global struggle against fascism. But recognizing the uncertainty of such calculations does not mean that one may ignore them; indeed, the Dutch surrendered and concluded that the costs of continuing war became too high after the

Germans indiscriminately bombed Rotterdam and threatened to do the same to other Dutch cities.

The upshot is that the NMA thesis still stands, for applying the "prudential" norms to military conflicts between the United States and its potential adversaries in the South does not pose doubts of outcome and moral dilemmas similar to the ones faced by the small countries of Europe in the Second World War. The certainty of defeat for most countries in the South is much more definite because they are not united in a common struggle and they are faced with a much greater asymmetry of military capabilities.[10] Moreover, risking numerous civilian and combatant lives to fight off defeat is morally much more difficult to defend because the price of military inaction is not remotely as grim for both the surrendering country and the world at large.

III. WAGING WAR IN A SUPREME EMERGENCY SITUATION

The second way to contest the NMA thesis rests on the "supreme emergency" doctrine. Michael Walzer argues that when a country at war is faced with a supreme emergency or imminent catastrophe it may justifiably set aside the rules of just war conduct—notably, the principle of noncombatant immunity—if doing so would be truly necessary to avert the threat.[11] The doctrine is widely accepted and by its logic weaker states would have the option, or even the duty, of fighting indiscriminately against the United States, assuming that they would be in a supreme emergency situation and that such tactics would greatly raise their chances of avoiding the threat.

In response, two questions need to be addressed: Is the supreme emergency doctrine actually convincing? And, does it apply to the wars that the United States might fight against countries of the South?

In regard to the first question, my own moral intuition is that we must be absolutists with respect to noncombatant immunity because wars fought in accordance with this principle (as commonly interpreted) already push the limits of what rightfully may be done to innocent human beings. Nonetheless, I do not wish to deny that the emergency doctrine has some prima facie moral plausibility once strong constraints are placed on its applicability so as to prevent that almost any war may lead to a bracketing of the laws of war. Henry Shue argues that we can find in Walzer three types of threats that can create a supreme emergency condition, the general threat of the rule of barbarism replacing the rule of law, as would have occurred if the Nazis had triumphed, and the more specific threats of the extermination or enslavement of a people and the destruction of a community and its mode of life. Shue accepts only the first two threats as potential supreme emergencies, rightly noting that once the third type of threat is counted the setting aside of the war convention would become the rule rather than a true exception.[12] In my view, we can further improve the emergency doctrine by combining the first two threats into one definition with a more precise (and, presumably, also in practice more narrow) scope: a country is faced with a supreme emergency when its imminent defeat will lead to the extermination or enslavement of its own people *or* the massive killing or enslavement of other populations. It is further important to stipulate that the laws of war may be violated only if there are solid grounds for believing that this will be effective and absolutely necessary for preventing a supreme emergency threat from materializing. The harm inflicted by indiscriminate warfare should also not be disproportionate to the harm one seeks to avoid. Incorporating the constraints, it is easy to construct situations in which the emergency doctrine appears as morally plausible, if not necessarily morally compelling. It seems, for example, morally defensible for a wrongly attacked country to aim at the widespread killing of enemy civilians, say, through a bombing of a city, if this would be the only way to prevent the genocide of its own civilians by the ruthless enemy. What proponents of the doctrine typically neglect, however, is that hypothetical scenarios are not enough to make their case. It needs to be shown on the basis of actual historical examples that there is genuine need for the doctrine, for its acceptance by states surely carries with it the price that it will be abused at great human costs.

Remarkably, the only example provided by Walzer (and other defenders of the emergency doctrine) is the British bombing of German cities during the early years of the Second World War.[13] One problem with the example is that it is far from obvious that the British were ever in a supreme emergency situation (as I have defined it). Their defeat by Germany would not have led to their physical annihilation, and it is debatable that they were in a position to claim that they were the only effective barrier left against the unleashing of the Nazi's genocidal plans. Another problem is that it is doubtful that the British believed, or had good reasons to believe, that terror bombing was essential to avoiding defeat. Walzer correctly notes that the British from the onset of the war were prepared to resort to terror bombing so as to break German civilian morale, but he wrongly argues that this strategy was adopted during 1940–1941 with the intent of avoiding defeat by the Nazis. In fact, as Robert A. Pape has shown, the main British air strategy during this time was first to avert the threat of a German invasion by attacking their airfields, plane factories, ports, and so forth, and then to reduce German fighting capacity by bombing transport and oil supplies. To be sure, some terror bombings took place (that were legitimated as reprisals), but it was not until mid-1941, when the British began to bomb railroad yards in city centers at night to prevent huge losses of their planes and knew that their bombs often missed their targets, that undermining civilian morale became an additional stated objective.[14] Terror bombing became the main policy in February 1942 and remained so until the end of the war.[15] At this juncture, however, the issue was to hasten victory rather than avoid defeat. Ironically, the campaign to shorten the war by breaking German morale through terror bombing may actually have lengthened it by leaving many vital industries, typically located outside city centers, untouched.[16] British leaders also should have been more skeptical of the campaign's aim in light of the fact that the morale of their own civilian population had not been weakened by the terror bombing of the Luftwaffe in 1940–1941.[17]

On Walzer's own account, most German civilians were killed by terror bombing after a supreme emergency ceased to exist—some time during the first half of 1942.[18] He further grants that the terror bombing by the British set a bad precedent for the incendiary bombing of Japanese cities and facilitated the decision to drop the atomic bombs on Hiroshima and Nagasaki.[19] What Walzer fails to fully appreciate, though, is that these facts count heavily against his supreme emergency doctrine, for they illustrate that once the rules of war are set aside as a matter of policy in a given conflict it is improbable that they will be restored at a later time during the same conflict. Of course, this is an abuse of Walzer's doctrine, but in arguing for the doctrine one must take into account that such abuses are bound to occur. Add to this that governments are predisposed to declare all sorts of emergencies where none exist so that they can break the rules if it is in their interest to do so, and it is clear that Walzer has not made a historical case for the supreme emergency doctrine strong enough to carry the burden of abuse that its general adoption invites.[20] In practice, then, non-absolutists with regard to the rules of war should on grounds of long-term consequences alone join moral absolutists in rejecting emergency exemptions to just war conduct rules.

What makes Walzer's claim that the British were justified in taking supreme emergency measures at the outset somewhat plausible is that the Nazi's military strength, even though superior, was sufficiently close to that of Britain to hold that such measures conceivably could make the difference between defeat and setting the stage for eventual victory. The same cannot be said at all of wars covered by the NMA thesis. In recent American wars, the opponents of the United States have violated the rules of war in rather minor and ineffective ways by using such tactics as surrounding bombing targets with civilians and hiding their forces behind human shields. The acts might have been partly motivated by the hope that public opinion would turn against the United States if it killed the innocent.[21] At any rate, the United States is aware of the power of public opinion and such acts can at most modify the military strategy of the United States and somewhat delay its victory. More effective scenarios are conceivable, such as weaker states engaging in terrorist acts against American civilians and using biological or chemical weapons against U.S. soldiers and civilians, but no political leaders guided by JWT, and thus motivated by seeking to protect their communities from American aggression, would opt for such scenarios. There is little doubt that the United States would in response unleash its full arsenal of destruction, including perhaps even its nuclear weapons, if the enemy would resort to indiscriminate fighting on a very large scale.[22] To run such risks would be morally indefensible, the more so since the United States has no intent of seeking to destroy or enslave the people of the countries it attacks militarily.

This points to a final reason for rejecting the emergency doctrine argument against the NMA thesis: the doctrine does not apply to the United States because its adversaries do not face a supreme emergency situation. Here it might be objected that even though the United States does not seek to exterminate enemy civilians on a wide scale, the long-term results of its victories might still be a great number of civilian deaths in the defeated countries, adding up to a supreme emergency. More specifically, it might be argued that the United States might cause many civilian deaths in the long run by destroying the economic infrastructure of a country, as happened after the Gulf War to the Iraqi people, a humanitarian catastrophe that was greatly worsened by the continued economic sanctions. The objection in this form does not succeed, for the harm here can be avoided by quick surrender or by not fighting in the first place (as, I have argued, JWT recommends). Supreme emergencies, on the contrary, involve unavoidable threats. A more challenging variant of the objection is that the very loss of political independence may lead to long-term harms so great that countries facing this prospect might conclude that they are in a supreme emergency. Consider, for example, that the United States would force the defeated country to undergo economic liberalization leading to greatly increased economic inequality and fewer public services available to the poor. The outcome might be higher infant mortality rates and a reduced life expectancy among the poor. Are such threats not great enough to fall under the supreme emergency doctrine? In my view, it would be a mistake to ignore or underestimate such threats, even though they might not add up to the scale of catastrophe that defines a supreme emergency. However, the possible threats posed by losing political (and economic) independence are a long-term matter, leaving a variety of options open to trying to avert the threats so that it would be implausible to claim with any real confidence that only a war fought in violation of the rules of war would possibly succeed in avoiding the threats. In other words, these kinds of threats are not sufficiently imminent to count as true emergencies, and so they should not be included in the supreme emergency doctrine.

IV. MILITARY HEGEMONY FOR HUMANITY

In the introduction to the National Security Strategy of 2002, George W. Bush states: "Today, the United States enjoys a position of unparalleled military strength and great economic and political influence. In keeping with our heritage and principles, we do not use our strength to press for unilateral advantage. We seek instead to create a balance of power that favors human freedom: conditions in which all nations and all societies can choose for themselves the rewards and challenges of political and economic liberty." Here, in a rather toned down manner, an idea is expressed that is deeply embedded in American political culture and popular belief: the United States resorts to military force only for the good of humanity. Thus phrased, the idea is ambiguous. If we take it to mean that the United States engages in wars only when it is a victim of aggression, then the NMA thesis would be a mere theoretical possibility, not a practical dilemma that countries in the South may have to face. The historical record heavily counts against America's "goodness" in this regard. A somewhat more credible version is that the United States in its wars always seeks in the long run to promote freedom, democracy, and justice for defeated countries rather than aim at its own "unilateral advantage." But this version does not invalidate the practical relevance of the NMA thesis. JWT holds that war is only justifiable in order to right a serious wrong, not to bring about some good, and so the United States may in fact commit an act of aggression against a country in the South even if its overall aims are merely to promote democracy and other ideals in the country.[23] Other countries may rightfully refuse the good, and they may even have solid reasons for doing so because the good itself, notably, the model of economic development that the United States seeks to promote, is highly contested, a fact concerning which the National Security Strategy of 2002 shows its blindness by declaring (in the introduction) that recent history has shown that there is only "a single sustainable model of national success: freedom, democracy, and free enterprise." Moreover, all too often material or narrow national interests are to be found behind lofty words to the effect that the aim of intervention is to promote political and economic ideals, and the forceful imposition of such ideals further weakens their credibility in the eyes of those who are supposed to embrace them.

The notion that America's wars are (almost) always on the right side of history presumes that the United States has a privileged position with regard to discovering where justice is to be found in international conflict. The recent popular view that America as the sole remaining superpower should play "international sheriff" or "global cop" rests on a similar assumption.[24] The world community has not appointed the United States to this role; in fact, most countries oppose that the United States acts like a global cop, but many Americans still view it as legitimate because they think that the global cop invariably only goes after the "outlaws." But how do we know that the global cop is not at times incompetent or even a rogue cop? After all, in most wars both parties fight in good faith and their people believe in the justice of their cause. Democratic debate and decision making in one's country are conducive to transcending subjective justice, but they do not suffice. In times of war preparation, opposition is typically stifled and the national media tend to embrace the prevailing sentiments and interests. A discourse beyond the national community is needed to arrive at a convincing assessment of where objectively the balance of justice is to be found in a violent conflict.[25] The formation of the United Nations may be seen as an attempt to address the problem of distorted perspectives within national communities by placing the authorization of the resort to force in the hands of the Security Council except in the case of strict, that is, reactive, self-defense. The Security Council permits dialogic interaction conducive to arriving at objective justice, even though a larger and more democratic Security Council less beholden to the interests of its permanent members would be much better suited for this purpose. The United States nonetheless holds that it can safely ignore or sidestep opinion formation in the United Nations if the decision does not go its way, thus assuming that it has privileged access to objective justice. It is hard to tell to what extent U.S. political leadership believes in its own moral infallibility, but the prevalence of the notion among the American public enables the United States to "act alone" without incurring vehement protest by most of its citizens. Even the broadest forum, world public opinion, can be safely ignored, as was illustrated by how the United States went to war against Iraq notwithstanding unprecedented and persistent protest across the world, involving a march of more than ten million people on February 15, 2003, alone. Clearly, the more the United States embraces such unilateralist moral certainty the more the NMA thesis becomes practically relevant.[26]

V. NONCONVENTIONAL RESPONSES TO HEGEMONIC AGGRESSION

Granted that JWT demands that most countries in the South do not respond militarily to U.S. aggression, it does not follow that JWT requires an unbearable political quietism and submission to aggression. Consider the worst case scenario of an unjust occupation. After surrender, JWT might quite well approve of guerila or insurgent warfare against the American occupiers because this warfare has a greater chance of success than conventional war by forcing the American military to fight without all its huge technological advantages. JWT insists that nonconventional fighters respect noncombatant immunity, but this may actually help to sustain popular support crucial for success. American casualties may mount in a well-organized popular violent resistance and the conflict may be drawn out over many years, making compromise and even withdrawal attractive for the United States. Widespread nonviolent resistance may lead to a similar outcome, but such resistance is more difficult to realize because it presupposes a more highly motivated, well-organized, and deeply united population. Also, governments generally do not prepare their people for such resistance because, unlike the creation of armed forces, it weakens their hold on power.[27]

In my view, the nonconventional options outlined thus far are the only options—other than protest and appeals to the international community to condemn U.S. aggression—that are compatible with JWT. I also think that they are the only morally defensible ones. It must be acknowledged, though, that morality (JWT) here exacts a great price: it demands that countries faced with hegemonic aggression surrender their sovereignty and then engage in a long struggle to regain it. Or, in the case of hegemonic acts of war rather than full-scale war, violations of sovereignty are to be tolerated without any resort to force. Accordingly, it is not surprising that an increasing number of countries in the South seek nuclear weapons, for these weapons seem to be the only effective deterrence against hegemonic aggression. Surely, possession of nuclear weapons greatly reduces the chance of conventional military conflict with the United States. It also enables an adversary of the United States to respond in limited fashion to an American military act of aggression because both parties have an interest in avoiding escalation that may lead to the use of nuclear weapons. U.S. national security policy recognizes that nuclear weapons are sought in order "to overcome our nation's advantage in conventional forces," but the policy is blind with regard to the possibility that fear, justified or not, of U.S. aggression might be an issue. Instead, the weapons are sought "to deter us [America] from responding to aggression against our friends and allies in regions of vital interest."[28] Similarly, the development of chemical and biological weapons by some countries in the South seems partly motivated by U.S. military hegemony, for even though such weapons cannot really prevent American military action, let alone meet it successfully, their existence may make U.S. leadership a bit more hesitant to opt for it. By the same token, it is not surprising that some countries in the South support or tolerate terrorist groups that seek to strike at American hegemony wherever they might be able to do so. The overall result is a vicious circle in that the National Security Strategy of 2002 views any challenge to American military hegemony anywhere as a reason to further expand its military presence across the globe and even into outer space.

VI. REVISING JUST WAR THEORY

In sharp contrast to Chomsky's assessment, Walzer has recently argued that JWT since the Vietnam War has gradually become a real limiting constraint on how the United States decides to go to war and executes war. He writes: "The triumph of just war theory is clear enough; it is amazing how readily military spokesmen during the Kosovo and Afghanistan wars used its categories, telling a causal story that justified the war and providing accounts of the battles that emphasized the restraint with which they were being fought."[29] Walzer holds that two factors account for JWT's great success: the Vietnam War taught the military that fighting with moral constraint is important for gaining the local civilian support needed for ultimate victory, while the growing impact of the media requires that violations of the laws of war be avoided so as not to arouse opposition to American wars across the globe and especially at home. As he puts it, today "the whole world is watching, [and] war has to be different in these circumstances."[30]

While Chomsky may be faulted for claiming that just war pronouncements lack any credibility, Walzer errs in overstating the degree to which U.S. leadership has been guided by JWT norms and has acted in accordance with them. The utter devastation inflicted on Iraq during and after the Gulf War belies, for example, the rosy picture he paints. Moreover, he fails to address that the U.S. military restricts media access and that the global media tend to underreport in the first place events that poorly reflect on American political and economic interests.[31] It may also be noted that more recently the Pentagon has engaged in "perception management" of the ongoing conflicts in Afghanistan and Iraq, creating, for example, public misunderstandings about the scope and nature of civilian casualties, and thus reducing the possibility of informed moral assessments of such conflicts.[32] Still, Walzer, to his merit, warns that just war theorists must always remain on their guard and not leave just war thinking up to politicians and the military alone. Indeed, Walzer himself argued shortly after his remarks on the great success of JWT that the United States had wrongly started the 2003 Iraq War.[33]

Walzer's more important error is that he proclaims a "triumph" of JWT without much reflection on the significance of JWT for countries other than the United States. He mentions in passing that all Western counties have made "justice" part of their military decision making, but neglects to assess the merits of JWT from the perspective of those who militarily face the United States and its closest allies.[34] The more universalistic approach, as exemplified by the argument for the NMA thesis, suggests a serious credibility problem for JWT. A minor difficulty is that it is clearly in America's military advantage to insist that especially *jus in bello* standards are upheld by all. "Dirty" fighting by America's opponents does not change the balance of power, but it makes U.S. victory more costly, and so weaker countries in the South may look with some skepticism at the United States claim that wars are to be fought on the moral high ground. The major difficulty is that JWT demands of most countries in the South the high price of surrendering to U.S. aggression. The demand, I think, is morally correct, but has little force as long as JWT does not make America's very pursuit of military hegemony a central critical concern. In other words, it is not enough that JWT would condemn individual U.S. (-led) aggressive wars or acts of war; rather, a credible JWT must at least make the very fact that we live in a unipolar military world part of the application of *jus ad bellum* norms whenever the issue is one of deciding whether the United States may rightfully resort to force.

In support of this claim, consider how military hegemony affects the norm of macro-proportionality. Conventional wars fought by the United States against weaker states in the South tend to further strengthen its military hegemony. Victory likely means an expansion of America's global network of military bases, while it also adds to the perception that its military might is irresistible—a perception that the United States deliberately seeks to strengthen, as shown by the fact that the United States widely proclaimed that it would launch a "shock and awe" campaign against Iraq.[35] Moreover, war is a crucial testing ground for new weapons, and so each war contributes to increasing American technological military superiority. We have seen that the costs of strengthened U.S. military hegemony are the proliferation of nuclear weapons, increased support for global terrorism, and the spread of chemical and biological weapons. These costs are more likely to emerge in response to aggressive wars by the United States, but since strengthened hegemony also occurs as a result of a just war and may be used to more effectively fight subsequent unjust wars, the costs should be considered in assessing any U.S. war decision. Accordingly, the norm of macro-proportionality should take into account the costs of hegemony whenever the issue is American resort to force. These costs do not preclude the use of American force for a just cause, such as a humanitarian rescue operation, but even in such a situation the costs make it preferable (other things being equal) that a military force other than the U.S. military pursues the task.[36]

Military hegemony also impacts the application of the norm of legitimate authority. We have noted that collective international deliberation and decision making is important in order to transcend subjective justice. This constitutes a moral ground for holding that, except in the case of strict self-defense, the legitimate authority to decide war is to be placed in some representative collective body rather than in national governments. Of course, international law requires this, but the moral issue remains pertinent in light of the track record of the UN Security Council. The moral case for a collective authority becomes even more compelling once we are dealing with the United States as military hegemon. The more the United States moves toward monopolizing the instruments of war the greater the need to subject its military force to collective control. A global cop must be supervised by a global community. JWT fails when it applies a notion of legitimate authority suitable for a Westphalian world of equal powers to a unipolar world. The problem will become still more acute if the U.S. Space Command succeeds in its self-described task of "dominating the space dimension of military operations to protect U.S. interests and investment."[37] Space weapons will make it even more futile for most nations to respond militarily to the United States and will even further reduce the human costs for America to engage in acts of war. Here Michael Ignatieff's concern, expressed in response to the fact that the successful "virtual war" against Serbia had no NATO combat fatalities, is pertinent: "If war in the future is sold to voters with the promise of impunity they may be tempted to throw caution to the winds. If military action is cost-free, what democratic restraints will remain on the resort to force?"[38] The answer seems that too few restraints will remain in place, especially if space weapons are used so that American soldiers do not even have to leave their bases to fight their battles. An additional concern is that the development of high-tech weapons as well as their continuous replacement serves the economic interests of many people in the United States. The solution is for JWT to insist that the authorization of America's wars is the world's concern.

Other *jus ad bellum* norms should be revised along similar lines. Considering the economic interests driving U.S. military hegemony the bar must be raised for what counts as a last resort. Another round of diplomatic negotiations might be required when we know that some of the parties engaged in the negotiations stand to gain financially from the impending armed conflict, say with additional mediators and negotiators who do not have a similar financial stake in the war. Or, we might demand a higher level of proof that nonmilitary alternatives (e.g., limited economic sanctions) are not going to be effective in containing a growing injustice or an act of aggression. Likewise, on the assumption that "success" in the norm of "reasonable chance of success" norms means lasting peace and stability rather than mere victory, it follows that it is more difficult for the United States to satisfy the norm due to the adverse impact of increased military hegemony.

But perhaps such revised applications of *jus ad bellum* norms are not enough to make JWT fully credible in light of the NMA thesis. What might be required is that just war theorists seek to develop criteria of what counts as just preparation for the possibility of war (armed conflict) and articulate how violation of these criteria impacts the *jus ad bellum* decision. These criteria may include whether the actual amount of military spending accords with its purpose of protection against aggression and massive human rights violations, whether there is a reasonable balance between military and nonmilitary spending on seeking to meet security threats, and whether military research and development is subject to democratic control and focused on seeking to reduce the probability of conflict.[39] On the assumption that the United States would fail such criteria due to its pursuit of military hegemony,[40] it would follow that the United States would be in violation of "just preparedness" and thus would be in a much more difficult position to satisfy the *jus ad bellum* decision.

More far-reaching, it might be necessary for the credibility of JWT to subsume just war thinking under a vision of how to create a peaceful global order. In a way, this was the intent of the United Nations, as reflected in the opening statement of its Charter that it aims "to save succeeding generations from the scourge of war." Even more visionary, Immanuel Kant sought to formulate a theory of how to abolish war, proposing such measures as doing away with standing armies and international credit for war preparation. Yet, he held that wars can (temporarily, at least) still rightfully be fought if they keep the goal of "perpetual peace" in view.[41] This is not the place to try to outline a theory of peace suitable for our own time and predicament. It is clear, however, that America's relentless pursuit of military dominance across the globe and into space runs counter to any conceivable way of realizing a peaceful world and so once JWT is subsumed under an adequate theory of peace we would have to conclude that few, if any, wars of the United States as military hegemon would be justified.

NOTES

1. I would like to thank Michael Brough, Milton Fisk, and John Lango for their detailed comments on this chapter. An earlier version was presented on April 29, 2005, at a session of the Concerned Philosophers for Peace at the Central Division meeting of the American Philosophical Association. I would like to thank the commentator, Duane Cady, for his engaging criticisms. Some of the main ideas of this chapter were first presented at the Sixth Biennial Conference of the Radical Philosophy Association at Howard University, November 4–7, 2004. I would like to thank the audience for its supportive feedback.

2. Chomsky, *Hegemony or Survival: America's Quest for Global Dominance* (New York: Metropolitan Books, 2002), 198.

3. Ibid., 187.

4. Ibid., 202.

5. Controversies include whether the common interpretation of the principle as demanding that the goods of war outweigh its evils is too restrictive, which specific goods and evils are to be counted, and whether partiality may play a role in weighing goods and evils. See Thomas Hurka, "Proportionality in the Morality of War," *Philosophy and Public Affairs* 33 (2005): 34–66. In my estimate, a wide variety of interpretations will accord with my minimal demand stated here.

6. See http://www.globalissues.org/Geopolitics/ArmsTrade/Spending.asp. The United States and its closest allies spend more than two-thirds of the global military expenditure. More than 80 percent of all countries have a military budget less than 1 percent of the U.S. military budget. What illustrates U.S. global military presence is that the Department of Defense owns or leases 902 sites in 46 foreign countries. See Department of Defense, 2004 Base Structure Report, at http://www.defenselink.mil/pubs/20040910_2004BaseStructure Report.pdf.

7. Johnson, *Morality and Contemporary Warfare* (New Haven: Yale University Press, 1999), 43.

8. Cited in Ronald Beiner, "Hannah Arendt on Judging," in Hannah Arendt, *Lectures on Kant's Political Philosophy*, ed. Ronald Beiner (Chicago: University of Chicago Press, 1982), 127. Beiner cites Wilner's words from an article by Leopold Unger in *International Herald Tribune* (December 1942). See also my *Kantian Ethics and Socialism* (Indianapolis: Hackett, 1988), 122–123, where I argue that the Warsaw Ghetto struggle upheld Kantian dignity.

9. See "Call to Resistance in the Warsaw Ghetto," from the Yad Vashem, reprinted at http://www.jewishvirtuallibrary.org/jsource/Holocaust/call.html. The initial call for resistance was launched in January 1943; the main armed struggle began in April and ended in May.

10. Due to its political, economic, and military dominance, it is much easier for the United States (especially, in collaboration with its allies) to prevent effective military cooperation between countries of the South than for these countries to overcome the cultural, economic, and political obstacles standing in the way of a united front. Significant military cooperation between Southern countries would weaken the NMA thesis, but since this is unlikely to occur I will not explore its theoretical significance here.

11. Walzer, *Just and Unjust Wars: A Moral Argument with Historical Illustrations* (New York: Basic Books, 1977), chapter 16. See also his essay "Emergency Ethics," 1988, reprinted in *Arguing About War* (New Haven: Yale University Press, 2004), chapter 3. The supreme emergency doctrine illustrates the need for "temporalizing" just war principles, as this idea is explained by John Lango in chapter 4.

12. See Shue, "Liberalism: The Impossibility of Justifying Weapons of Mass Destruction," in *Ethics and Weapons of Mass Destruction: Religious and Secular Perspectives*, ed. Sohail H. Hashmi and Steven P. Lee (Cambridge: Cambridge University Press, 2004), chapter 7, 145–154.

13. In *Just and Unjust Wars*, Walzer claims that the U.S. nuclear policy of mutual assured destruction (MAD) has made "supreme emergency [into] a permanent condition" (274). It would be an error to view the MAD policy as a second historical example of the emergency doctrine, for, as Shue argues, Walzer here distorts his own original supreme emergency doctrine. Among other reasons, this is so because neither during the Cold War nor at present is it true that we can only prevent our physical annihilation by threatening to obliterate tens of millions of people by the use of nuclear weapons. Walzer more or less grants the criticism in his response to Shue in *Ethics and Weapons of Mass Destruction*. See 155–158 and 163–164, respectively.

14. Pape, *Bombing to Win: Air Power and Coercion in War* (Ithaca: Cornell University Press, 1996), 267–268 and 269 n. 37.

15. The following data reflect the change in policy: In 1940, the RAF dropped 1 percent of its bombs on towns; it was 39 percent in 1941, and 74 percent in 1942. The number of square miles of destroyed urban areas in Germany's major cities was minimal prior to 1942 and doubled every year thereafter. See ibid., pages 268 and 271–272. Between October 1940 and February 1942 the RAF killed a few thousand German civilians, less than 1 percent of the eventual death toll. See Hermann Knell, *To Destroy a City: Strategic Bombing and its Human Consequences in World War II* (Cambridge: Da Capo Press, 2003), 188.

16. See *Bombing to Win*, 273.

17. Cf. Douglas P. Lackey, *The Ethics of War and Peace* (Upper Saddle River: Prentice Hall, 1989), 73.

18. Walzer is not entirely consistent about the turning point. In *Just and Unjust Wars*, he suggests that a supreme emergency existed until the summer

of 1942 (see 255 and 261). In *Arguing About War*, he writes: "My claim that the British bombing of German cities might have been defensible in 1940 and '41 extends no further than those years" (46).

19. See, respectively, *Just and Unjust Wars*, 261 and 255.

20. Walzer seeks to prevent the "normalization" of the doctrine by claiming that the leaders executing it have "dirty hands." See *Just and Unjust Wars*, 323–335, and *Arguing About War*, 45. It is doubtful that leaders are much constrained by the prospect of receiving some dishonor after the fact. Moreover, the logic of Walzer's argument is that leaders executing supreme emergency measures actually do what is morally right. This is Shue's view. It is also the view of John Rawls in his *The Law of Peoples* (Cambridge: Harvard University Press, 1999), 98–99. See also Frederik Kaufman, chapter 5.

21. Cf. Michael Skerker, "Just War Criteria and the New Face of War: Human Shields, Manufactured Martyrs, and Little Boys with Stones," *Journal of Military Ethics* 3 (2004): 27–39, p. 29.

22. According to current U.S. policy nuclear weapons may be used in response to the use of chemical and biological weapons by other states, but whether the United States would actually resort to this is debatable in light of how a world with a lesser inhibition against the nuclear option in general may harm its long-term interests. Cf. Scott D. Sagan, "Realist Perspectives on Ethical Norms and Weapons of Mass Destruction," in *Ethics and Weapons of Mass Destruction*, chapter 3, 91. One would hope that basic moral inhibitions in the first place would also prevent the use of nuclear weapons in such situations.

23. An increasing number of policy makers are willing to argue that the United States as benevolent hegemon is not bound to the same international norms, including *jus ad bellum* principles, as other countries. For a rebuttal of their view, see David Luban, "Preventive War," *Philosophy and Public Affairs* 32 (2004): 207–248, pp. 236–248. My analysis in this section has profited from his discussion.

24. Robert Kagan popularized the notion in *Of Paradise and Power: America and Europe in the New World Order* (New York: Vantage Books, 2004).

25. A demand for complete justice would imply that few wars, if any, would ever be justly initiated. See A. J. Coates, *The Ethics of War* (Manchester: Manchester University Press, 1997), 147–156.

26. As this book goes to press, the American public and many of its politicians increasingly have second thoughts about the war against Iraq. There is no clear indication, however, that this signifies a real turning away from what I describe here as the belief in "Military Hegemony for Humanity." Rather, the prevailing attitude seems that we got it wrong just this one time, that our mistake is getting rather costly to us, and so we must find a way out.

27. The current occupation of Iraq illustrates to some extent the points made here. However, there are also essential differences: among others, the

Iraqi army did not immediately surrender, the insurgency lacks clear legitimate authority, and the insurgency frequently commits war crimes.

28. National Strategy to Combat Weapons of Mass Destruction (December 2002): 1. Online at www.whitehouse.gov/news/releases/2002/12/WMDStrategy.pdf.

29. "The Triumph of Just War Theory (and the Dangers of Success)," in *Arguing About War*, 11.

30. Ibid.

31. This is putting the matter rather mildly. For a much sharper criticism of the media, see Norman Solomon, *War Made Easy* (Hoboken, NJ: John Wiley and Sons, 2005).

32. See Carl Conetta, *Disappearing the Dead: Iraq, Afghanistan, and the Idea of a "New Warfare,"* Research Monograph 9, Project on Defense Alternatives. Posted online on February 18, 2004, at http://www.comw.org/pda/usdefpos.html.

33. *Arguing About War*, 14–15 and 143–162, respectively.

34. Ibid., 12. In his later assessment of the second war with Iraq, Walzer synoptically discusses whether the war was just from Iraq's perspective, concluding that "Saddam's war is unjust." It is a step in the right direction. See Ibid., 160.

35. Following the recommendations of Harland K. Ullman and James P. Wade Jr., *Shock and Awe: Achieving Rapid Dominance* (Washington, DC: National Defense University Press, 1996). Reprinted by Pavilion Press, 2003. It is a contested issue whether the actual campaign matched its billing.

36. For a more detailed defense of this claim, see my "The Left and Humanitarian Intervention as Solidarity," in *The Liberation between Selves, Sexualities, and War*, Radical Philosophy Today, volume 3, ed. Greg Moses and Jeffrey Paris (Charlottesville, Virginia: Philosophy Documentation Center, 2006).

37. See its *Vision for 2020*, issued in 1997 and reprinted at numerous websites.

38. *Virtual War: Kosovo and Beyond* (New York: Metropolitan Books, 2000), 179. Consider also Ignatieff's claim after the invasion of Iraq—which he supported—had begun: "How will we oblige military hegemony to pay 'decent respect to the opinions of mankind'? I don't know." In "Friends Disunited," *The Observer* (March 23, 2003).

39. For some valuable suggestions of how the last criterion may be further developed, see Hans G. Brauch, Czeslaw Mesjasz, and Björn Möller, "Controlling Weapons in the Quest for Peace: Non-offensive Defence, Arms Control, Disarmament, and Conversion," in *The Future of the United Nations System: Potential for the Twenty-first Century*, ed. Chadwick F. Alger (Tokyo: United Nations University Press, 1998), chapter 1, 39–47. The need for developing criteria for determining what counts as just preparations for the possibility of war is also noted by Mark Woods in chapter 1 of this volume.

40. To illustrate, the National Security Strategy of 2002 maintains in chapter 7 that reducing global poverty is important for improving security; yet, the U.S. ratio of military spending to official development aid is about 25 to 1, while it ranges in Western Europe from a high of 7 to 1 in Britain to a low of less than 2 to 1 in Holland, Belgium, and Denmark. See Jeffrey D. Sachs, *The End of Poverty: Economic Possibilities for Our Time* (New York: Penguin, 2005), 330. We may wonder, then, whether in this regard the United States fails in "just military preparedness."

41. For a more detailed discussion, see my "Kant, the Duty to Promote International Peace, and Political Intervention," in *Proceedings of the Eighth International Kant Congress*, volume II, part 1, ed. Hoke Robinson (Milwaukee: Marquette University Press, 1995): 71–79, especially p. 75.

CHAPTER 4

Generalizing and Temporalizing Just War Principles: Illustrated by the Principle of Just Cause

John W. Lango

I. INTRODUCTION

In order to make moral judgments about such nontraditional forms of armed conflict as military campaigns against terrorists and armed humanitarian interventions, is a largely new ethics of armed conflict required, or would an appropriately revised just war theory be sufficient? In this chapter, I shall propose an answer to this question. First, I shall propose that just war principles should be generalized, so that they are applicable to military actions generally. Consequently, they would be applicable not only to military actions in paradigmatic interstate wars but also to military actions in civil wars, military actions in UN peacekeeping operations, military actions by and against terrorists, and so forth.[1] Second, I shall propose that just war principles should be temporalized.[2] Typically, a military action (e.g., a war) has temporally successive phases, and each of the phases (e.g., a battle) is itself a military action. Accordingly, the process of applying the principles to cases should be understood as a temporal process. For example, a war that initially had a just cause might at some critical juncture while it is being waged cease to have a just cause. In summary, my proposal is that just war principles should be, in senses that need to be explained, generalized and temporalized. To concretize the proposal, I shall examine particularly the most fundamental of the just war principles, the principle of just cause. For lack of space, I cannot provide comparable discussions of other just war principles.

Writers as diverse as Paul Ramsey and Michael Walzer have theorized about just war principles. Instead of a single unanimously accepted just war theory, there are various overlapping just war theories. However, my purpose is not to study the history of just war theories, but rather to propose how just war principles as I understand them should be generalized and temporalized. Let me suggest that, when the principles are appropriately revised, so as to be applicable to every form of armed conflict—not only wars but also forms of armed conflict that are not wars (e.g., armed conflict between a robust UN peacekeeping operation and peace-agreement spoilers)—they should be renamed *just armed-conflict principles*. Although I am strongly influenced by various just war theories, what I am advocating here is better termed a *just armed-conflict theory*. Ideally, such a theory should function as a theoretical framework within which the justice or injustice of particular cases of armed conflict may be debated rationally.[3]

Although just war principles have been used retrospectively to make moral judgments about past wars, it is most important that they be used prospectively to make moral judgments about future wars, or future phases of wars that are presently occurring. To generalize, it is most important that just armed-conflict principles be used prospectively to make moral judgments about future military actions, or future phases of military actions that are presently occurring. For a basic purpose of the principles should be to morally constrain agents from performing unjust military actions. Accordingly, the principles should function primarily as agent-centered moral (or deontological) constraints on military actions. Thomas Nagel calls a moral reason "agent-centered" when it applies "primarily to the individual" for whom it is a moral reason.[4] In addition to having such a moral reason for not doing something (e.g., not committing a murder), I think that sometimes an agent can have such a moral reason for not allowing someone else to do something (e.g., not allowing someone else to commit a murder). Since often there can be strong moral reasons for preventing grievous harm from occurring, another basic purpose of just armed-conflict principles should be to constrain agents to perform some just military actions (e.g., to prevent genocide).[5] For brevity, I shall focus on the principles as blocking injustice, but it should be recognized that they also are standards for justice.

It is customary to distinguish between *jus ad bellum* principles (e.g., the just cause principle) and *jus in bello* principles (e.g., the noncombatant immunity principle). The former establish "the right to go to war," it is said, whereas the latter determine "right conduct within war."[6] In generalizing and temporalizing just war principles, I shall challenge this customary distinction. Admittedly, we must establish the right to perform a military action by applying just armed-conflict principles prospectively to it. Additionally, at some critical juncture while we are in the midst of performing it, we might have to establish the right to continue to perform it by applying just armed-conflict principles prospectively to the remainder of it (i.e., that part of it that is still in the future). For example, a military action that initially was a last resort might—because at some critical phase there is a new opportunity for negotiation—cease to be a last resort.

Just armed-conflict principles are moral principles, and so a theory of just armed-conflict principles is a moral theory. Should such a theory be foundationalist or coherentist? According to foundationalism, just armed-conflict principles are fixed premises by means of which moral judgments are made about cases. In contrast, according to coherentism, just armed-conflict principles are not fixed: indeed, they can be used to make moral judgments about cases, but cases can be used to revise them. Furthermore, insofar as they are grounded on moral principles of greater generality (e.g., a principle of utility or a categorical imperative), they can be revised by recurring to such principles. Coherentism extends to the meanings of key terms: rather than having fixed definitions, terms such as *noncombatant* can be revised (e.g., by examining new cases). Coherentism also extends to links between ethics and other fields—for instance, the philosophy of action and the philosophy of time. For military actions are human actions, and the process of applying just armed-conflict principles to them is a temporal process. In theorizing about the ethics of armed conflict, I shall presuppose coherentism.[7]

It is essential to distinguish between a moral principle and its specifications.[8] Coherentism also encompasses the specifications of moral principles. Roughly speaking, to specify a moral principle is to particularize it in terms of morally relevant circumstances. But specification is different from casuistry. No matter how specific the morally relevant circumstances, a specification is still universalizable.[9] There is widespread agreement among just war theorists that, for a war to be just, there must be a just cause. Nevertheless, there is considerable disagreement about how this just cause principle should be specified. There is broad agreement about one type of specification—namely, that, when invaded by the armed forces of an aggressor, a state has a just cause for a war of self-defense. But other types of specification are controversial—for example, whether the possession of weapons of mass destruction by a bellicose state furnishes a just cause for a preventive war. It is crucial to recognize that, in applying just armed-conflict principles to cases, we usually have to be far more specific. (This specificity requirement is illustrated later by means of the just cause principle.) For, in order to apply a just armed-conflict principle to a case correctly, we have to specify it appositely for that case—that is, we have to particularize it fully in terms of all of the circumstances of the case that are morally relevant.

I am proposing that just war principles should be generalized, so that they are applicable to all forms of armed conflict, but I am also claiming that the resultant just armed-conflict principles should be specified. Alternative to generalizing is analogizing. For instance, instead of generalizing just war principles, so that they are applicable to armed humanitarian interventions, closely similar principles might be formulated—for example, George Lucas's criteria of *jus ad interventionem* and *jus in interventione*.[10] Closely similar principles might also be formulated for other forms of armed conflict—for example, just peacekeeping principles, just civil war principles, just insurrection principles, and just counterterrorism principles.[11] That such principles would be closely similar to just war principles indicates, I submit, that they could be understood as specifications of just armed-conflict principles. Moreover, in order to apply them to cases correctly, they usually would have to be specified further, that is, they would have to be particularized fully in terms of all of the morally relevant circumstances. As an additional complication, some cases might be hybrids of stock forms of armed conflict, for example, a robust UN peacekeeping operation amid a civil war the parties to which commit acts of terrorism. Since there is a kaleidoscope of circumstances that might prove morally relevant, there also is need for sufficiently general just armed-conflict principles, so that diverse cases can be compared more coherently.

In order to morally constrain agents from performing unjust military actions effectively, there has to be a strong moral presumption against the use of military force. When agents apply just armed-conflict principles prospectively to military actions, they have to make the moral presumption that those military actions are unjust. To override this moral presumption, they have the burden of proving that the military actions satisfy just armed-conflict principles.[12] More exactly, they have the burden of proving that the military actions satisfy apposite specifications of the principles, that is, full particularizations of the principles in terms of the morally relevant circumstances.[13] In accordance with coherentism, this burden of proof might be grounded on an ethical principle of greater generality, for example, a prima facie obligation not to knowingly cause or seriously risk causing injury or death. Frequently, when agents use military force, they knowingly cause or seriously risk causing injuries or deaths. Hence, because of the stated prima facie obligation, there is a more specific prima facie obligation not to use military force. And so, when agents engage prospectively in moral deliberation about whether to perform military actions, they have to presume that they must not.[14]

II. MILITARY ACTIONS

I am proposing that just war principles should be generalized, so that they are applicable to military actions generally. But what are military actions? And who (or what) are the agents?

With regard to interstate wars, states are agents, and within each state there are governmental agencies or departments (e.g., the White House and the Pentagon) that are agents. A state's military forces (e.g., its army) are agents, as are constituent groups within a military force (e.g., battalions and companies). Furthermore, with regard to nontraditional forms of armed conflict, various nonstate actors (e.g., terrorist groups) are agents, and so are their constituent organizations (e.g., terrorist cells). To generalize, it should be the purpose of just armed-conflict principles to morally constrain such organizations from performing unjust military actions.

But the primary agents are human beings who belong to these organizations (e.g., the president in the White House, the secretary of defense in the Pentagon, each officer in an army, and each terrorist in a terrorist group), and the primary purpose of just armed-conflict principles should be to morally constrain these human agents from performing unjust military actions. Actions of an organization are derivative from actions of human beings, and moral constraints on the organization are derivative from moral constraints on these human beings. Morally constraining the United States from invading a country involves morally constraining the president from deciding to invade, his advisers from advising him to invade, members of the Senate from concurring, and so forth. It is useful to distinguish three overlapping categories of human agents: leaders who plan, authorize, or command military actions, combatants who fight in them, and noncombatants. In generalizing and temporalizing just war principles, I shall focus on human agents and their military actions.

In accordance with coherentism, I shall presuppose a planning theory of human actions, which includes (among other things) the following ingredients.[15] A voluntary action can be performed intentionally, knowingly, recklessly, or negligently. An intentional action is performed for the sake of some goal. For instance, in intentionally bombing a munitions plant with the goal of destroying it, a tactical bomber could knowingly or recklessly or negligently kill noncombatants. Typically, an intentional action is part of a planned course of actions—that is, a course of actions that is followed for the sake of some goal. The actions in a planned course of actions are causally interlinked and have interlinked goals (e.g., by relations of means to ends). A planned course of actions is mutable: at any juncture, while carrying it out, its plan could be revised, and so could its goal. Some plans are well-formulated in advance, and others are partly or wholly improvised; some are expressly formulated, and others are partly or wholly implicit. Although the intention to perform an action is determinate, insofar as the propositional content of the intention is determinate, a plan to follow a course of actions is indeterminate. For the plan does not determine every action to be performed in realizing its goal. Also, a group of interrelated plans is itself a plan, and such a plan could be indeterminate, insofar as the component plans are incompletely interrelated. Furthermore, in anticipation of contingencies, there is need to provide for alternative courses of action, each of which might be followed to realize the goal.

This planning theory of human actions encompasses the actions of organizations. For organizations have plans, which are formulated by human agents and devolve upon human agents. A plan of one organization can be subordinate to a plan of another organization. For instance, a military campaign has been defined as "a group of military operations within a limited period of time connected by a strategic plan under the control of a single command."[16] For each of these military operations, there is an operational plan, which is subordinate to the strategic plan. And subordinate to each operational plan are tactical plans. (Also, military plans are usually subordinate to more comprehensive plans—e.g., to obtain access to natural resources, or to achieve world hegemony.) Let us have a case. At the close of the Second World

War, the U.S. military campaign against Japan included the military operation of atomic bombing Hiroshima and Nagasaki. Such organizational plans are necessarily indeterminate, and ordinarily require contingency planning (e.g., Nagasaki was a secondary target). Some plans of human agents (e.g., soldiers) are subordinate to an organization's plan, but others (e.g., of leaders) are superordinate. In this case, President Harry Truman's military planning was most superordinate, and the military plans of the crews of the bombers with the atomic bombs were subordinate. In general, a planned course of actions followed by an organization is derivative from planned courses of actions followed by human agents. It should be the purpose of just armed-conflict principles to morally constrain planned courses of military actions.

To generalize just war principles sufficiently, it is essential to utilize a sufficiently general conception of military actions. Waging a war is a military action. And carrying out a military campaign is a military action, as is engaging in a military operation. These concepts of military campaign and military operation hold not just of interstate wars but also of other forms of armed conflict. For example, even if the U.S. "Global War on Terrorism" is inappropriately labeled a war, the United States is carrying out a military campaign against Al Qaeda that involves engaging in military operations. Even if because Al Qaeda is not a state it cannot be said to be waging a war against the United States, it is carrying out a military campaign that involves engaging in military operations. In carrying out its military campaign in 1994 against the Hutu-dominated government of Rwanda, a Tutsi-dominated rebel group engaged in military operations. If a military force authorized by the United Nations had intervened to stop the genocide in Rwanda, and if it had been given robust rules of engagement, it might have carried out a military campaign—and thus engaged in military operations—against both the government and the rebel group.[17]

In a standard military operation, there are combats (i.e., battles or lesser combats). For each combat, there is a (perhaps implicit or improvised) tactical plan, which is subordinate to the operational plan. Fighting a combat is a military action. In participating in a combat, human agents use armed force. Any such use of armed force is a military action. Often, in performing such a military action, a human agent is following a course of military actions, the (perhaps implicit or improvised) plan of which is subordinate to the tactical plan for the combat.

Arguably, for an action to be military, it has to involve the actual use of military force, but my conception of military actions is more general. An action can be military, even if it only involves the threat—whether deterrent or compellent—to use military force. For example, during the Cold War, acts of nuclear deterrence were military actions. A UN peacekeeping operation could be a military action, even if it only were to involve the threat to use military force (e.g., to deter the parties to an armed conflict from violating their peace agreement, or to compel them to keep it).

Finally, in discussing how just war principles should be temporalized, I shall maintain that each temporal phase of a military action is itself a military action. For instance, in the Korean War, there were three principal phases, each of which was a military action—namely, defending South Korea, invading North Korea, and defending against China. In accordance with this concept of temporal phase, a course of military actions is itself a military action, and the temporal series of military actions comprising it are its temporal phases. (In general, an action is typically divisible into component actions. And several actions are sometimes combinable into a single action of which they are the component actions. But the presupposed relation of part to whole is not mereological.[18])

In summary, there is a continuum of military actions, from large-scale (e.g., waging the Second World War) to small-scale (e.g., firing a cruise missile at a terrorist training camp). Presumably, my incomplete survey of types of military actions suffices to convey provisionally my general conception of military actions. In accordance with coherentism, I shall not attempt to state a fixed definition (e.g., in terms of necessary and sufficient conditions). Additionally, I have to ignore philosophical disputes about how actions are individuated. A major in the U.S. Marines, Glen G. Butler, in discussing his experiences in the Iraq War, said, "I have not shot one round without good cause."[19] Let us imagine that he meant by "good cause" a cause that is morally good, although he might have meant something different. In this chapter, I am endorsing such a moral intuition about the need for a good cause. It should be the purpose of the just cause principle—and the other just armed-conflict principles—to morally constrain his shooting of each round. Every military action, no matter how large-scale or small-scale, must satisfy these principles.

Therefore, at each critical phase of any military action, relevant agents have the moral responsibility of determining whether the principles are satisfied. Let me emphasize that this claim holds of phases that are critical. (Throughout this chapter, the adjective "critical" is used similarly.) As one phase is succeeded by another phase—and if the morally relevant circumstances remain unchanged—the new phase is not one that is critical. On the other hand, as one phase is succeeded by another phase—and if some morally relevant circumstances have changed or if new morally relevant circumstances have emerged—the new phase is one that is critical. Hence relevant agents need not find just armed-conflict principles unduly burdensome.[20] (Eventually, while discussing the principle of competent authority, the qualification meant by the term "relevant agents" is clarified.)

III. GENERALIZING THE JUST CAUSE PRINCIPLE

I have been discussing just armed-conflict principles collectively, but they also need to be discussed separately, for each of them raises distinct issues. In what follows, I shall examine particularly the just war principle that is most fundamental, the just cause principle. For lack of space, I cannot provide comparable discussions of the others.

Just armed-conflict principles are agent centered. Most importantly, they morally constrain agents from intentionally performing unjust military actions. In particular, the just cause principle morally constrains agents from intentionally performing military actions that have unjust goals. For the concept of just cause should be understood teleologically, I submit, and the term *cause* should be construed to mean *goal*. Accordingly, insofar as the concept of just cause has been understood differently in the just war tradition, my understanding of it is revisionary. Traditionally, the just cause principle has been applied to wars. Roughly speaking, one just cause for war is attack by an aggressor. But the just cause here is not a state of affairs (i.e., that there was the attack) or an event (i.e., the occurrence of the attack). Indeed, the harms caused by the attack may be evaluated as morally bad, but such a moral evaluation of consequences is different from an agent-centered moral constraint on action. Instead, the just cause is the just goal of countering the attack. More explicitly, the agent, the attacked state, has as its just cause for waging a war its just goal of countering the attack.

But how is the attack to be countered? When the attacked state plans its war of self-defense, this question has to be answered more specifically. The attacked state's planned course of military actions needs to have a more specific goal. To apply the just cause principle correctly to the waging of a war by a state, the state's specific war goal has to be ascertained. In general, to apply the principle correctly to any military action, the specific goal has to be discerned. This requirement of goal specificity can be elucidated in terms of the ideas of moral presumption and burden of proof. In order to morally constrain agents from performing an unjust military action effectively, there has to be a strong moral presumption against the use of military force. When agents apply the just cause principle prospectively to a military action, they have to make the moral presumption that it does not have a just cause. To override this moral presumption, they have the burden of proving that the military action satisfies the just cause principle. More exactly, they have the burden of proving that it satisfies the apposite specification of the principle—that is, the full particularization of the principle in terms of the morally relevant circumstances.

Returning to the aforementioned case, let me illustrate this requirement of goal specificity. In so doing, I shall illustrate how the just cause principle should be generalized, so as to hold of military campaigns. The goal of the U.S. military campaign against Japan was to counter Japan's attack. More specifically, the goal was to force Japan to surrender. Even more specifically, the goal was to force Japan to surrender unconditionally. Let us suppose that this last goal fully particularizes the just cause principle in terms of all of the circumstances of this case that are morally relevant. Also, let us suppose that forcing surrender was a just cause, whereas forcing unconditional surrender was not. (Note that I am making these suppositions—and other suppositions about this case and other cases—for the sake of illustration. Sometimes I agree with a supposition, and sometimes I do not. In this chapter, there is no space for a thorough moral appraisal of any case.) Accordingly, if we were to judge that, because the U.S. military campaign against Japan had as its goal forcing surrender, it had a just cause, we would apply the just cause principle incorrectly. This case also illustrates how the principle is an agent-centered moral constraint, for it should have morally constrained the United States from carrying out a military campaign the specific goal of which was to force Japan to surrender unconditionally.

The goal of the military operation of atomic bombing Hiroshima and Nagasaki was to destroy (military targets in) them. Traditionally, only *jus in bello* principles (e.g., the noncombatant immunity principle) are applied to military operations, but my view is that the just cause principle should also be applied. Let us suppose that this military operation of atomic bombing satisfied the *jus in bello* principles. (Of course, this supposition is highly controversial, and I believe it to be erroneous, but I am only making it for the sake of illustration.) The goal of the military operation was, more specifically, to destroy the two cities, in order to force Japan to surrender. Even more specifically, the goal was to destroy them, in order to force unconditional surrender. Destroying them was the means, and forcing unconditional surrender was the end. In general, the specific goal of any planned course of military actions includes all of the ends for which that course of military actions is a means. Moreover, it is unjust to employ a means for the sake of an end, when it is unjust to pursue that end.[21] Therefore, because the goal of forcing unconditional surrender was (it is supposed) unjust, it was unjust to have as a goal destroying Hiroshima and Nagasaki, in order to force unconditional surrender. In accordance with the requirement of goal specificity, the just cause principle should have morally constrained the United States from engaging in that military operation of atomic bombing.

More particularly, since the primary agents are human beings, the just cause principle should have morally constrained Truman, the most superordinate human agent, from authorizing the military operation of atomic bombing, but it also should have morally constrained other human agents. For example, it should have morally constrained Major Thomas Ferebee, bombardier of the B-29 *Enola Gay*, from atomic bombing Hiroshima. However, suppose that Ferebee did not understand that the specific goal of the military campaign against Japan was to force unconditional surrender, and suppose that his own goal in this atomic bombing was to destroy Hiroshima, in order to force surrender. Then, given the earlier suppositions, he should not be morally blamed for intentionally performing a military action that violated the just cause principle. Nevertheless, suppose that a reasonable person who had this role of atomic bombardier in the military operation ought to have understood the specific goal. Then Ferebee should be morally blamed for negligently performing a military action that was part of a planned course of military actions the plan of which violated the just cause principle. The just cause principle also morally constrains agents from negligently performing military actions that have unjust goals.

How should the just cause principle be generalized, so as to be applicable to other forms of armed conflict? For instance, I shall presuppose that genocide provides a just cause for armed humanitarian intervention. Rather than being the occurrence of the genocide, the just cause is the just goal of stopping the genocide. But how is the genocide to be stopped? When a plan for armed humanitarian intervention is formulated, this question has to be answered more specifically. The planned course of military actions needs to have a more specific goal. To apply the just cause principle correctly to the armed humanitarian intervention, the specific goal of the military campaign against the genocide has to be ascertained. Let us imagine a hypothetical case. If a UN military force had intervened to stop the genocide in Rwanda, what would have been the specific goal of its military campaign? Let me distinguish four answers to this question: (1) only to guard Tutsis in secure areas, (2) to guard Tutsis in secure areas and also to prevent Hutus from killing Tutsis, (3) not only to guard Tutsis in secure areas and to prevent Hutus from killing Tutsis but also to terminate the armed conflict between the government and the rebel group, and (4) to guard Tutsis in secure areas, to prevent Hutus from killing Tutsis, to terminate the armed conflict between the government and the rebel group, and to remove that government and establish a more democratic government.

In addition to an armed humanitarian intervention's military campaign, my view is that the just cause principle should also be applicable to its military operations. In support of this view, let me illustrate how the following question might be answered. In a military operation, could there be a just cause for preventive military actions? Suppose that, in my hypothetical Rwanda case, the UN military campaign would have had as its specific goal only to guard Tutsis in secure areas. And suppose that it would have engaged in a military operation the goal of which was to guard a particular secure area (e.g., near Kigali). But how would the secure area have been guarded? To apply the just cause principle correctly to this military operation, this question has to be answered more specifically. Let me distinguish two answers: (1) only to defend the secure area against actual attacks, for example, by Hutu militias, and (2) not only to defend the secure area against such attacks but also to fight offensive combats that would prevent such attacks from occurring. Arguably, a just cause for this UN military operation would have been the specific goal of both fighting defensively against such attacks and forcibly preventing such attacks from occurring, in order to guard the secure area, for the sake of stopping the genocide.

IV. TEMPORALIZING THE JUST CAUSE PRINCIPLE

Having discussed how the just cause principle should be generalized, I want now to discuss how it should be temporalized. Just armed-conflict principles should function primarily as agent-centered moral constraints on military actions. And the concept of being centered on the agent includes the concept of *being centered from the agent's temporal standpoint*. Military actions usually have temporally successive phases. Each temporal phase of a military action is itself a military action. Indeed, before a military action is performed, the just cause principle has to be applied prospectively to it. But also, while it is being performed, the principle has to be applied prospectively at each phase of it. For a planned course of actions is changeable: at any critical point in time, while it is being carried out, its plan could be revised, as could its goal. To be more exact, even if its generic goal remains constant, its specific goal could be revised. Especially because of the requirement of goal specificity, we should expect (with whatever likelihood) the specific goal of a military action to be revised, and we should strive to anticipate new specific goals in future phases.

For an illustration, let us turn to the Korean War. On June 24, 1950, advancing across the 38th parallel, North Korea invaded South Korea. On June 27, Truman authorized a U.S. military campaign to counter the invasion. But how would he have it be countered? In terms of a UN Security Council resolution of that date, his goal was to "repel the armed attack"—that is, to force the North Korean army to withdraw to the 38th parallel. Let us suppose that this goal of repelling the invasion was a just cause. By the end of September, the North Korean army had been driven across the 38th parallel. However, by that time, Truman had changed his plan for the U.S. military campaign: his goal had become to destroy the North Korean army. But what was his goal more specifically? In light of current interest in the topic of preventive war, one answer is that his goal was to destroy the North Korean army in order to prevent North Korea from invading South Korea again. In light of current interest in the topic of regime change, another answer is that his goal was to destroy the North Korean army not only in order to prevent North Korea from invading South Korea again, but also in order to unite the two Koreas.[22] Let us suppose that, at this juncture, the United States ceased to have a just cause for waging the Korean War. Accordingly, if we were to judge that, because the U.S. military campaign had as its generic goal countering the North Korean invasion, the United States had a just cause for waging the Korean War in its entirety, we would apply the just cause principle incorrectly. Instead, because the specific goal of the U.S. military campaign had been revised, and because the new specific goal was (it is supposed) unjust, the just cause principle should have morally constrained the United States from continuing the military campaign.[23]

How should the just cause principle be temporalized, so as to be applicable to other forms of armed conflict? For an illustration, let us return to the hypothetical Rwanda case. In early April 1994, the genocide began. On May 17, with the generic goal of stopping the genocide, the Security Council authorized a UN military force of "up to 5,500 troops," gave it a mandate that included as a specific goal "the establishment and maintenance, where feasible, of secure humanitarian areas," but only allowed it to "take action in self-defence."[24] But UN member states failed to provide sufficient troops and logistical support. Had such a UN military force intervened to stop the genocide, its initial specific goal would have been only to guard Tutsis in secure humanitarian areas. Let us imagine how, while carrying out its military campaign, this initial specific goal might have been revised. At some critical juncture, the specific goal might have become to guard Tutsis in secure humanitarian areas and also to prevent Hutus from killing Tutsis. At a later critical phase, the specific goal might have become not only to guard Tutsis in secure humanitarian areas and to prevent Hutus from killing Tutsis but also to terminate the armed conflict between the government and the rebel group. Still later, the specific goal might have become to guard Tutsis in secure humanitarian areas, to prevent Hutus from killing Tutsis, to terminate the armed conflict between the government and the rebel group, and to remove that government and establish a more democratic government. To apply the just cause principle correctly, it would have to be applied prospectively to the initial specific goal, and in temporal succession it would have to be applied prospectively to each of the three revised specific goals.

Note that these four temporally successive phases are tantamount to a slippery slope, reminding us that, had a UN peacekeeping operation intervened, there might have been dangerous "mission creep." This illustrates an essential reason for temporalizing the just cause principle: to morally constrain agents from unjustly altering the specific goals of their military actions.

V. CONCLUDING REMARKS

Having examined particularly the just cause principle, I only have space for some brief remarks about other just armed-conflict principles. The traditional *jus ad bellum* proportionality principle requires that the benefits of a war must outweigh the harms, and the traditional *jus in bello* proportionality principle requires that the benefits of each engagement within a war must outweigh the harms. But I am challenging the traditional distinction between *jus ad bellum* and *jus in bello* principles. When appropriately generalized and temporalized, there is only one proportionality principle—namely, that the expected benefits of any military action must outweigh the expected harms.[25] To apply this principle correctly to a military action, the specific goal has to be ascertained. In light of the requirement of goal specificity, the principle morally constrains an agent from performing a military action, if the expected benefits of (the process of) achieving the specific goal of the military action are outweighed by the expected harms. In this way, the moral assessment of the proportionality of the military action is affected by the moral evaluation of the specific goal.

Furthermore, a military action that initially satisfied this proportionality principle might at some critical phase cease to satisfy it. For a military action usually has temporally successive phases, and at any of its phases its specific goal might be revised. Consequently, when its specific goal is revised at some critical phase, the proportionality principle morally constrains an agent from continuing to perform it, if the expected benefits of achieving its revised specific goal are outweighed by the expected harms. Because the specific goals of military actions are mutable, proportionality judgments about them are mutable. Additionally, proportionality judgments are mutable, because expectations of benefits and harms are mutable. As new eventualities necessitate alterations of earlier assessments of expected benefits or harms, proportionality judgments have to be revised. Thus, at some critical phase of a military action, even if the specific goal remains unaltered, a judgment that expected benefits outweigh expected harms might have to be replaced by a judgment that expected harms outweigh expected benefits.

The traditional principle of noncombatant immunity prohibits (intentionally) harming noncombatants (but permits foreseen but nonintended harm to them). During the Cold War, it was often claimed that, because of the indiscriminate destructiveness of nuclear weapons, the principle prohibits the waging of any nuclear war.[26] Hence, although the principle has been categorized as a *jus in bello* principle, it also can plausibly be categorized as a *jus ad bellum* principle. When appropriately generalized, it should govern any military action, no matter how large-scale or small-scale. And, when appropriately temporalized, it should govern each phase of any military action.

In challenging the customary distinction between *jus ad bellum* principles and *jus in bello* principles, I am also challenging the claim that combatants on both sides of an armed conflict "face one another as moral equals."[27] When combatants violate the principles of proportionality and noncombatant immunity, they are morally blameworthy; but it does not follow that, when they do not violate those principles, they are not morally blameworthy. In particular, combatants who embrace unjust goals are especially morally blameworthy; but even combatants who are oblivious to those unjust goals—and given that a reasonable person should have known about them—also are morally blameworthy. Nevertheless, all combatants are moral equals, in that they are human beings having human rights (e.g., the right not to be tortured).

Traditionally, the last resort principle requires that measures other than war must be tried sufficiently first.[28] A standard assumption is that such measures are nonmilitary measures—for example, negotiations, judicial settlements, and economic sanctions. However, when the principle is correctly generalized and temporalized, so as to be applicable to military actions generally, there can be no such assumption. For, even when there is no nonmilitary measure that ought to be attempted first, the principle still should morally constrain an agent from performing a military action, when there is a morally better alternative military action (e.g., one that is less destructive) that ought to be attempted first. In this way, the principle should incorporate (something like) the military principle of "economy of force."[29] Note also that the standard assumption as previously stated is misleading (or hypocritical). For some nonmilitary measures (e.g., economic sanctions) are more coercive than others (e.g., voluntary judicial settlements). In particular, some (so-called) nonmilitary measures are highly coercive—for example, acts of coercive diplomacy that involve (implied or explicit) threats to use military force. However, according to my conception of military actions, an action can be military, even if it only involves the threat—whether deterrent or compellent—to use military force. A main point is that the last resort principle should sometimes allow military measures to be used in support of nonmilitary measures. For example, the use of armed force to demonstrate resolve—or the credible threat of using armed force—might help to bring about negotiations. On April 9, 1994, Lieutenant-General Roméo Dallaire, force commander of the

UN peacekeeping operation in Rwanda (UNAMIR), attempted unsuccessfully to obtain additional troops and logistical support. "If we were given a new mandate and the necessary force," he remarked, "we might be able to get the two parties back to the negotiating table."[30]

Traditionally, the competent authority principle requires that an interstate war must be undertaken and controlled by a state's rulers.[31] When suitably generalized (and temporalized), so as to be applicable to the military actions of organizations generally, the principle should require that (each phase of) a military action performed by an organization must be undertaken and controlled by that organization's leaders. Typically, within such an organization, there are hierarchies of subordination and superordination, and so the conception of competent authority needs to be understood as distributed hierarchically among the various leaders in the organization. Each subordinate leader has his or her own authority within his or her own sphere of competence. Accordingly, the principle should require, for example, that a military campaign (or military operation or combat) must be undertaken and controlled by the military campaign's (or military operation's or combat's) leaders.

According to James Childress, the traditional competent authority principle "determines *who* is primarily responsible for judging whether the other criteria [i.e., just war principles] are met."[32] Nonetheless, a war waged by a state is not made just because the state's rulers have judged that it is just. Instead, the just cause principle is the more fundamental just war principle, for a state's rulers lack the moral authority to wage a war for which there is no just cause. (Similar remarks hold of the other just war principles.) With these qualifications, I shall accept Childress's claim, and generalize it as follows. It is the moral responsibility of each of a military action's leaders—no matter how subordinate—to judge at each critical phase of the military action whether the other just armed-conflict principles are satisfied. If the leader judges that one of them fails to be satisfied, it becomes his or her moral obligation to oppose an unjust military action.

Indeed, leaders have competent authority, but then so do the lowliest of combatants. In any combat, each combatant has his or her own personal (albeit subordinate) planned course of military actions, however implicit or improvised that plan might prove to be. Each combatant has his or her own authority within his or her own sphere of competence. Therefore, the competent authority principle should require that each combatant must undertake and control his or her own planned course of military actions. It is the moral responsibility of each combatant to judge at each critical phase of the combat whether the other just armed-conflict principles are satisfied. In this way, just armed-conflict principles should help to ground ethical standards for, for example, whistle blowing and disobeying unjust orders.

Finally, I want to append a few remarks about noncombatants as agents. Those noncombatants who would aid or abet a military action—whether by their acts or by their omissions—are morally responsible for judging whether that military action satisfies just armed-conflict principles. And noncombatants are morally blameworthy if they knowingly or negligently fail to oppose (as much as they reasonably are able) an unjust military action.[33]

In conclusion, I have been discussing how just war principles should be generalized and temporalized, and the resultant just armed-conflict principles fully specified for cases; but I have only been able to outline some ingredients of a just armed-conflict theory, and so much remains to be accomplished.[34]

NOTES

1. I discuss how just war principles are applicable to UN military actions in "Preventive Wars, Just War Principles, and the United Nations," *Journal of Ethics* 9 (2005): 247–268. Reprinted in *Current Debates in Global Justice*, ed. Gillian Brock and Darrel Moellendorf (Dordrecht: Springer, 2005).

2. I discuss the temporalization of just war principles in "Process Thought and Just War Principles," *Concrescence: The Australasian Journal of Process Thought* 5 (2004): 42–45. Available at http://concrescence.org.

3. Just war principles "constitute a formal framework and structure for moral debates about the use of force," according to James F. Childress, "Just-War Criteria," in his *Moral Responsibility in Conflicts: Essays on Nonviolence, War, and Conscience* (Baton Rouge: Louisiana State University Press, 1982), 90.

4. See Thomas Nagel, *The View from Nowhere* (Oxford: Oxford University Press, 1986), 175–180.

5. I discuss this sort of topic in "Is Armed Humanitarian Intervention to Stop Mass Killing Morally Obligatory?" *Public Affairs Quarterly* 15 (2001): 173–191.

6. Childress, "Just-War Criteria," 65.

7. See, for example, R. M. Hare, "Foundationalism and Coherentism in Ethics," in *Moral Knowledge? New Readings in Moral Epistemology*, ed. Walter Sinnott-Armstrong and Mark Timmons (New York: Oxford University Press,

1996). Cf. the idea of reflective equilibrium in John Rawls, *A Theory of Justice* (Cambridge: Harvard University Press, 1971).

8. My conception of specification is especially indebted to the discussion of specification in bioethics in Tom L. Beauchamp and James F. Childress, *Principles of Biomedical Ethics*, fifth ed. (New York: Oxford University Press, 2001).

9. See R. M. Hare, *Moral Thinking: Its Levels, Method, and Point* (Oxford: Clarendon Press, 1981), 41.

10. George R. Lucas Jr., *Perspectives on Humanitarian Military Intervention* (Berkeley: Berkeley Public Policy Press, 2001) and "From *Jus ad Bellum* to *Jus ad Pacem*: Re-thinking Just-war Criteria for the Use of Military Force for Humanitarian Ends," in *Ethics and Foreign Intervention*, ed. Deen K. Chatterjee and Don E. Scheid (Cambridge: Cambridge University Press, 2003), 72–96.

11. In a recent report to the United Nations, it is recommended that the Security Council, when deliberating about authorizing the use of armed force, should utilize five criteria of legitimacy, which closely resemble just war principles. See *A More Secure World: Our Shared Responsibility*, Report of the High-level Panel on Threats, Challenges and Change (United Nations, 2004), par. 207.

12. For an interpretation of just war principles in terms of W. D. Ross's conception of prima facie duties, see Childress, "Just-War Criteria."

13. To satisfy this burden of proof, there must be sufficient evidence. Accordingly, my view is that intelligence collection and analysis could often be critical to the process of determining whether just war principles are satisfied. See my "Collective Security and the Goals of Intelligence," *Defense Intelligence Journal* 15:3 (Winter 2006) (a special issue entitled *Ethics and Intelligence*).

14. On the other hand, in order to morally constrain agents to perform just military actions effectively (e.g., to prevent genocide), it might be contended that there also should be a strong moral presumption to use military force. Such a presumption could be grounded on a prima facie obligation of beneficence. W. D. Ross claimed (in *The Right and the Good* [Indianapolis: Hackett, 1988], 21) that prima facie duties of nonmaleficence are "more stringent" than prima facie duties of beneficence. In accordance with his priority claim, I am presupposing that the strong moral presumption against the use of military force has priority. For further discussion of this priority claim, see my "Is Armed Humanitarian Intervention to Stop Mass Killing Morally Obligatory?"

15. For a discussion of the role of a concept of plan in a theory of intention, see Michael E. Bratman, *Intention, Plans, and Practical Reason* (Cambridge: Harvard University Press, 1987).

16. Quincy Wright, *A Study of War*, vol. II (Chicago: University of Chicago Press, 1942), 687.

17. For a study of the case of genocide in Rwanda, see Alison Des Forges, *Leave None to Tell the Story: Genocide in Rwanda* (New York and Paris: Human Rights Watch and International Federation of Human Rights, 1999).

18. For example, see my discussion of "connected wholes" in "Overlapping Networks of Tropes," *Modern Schoolman* 79 (2002): 217–234, pp. 227–232.

19. Quoted in "Over Najaf, Fighting for Des Moines," *New York Times*, 23 August 2004, A23.

20. To ensure that utilitarianism is not unduly burdensome, R. M. Hare distinguished two levels of moral thinking, "the intuitive and the critical" (*Moral Thinking*, 25).

21. This principle is compatible with the rejection of the principle that the end justifies the means. For, even if agents are not morally constrained from employing a means because of the just cause principle, they still could be morally constrained from employing it because of another just armed-conflict principle (e.g., the proportionality principle).

22. Relevant documents can be found at the website of the Truman Presidential Museum and Library: http://www.trumanlibrary.org/whistlestop/study_collections/korea/large/index.htm.

23. To indicate the practical relevance of this conception of a temporalized just cause principle, let me comment briefly on a more controversial illustration: the Iraq War. The U.S. Joint Chiefs of Staff may have construed "the war against Iraq as a continuation of the 1991 Desert Storm war," according to Franklin Eric Wester, "Preemption and Just War: Considering the Case of Iraq," *Parameters: US Army War College Quarterly* 34 (2004–2005): 20–39, p. 21. As a consequence, Admiral Vernon Clark, Chief of Naval Operations, asserted that "it was my belief that this cause was just" (as reported by Wester, 38 n. 4). I have said that I am ignoring philosophical disputes about how actions are individuated. Evidently, there can be disputes, in particular, about how wars are individuated. However, even if the 2003 Iraq War and the 1991 Gulf War are construed as two major phases of a single war (with intermediate episodic phases of combats), the temporalized just cause principle still is applicable to each of these phases.

24. United Nations Security Council Resolution 918 (1994).

25. The terms *macro proportionality* and *micro proportionality* misleadingly dichotomize. Between the extremes of total wars and minor uses of military force, there is a gamut of intermediate cases, with their various amounts of benefits and harms.

26. I make such a claim in "Is It Wrong to Intend to Do That Which It Is Wrong to Do?" *Monist* 70 (1987): 316–329.

27. The quotation is from Michael Walzer, *Just and Unjust Wars*, third ed. (New York: Basic Books, 2000), 127.

28. See John W. Lango, "The Just War Principle of Last Resort: The Question of Reasonableness Standards," *Asteriskos: Journal of International and*

Peace Studies 1:1–2 (2006): 7–23. Portions of earlier drafts of that article were presented at the 2006 Joint Services Conference on Professional Ethics (JSCOPE 2006) and at the "Ethics and Africa" Conference, University of Cape Town (May 2006).

29. See William V. O'Brien, *The Conduct of Just and Limited War* (New York: Praeger, 1981), 225–228.

30. Lieutenant-General Roméo Dallaire (with Major Brent Beardsley), *Shake Hands with the Devil: The Failure of Humanity in Rwanda* (New York: Carroll and Graf, 2004), 276.

31. I prefer the term *undertaken* to the term *declared*. Cf. the phrase *undertaken and waged* in the formulation of the principle by Gorden Graham, *Ethics and International Relations* (Oxford: Blackwell, 1997), 57.

32. Childress, "Just-War Criteria," 74.

33. My parenthetical qualification is influenced by Kant's qualification of the duty of beneficence: "To be beneficent, that is, to promote *according to one's means* the happiness of others in need, without hoping for something in return, is every man's duty." See Immanuel Kant, *The Metaphysics of Morals*, trans. Mary Gregor (Cambridge: Cambridge University Press, 1991), 247 (emphasis added).

34. I wish to thank my coeditors, Michael Brough and Harry van der Linden, for their extensive and very helpful comments on this chapter. Part of an earlier draft (entitled "The Theory of Just War Principles") was presented on April 29, 2005, in a Group Session of the Concerned Philosophers for Peace at the Central Division Meeting of the American Philosophical Association. I also wish to thank the commentator, Duane Cady, for a brief but equally helpful critique. This work was supported in part by a grant from The City University of New York PSC-CUNY Research Award Program.

PART 2

Noncombatants and Combatants

CHAPTER 5

Just War Theory and Killing the Innocent

Frederik Kaufman

I. KILLING IN WAR

In just war thinking the principle of discrimination is used to distinguish between legitimate and illegitimate military targets, it being morally wrong (analytically) to attack illegitimate targets. Since illegitimate military targets include inanimate objects such as places of worship, crops, hospitals, cultural artifacts, and so on, as well as innocent people, the principle of discrimination is broader than the combatant/noncombatant distinction. In this chapter I will focus on the principle of discrimination as it applies to killing innocent people. I consider how the right to life of innocent people is affected by war and whether it is ever legitimate to intentionally target innocent people.

According to the principle of discrimination, only those people who are relevantly involved in a war may be intentionally targeted. All other people are held to be innocent and thus immune from attack. In just war thinking *innocent* is not opposed to *guilty*, but rather is used to distinguish between those who harm (or threaten harm) and those who do not; *nocens*, we are told, is Latin for *harm* and so those who do not harm or pose a threat of harm are innocent in the relevant sense. Thus the teenage conscript who is scarcely aware of the war into which he has been drafted may well be morally innocent, but because he has been transformed into an armed soldier who submits to a chain of

I am grateful for comments on earlier versions of this chapter from Jeff McMahan, Steven Lee, Donna Fleming, David Suits, Michael McKenna, Craig Duncan, and Carol Kates.

command he now constitutes a threat (or it is at least reasonable to think that he does). He is not innocent in the sense used in just war theory because he now poses a threat and is therefore a legitimate target for attack. Similarly, the editorial writer who advocates for the war does not pose a threat of harm, at least not directly. Unlike the teenage conscript he is not morally innocent, since he speaks out vigorously in favor of his country's war, but he is innocent in the sense that he does not directly threaten harm and so is not a legitimate target for attack, at least according to just war thinking.

Irrespective of the many difficult problems surrounding exactly who poses a threat of harm and who does not, the degree of harm posed, how direct the harm must be, and so forth, the conceptual point seems clear enough: to fight with discrimination is to target for killing only those whom it is legitimate to kill and not to target those who are innocent in the specified sense. Respect for the distinction between people it is permissible to target for killing and those who are not legitimate targets is the cornerstone of morally acceptable warfare.

II. UNINTENTIONALLY KILLING THE INNOCENT

However, as we are painfully aware, often in war many innocent people are killed, borderline cases of innocence not withstanding. When deaths of the innocent occur as unintended side effects of an otherwise legitimate military operation, they become part of the frightful cost of war; regretted to be sure, but allegedly permissible given the context. Provided military action is directed against legitimate targets only, undertaken with due care for the innocent lives put at risk, and the military value of the targets is somehow proportional to the lives at risk, then the action is permissible, even though we foresee that innocent people will be killed.

Given the general distinction between intended and unintended consequences embraced by just war thinking, how, specifically, are we to understand the right to life of innocent people in war? The standard answer is that because the innocent pose no harm (by definition), their right to life is unaffected by war.[1] As mere bystanders to the fighting their rights remain fully intact. So killing the innocent intentionally violates their right to life, but their unintentional deaths in pursuit of legitimate military targets does not violate this right, assuming proportionality and serious attempts to minimize their exposure to risk by, among other things, soldiers assuming increased risk themselves. But I will argue, contrary to the standard view, that the right to life of innocent people during war changes considerably; it can become highly attenuated, sometimes so much so that one wonders whether it is appropriate to speak of it any longer as a right.

I follow Judith Jarvis Thomson and distinguish between violating a right and infringing a right. One infringes a right when one negates what the right protects; one violates a right by wrongfully infringing it.[2] In war, then, one infringes the right to life of the innocent whenever they are unintentionally killed, but their right to life is violated only when they are wrongfully killed. When in war are the innocent wrongfully killed? We are told that innocent deaths in war are wrongful when disproportional, useless, or when due care is not exercised by attackers in pursuit of legitimate military targets. But when due care is exercised there is no violation of the innocent victim's right to life; such deaths are tragic, not wrong, making them permissible infringements of the right to life. An official military spokesperson sometimes even expresses regret for the loss of innocent life caused by its action, but nevertheless defends the attack as a permissible military operation.

It is striking that permissible infringements of a right to life are so blithely accepted as more extensive in war than in peace. Peacetime actions by the state that might kill one's own citizens, such as dam construction or medical testing, would never be excused by a hand-waiving appeal to unintended consequences, insisting that those deaths, though clearly foreseen and useful, were, in any case, proportional to the ends sought. It is not that innocent people may never be unintentionally killed by state actions in peacetime, but what counts as exercising due care to avoid those deaths in peace is much more stringent than during war (and typically involves only one's own citizens). Evidently, the exigency of war changes what in peacetime would be negligent violations of a right to life to permissible infringements of that right.

The innocent, of course, retain their right that due care be exercised by those who expose them to risk in the pursuit of legitimate activities, but the degree of moral protection their right to life affords their interest in living varies depending on context, and this suggests that an innocent person's right to life is more robust in some situations than in others, since permissible infringements of it can vary. Permissible infringements can vary according to (among other reasons) the military value of the target: the more valuable the target, the more innocent deaths we are willing to accept in exchange for its destruction. But as permissible infringements of the right to life become ever more extensive (because a target is of such high military value), the right diminishes in strength, as it were, perhaps to the point at which the moral protection it affords one's interest in living is negligible. The difference between a right to life where extensive infringements are so readily permissible and not having a right to life at all makes little practical difference. This may well be a general feature of rights, not unique to the right to life and war; but war starkly reveals how rights—even our most fundamental rights—are flexible and context dependent rather than immutable moral bulwarks that guard our vital interests. So even if just war theorists are correct when they say that the innocent retain their right to life in time of war, due to the extensive infringements allowed in war, it is not credible to think that the right is unaffected.

The notion that moral protection conferred by the right to life can vary according to context should not be surprising. Michael Walzer holds that by becoming soldiers, people relinquish their right to life in exchange for war rights.[3] Hence killing soldiers does not violate their right to life, since they no longer retain it, in his view. But this overstates the case; rather than losing the right to life, becoming a soldier more plausibly redefines permissible infringements of that right, since even soldiers can be wrongfully killed depending upon the context. But if the range of permissible infringements of a right to life can fluctuate for soldiers, then it can do so for the innocent as well. Thus, another way to think about war and the right to life is that war profoundly affects the right to life of both combatants and noncombatants by redefining permissible infringements of that right. This is theoretically simpler than Walzer's view under which people can relinquish one set of rights for another, especially if the right to life is contingent upon intrinsic properties of personhood, such as autonomy and self-consciousness, and so cannot be relinquished.

It is obvious that permissible infringements of a right to life presuppose legitimate activity. This means that the deaths of innocents caused by combatants engaged in illegitimate actions are not permissible infringements of the right; these are wrongful infringements and thus violations of the right to life. Which actions by combatants are illegitimate? This is far too large a question for consideration here, but *if* unjust combatants—that is, combatants who fight without just cause—have no legitimate targets at all, then all unintended innocent deaths would violate the right to life because they would all be impermissible infringements of that right. Just war theory distinguishes between justice of war (*jus ad bellum*) and justice in war (*jus in bello*), so that even those who fight without just cause nevertheless have legitimate and illegitimate targets and hence can allegedly fight within the bounds of morality. Whether the distinction can carry the moral weight placed upon it is not clear; my only point is that if it cannot bear this burden, then it is unlikely that a contemporary war can be fought morally, since any innocent deaths caused by the unjust side will violate the right to life and thus be wrong rather than merely unfortunate.[4]

III. INTENTIONALLY KILLING THE INNOCENT: THE SUPREME EMERGENCY

So far our discussion has considered unintentionally killing innocent people in war; but what about *intentionally* killing innocent people in war? Here traditional just war thinking is clear: we are required to discriminate sharply between people we may intentionally attack and kill—combatants—and the innocent, people we may not intentionally attack and kill, even if their unintentional deaths are sometimes allowed. This precept against intentionally killing the innocent is often taken as a categorical prohibition. In *The Challenge of Peace* the National Conference of Catholic Bishops claim, "The intentional killing of innocent civilians or noncombatants is always wrong" and that "the lives of innocent persons may never be taken directly, regardless of the purpose alleged for doing so."[5] And Paul Ramsey's epic work, *The Just War*, finds noncombatant immunity equally sacrosanct. In a celebrated passage, Ramsey deduces noncombatant immunity from the same Christian brotherly love that supposedly justifies war: "The same considerations which justify killing the bearer of hostile force by the same stroke prohibit non-combatants from *ever* being directly attacked with deliberate intent."[6] Other just war theorists concur that noncombatant immunity is a moral bright line, never to be crossed.[7] This is a hard requirement; innocent people may *never* be treated as combatants and intentionally attacked, irrespective of the military advantages of doing so. Evidently, we may allow their deaths, but intending them is strictly and absolutely prohibited.

Christian influence on just war thinking is pervasive and if the categorical nature of noncombatant immunity is ultimately linked to claims about God's commands then, of course, we should raise

Socrates' penetrating questions: Does God forbid us to intentionally kill the innocent because it is wrong or is it wrong because God forbids it? The implications of each question are well known. However, an absolute prohibition on targeting innocent people need not rest on God's commands. Treating persons as less than ends can also ground the prohibition, as can views about the nature of basic human rights if they are taken as inviolable. Whether grounded in theology or a form of secular deontology, many just war theorists take the absolute immunity of innocent people from intentional attack as a necessary condition for morally acceptable conduct in war; and if proper conduct in war is necessary for war to be just, then respecting that immunity is necessary for war ever to be morally acceptable.

Other just war theorists break with the more traditional absolutists on this point. When faced with imminent danger by a monstrously evil enemy, where defeat would involve massacre or enslavement or a moral and humanitarian catastrophe beyond comprehension, "one might well be required to override the rights of innocent people and shatter the war convention [of noncombatant immunity]," writes Walzer.[8] Intentionally targeting civilians under these dire circumstances is a supreme emergency; in such desperate circumstances it is permissible to do what one must to ensure "the survival and freedom of political communities."[9] It is important to be clear about what must be at stake for this proposed break in a categorical commitment to noncombatant immunity: if losing a war means just a change of government or redrawing political boundaries or higher prices for oil, that is not enough for a supreme emergency; neither is the mere possibility of something terrible happening; only imminent and extreme danger to a great moral ideal, such as democracy or the survival or freedom of a people or civil society, can sanction these extreme and otherwise unthinkable measures.

As explained by Walzer, the phrase *supreme emergency* was originally used by Winston Churchill to describe the imminent prospect of Britain's defeat by Nazi Germany in the early days of World War II. Churchill argued that the looming and real possibility of a Nazi victory would be morally abhorrent; German cities must be bombed, he claimed, as the only way to avoid a disastrous triumph of evil. Walzer proposed this as an actual example of a supreme emergency, a case where Britain's "back was against the wall." The only way left to prevent a catastrophe, according to Churchill, was to kill innocent German civilians by indiscriminately bombing cities because, it was surmised, this would undermine German civilian support for the war. Whether this is a historically accurate account is not relevant to our discussion; the important theoretical point is that some just war thinkers are prepared to break with absolutists on the intentional targeting of innocent people.

The supreme emergency is supposed to be intellectually defensible, not merely a reflexive act of national self-preservation, as one might act impulsively and perhaps understandably but still shamefully in a life or death situation to preserve one's life. Just shy of absolutism, the supreme emergency is a threshold view; it requires that we refrain from intentionally killing innocent people until the costs of doing so become too high plausibly to do anything else. We then accept military necessity, but only because we have no realistic alternative to avoid a moral disaster. Thomas Nagel put forward a similar view in his now classic "War and Massacre": "Deliberately killing an innocent," he wrote, "is impermissible unless it is the only way to prevent some very large evil (say the death of fifty innocent people). Call this the *threshold* at which the prohibition against murder is overridden."[10] A threshold view allows us to hew to principle except when the consequences of doing so become absurd, in which case the religious absolutist falls back on faith, the secular absolutist clings pointlessly to principle in the face of those absurd consequences, and the practical minded swallow hard and violate what is ordinarily prohibited for the sake of a greater good.

John Rawls, who also allows for exceptions to noncombatant immunity in extreme situations (he calls them "exemptions"), takes this as the definitive difference between his view, the Law of Peoples, and Christian Natural Law on war: "Political liberalism allows the supreme emergency exemption; the Catholic doctrine rejects it, saying that we must have faith and adhere to God's command."[11] The supreme emergency exemption is thus the crucial divide between any absolutist just war theorist—Catholic or not—and deontological (but non-absolutist) thinkers such as Walzer, Nagel, and Rawls who embrace the moral restrictions in war imposed by individual rights, but only up to a point; they allow those rights to be overridden in extreme enough situations.

Who may appeal to a supreme emergency exemption? It is tempting to think that only the side objectively in the right may resort to this exemption to avert a moral catastrophe that would result from losing a war. But this cannot be correct. Suppose, wildly contrary to fact, that the Allies in World War II planned to murder all Germans once the Allies won the war. This would be a moral disaster beyond comprehension—

certainly worse than the criminality of the Nazis—and if that insane plan could only be averted by the Nazis intentionally killing innocent people, then why should their prior criminality mean that they may not do so to prevent an even greater crime? Even bad guys can prevent evil. The supreme emergency exemption is intended as the last resort to avert a moral catastrophe; it should therefore be available to any state (or, perhaps, individual) for that purpose regardless of moral culpability for an unjust war. But typically each side thinks that it is in the right and that losing a war will be a terrible catastrophe, so supreme emergency appeals are bound to be abused. If a way of thinking about war can be so readily twisted to serve one's ends, perhaps it should never be sanctioned. But abuse implies the possibility of proper use; all the more reason to be clear about when a supreme emergency may be properly used.

We can distinguish two versions of the supreme emergency exemption, one having to do with victory and the other with avoiding defeat. Achieving victory is different from avoiding defeat, even if one can sometimes avoid defeat by achieving victory. According to Walzer, the British decision to bomb German civilians was an attempt to win the war; he quotes Churchill as saying, "The bombers alone provide the means to victory."[12] And Walzer refers to "fighting and winning" and "victory" throughout his discussion of this case, as do other commentators.[13] But victory, understood as defeating the enemy militarily, is not the only way to avoid the imminent moral catastrophe that is supposed to warrant a supreme emergency exemption. If intentionally targeting fewer innocent people will halt an attack or conclude the war in a draw short of victory, then that seems preferable because of the moral gravity of intentionally targeting the innocent. Victory might be more than is needed to avert the pending disaster that was the original justification for a supreme emergency exemption. Therefore, contrary to Walzer's claim that "necessity knows no rules," even among monstrous choices it seems that some choices are morally better than others.[14]

The supreme emergency exemption is not the suspension of morality; it is "arguably justifiable" (Rawls[15]) because it is the lesser evil in situations where deontological commitments are overwhelmed by the consequences of maintaining them. So rather than targeting the innocent being merely permissible, it would be required, if we are to act morally. Walzer sometimes writes as if targeting civilians is just an option in a supreme emergency, permissible or excusable, but not required; yet he also says, "Can soldiers and statesmen override the rights of innocent people for the sake of their own political community? I am inclined to answer this question affirmatively, though not without hesitation and worry. What choice do they have? They might sacrifice themselves in order to uphold the moral law, but they cannot sacrifice their countrymen."[16] Assuming the term *cannot* has moral content, this implies that were soldiers and statesmen to sacrifice themselves and thus their countrymen "in order to uphold the moral law," they would have acted wrongly. The choice for soldiers and statesmen is not between upholding moral law and not upholding moral law, as Walzer seems to see it, but deciding which moral law to uphold. Which has priority, the moral law about not intentionally killing innocent people or doing what is required to avoid a terrible moral catastrophe? Exigency might drive us ever deeper into our moral commitments, but we remain within the realm of the moral in a supreme emergency because we still regard our action, however repugnant, as morally justified, rather than merely excusable.

If deliberately killing innocent civilians in a supreme emergency is morally justified, then they are not wrongfully killed. Walzer and other just war thinkers disagree. In their view, paradoxically, it is wrong to kill the innocent *and* yet the supreme emergency is justified.[17] Rather than accept this as a tragic paradox and declare killing the innocent in a supreme emergency an irreconcilable moral dilemma that we might face in war, we should recall the source of the problem. It is generated by our commitment to a moral ideal about communal life and an absolutist conception of the right to life such that it cannot be eroded or diminished by context. But *if* we really are morally justified in deliberately killing innocent people in a supreme emergency, then this would not violate their right to life; it is instead a permissible infringement of the right. Those who think a supreme emergency is a moral paradox evidently regard rights as inflexible; any action that negates what the right protects must be a violation of it. But once we allow for infringements of a right that do not violate it, the paradox disappears. So there is no longer any reason to think both that we are justified in intentionally killing the innocent and that doing so violates their right not to be killed.

If killing the innocent in a supreme emergency is morally justified, then their deaths do not violate their right to life, and so do not count as murders. The concept of murder is evaluative; it is the *wrongful* or *unjustified* deliberate killing of the innocent, not merely deliberately killing the innocent.[18] Not all infringements of the right to life are wrongfully done. Active euthanasia, for example, is the deliberate killing of an innocent person but not murder (or so many argue). The same might be true of assisted suicide and perhaps abortion. And capital punishment, if justified, is also the deliberate killing of an innocent person, not morally innocent, of course, but innocent in the sense that the incarcerated criminal poses no threat (and this is the sense of innocent at issue in just war thinking).

So the supreme emergency exemption is not an insoluble moral paradox or ethical blind alley, as is sometime thought.[19] It is a sudden shift of moral perspective, to be sure, but reaching the threshold does not remove us from the realm of the moral, for the threshold at issue is not between the moral and the amoral. And we beg the question to think that it is. Indeed, the very act of presenting arguments that we are morally justified in invoking the supreme emergency exemption in a particular instance thereby demonstrates that we still seek to do the right thing. We are still operating with moral concepts, rather than descending into a Hobbesian amoralism where one does not give moral reasons to justify action. The supreme emergency is thus not mere military necessity, if military necessity is an abrogation of all moral considerations.

That supreme emergency exemptions can be morally justified corroborates the conclusion reached earlier about the extent to which an innocent person's right to life is circumscribed in war. For if innocent people can be justifiably attacked to prevent a moral disaster from happening, then their right to life does not protect them from being deliberately attacked in a supreme emergency. This is not to say that innocent people lose their right to life, for there remain ways in which they may be wrongfully killed even in a supreme emergency—in excessive numbers, for example. But the justifiability of the supreme emergency exemption shows that permissible infringements of the right to life can be extensive indeed; in such a case, moral protection offered by the right is minimal.

Although he resists this conclusion, Walzer is committed to it, because he claims, "A legitimate act of war is one that does not violate the rights of the people against whom it is directed."[20] This is a significant observation. Since he allows that targeting innocent people in a supreme emergency is a legitimate (though extreme) act of war, it follows that killing those innocent people does not violate their right to life. Perhaps "legitimate act of war" refers only to acts that stay within traditional war conventions, so strictly speaking supreme emergencies are not legitimate acts of war. But this is a technicality. If a supreme emergency exemption is ever legitimate, meaning that one may justifiably do it, then so long as acting on a supreme emergency exemption stays within the bounds that justify it, a supreme emergency exemption does not violate the rights of the innocent people against whom it is directed. The supreme emergency exemption can thus be understood within the context of rights, once we realize that rights may be permissibly infringed without being violated.

In his more recent reflections on this topic, Walzer sees the supreme emergency as a way to maneuver between two broad features of our moral lives: the absolutism of rights and the "radical flexibility" of utilitarianism. Evidently each outlook has its problems. The absolutist is committed to respecting rights even if doing so means disaster, whereas the utilitarian can find nothing inviolable to hinder indiscriminate calculation. Especially in adversarial situations, like war, Walzer notes, we tend to discount the interests of those opposed to us; "even infant deaths bring pain and sorrow to adults and so undermine the enemy's resolve."[21] (But this is a psychological observation rather than a theoretical objection to utilitarianism; that it is hard to adopt the "benevolent spectator" point of view required by utilitarianism when our vital interests are at stake hardly shows that we should not still try.) And while rule utilitarianism might address some absolutist moral prohibitions, it does so inadequately, because those prohibitions are still derived from utility. In the end, according to Walzer, the problems with utilitarianism return us to a theory of rights, though a non-absolute one: "When our deepest values are radically at risk, the constraints [of rights] lose their grip, and a certain kind of utilitarianism reimposes itself. I call this the utilitarianism of extremity, and I set it against a rights normality."[22]

But Walzer's quasi-absolutist conception of rights for normality and utilitarianism for extremity still endorses a view about the inflexibility of rights in all but extremity. If rights can be infringed without being violated, then we abandon an absolutist conception of rights for normality too. In Walzer's view, short of extremity, all intentional infringements of the right to life are violations of it. But that does not seem correct, since, as we have seen, the stringency of a person's rights can vary with circumstance. Rather than keep utilitarianism in abeyance until extremity overwhelms us, as Walzer would have it, a more nuanced theory of rights incorporates utilitarianism's flexibility into a conception of rights from the start. Thus, the supreme emergency exemption could be understood according to a flexible theory of rights, rather than as an abandonment of rights in favor of utilitarianism.

IV. THE SUPREME OPPORTUNITY?

I wish to consider, finally, the worst fear of those who, however reluctantly, permit supreme emergency exemptions: a possible expansion of them. Could there be what we might call a "supreme opportunity," where a great good can be achieved only by targeting the innocent? If supreme emergency exemptions are subject to abuse, this is even more so. Yet if we are willing to give up absolute moral prohibitions to avoid catastrophe, then how can we cling to them here? Threshold views, it seems, can cut both ways. We might say that in general avoiding evil is more important than promoting good, but this still allows for a great enough good to overcome the presumption against achieving it by otherwise wrongful means. For Walzer, "Utilitarian calculation can force us to violate the rules of war only when we are face-to-face not merely with defeat but with a defeat likely to bring disaster to the political community."[23] And yet, "the survival and freedom of political communities—whose members share a way of life, developed by their ancestors, to be passed on to their children—are the highest values of international society."[24] It is a measure of Walzer's commitment to the (near) absolutism of individual rights that he is prepared to infringe them only to spare political community from moral disaster but not to infringe them to establish what he takes as the highest value of international society. Evidently this would be a wrongful infringement, a violation.

But why should this be so? As in the tired (but revealing) hypothetical example where we can cure cancer by doing lethal medical experiments on a few healthy individuals, so in war; what if by targeting the innocent we will achieve goods on the order required to sanction a supreme emergency, such as the establishment of a great moral ideal, like a democratic society, or begin the legacy of a decent form of communal life? The problem is not that individual rights rule out these calculations, for we have stipulated that the good achieved is so great that it makes clinging to them as difficult as it was when faced with catastrophe. Rather, the problem is practical: the burden to show that a great good will result from targeting the innocent is even higher than it is for a supreme emergency, since avoiding evil is more stringent than promoting good. So while not ruled out categorically, a supreme opportunity will remain largely hypothetical.

Yet a permanent state of supreme emergency is enshrined in nuclear deterrence policy: we intentionally target the innocent, presumably to stop evil. It is easy to imagine the policy changing from stopping evil to achieving good, such as allowing democracy to spread or permitting decent political communities to form and flourish under our nuclear umbrella. Such a change could take place by the stroke of a pen; nary a missile to be retargeted. In other words, we might not actually have to kill the innocent in order to achieve great moral goods; we might do it simply by threatening to kill the innocent. And to the extent that our nuclear policy could be interpreted as intentionally seeking any moral good whatsoever rather than simply avoiding evil, what I have called the supreme opportunity would be reality, rather than just a wild hypothetical possibility. Some argue, for example, that under our nuclear protection democracies like Germany and Japan flourish, thus achieving great moral good because we threaten to kill the innocent. But how could we condone either the supreme emergency or supreme opportunity interpretation of our nuclear policy? Nuclear war would be insanity; it spectacularly violates proportionality, and because it is immoral to threaten to do what is immoral, any positive goods obtained or evils avoided by our policy are ill-gotten.

If a supreme opportunity is ever warranted, it will likely be in carefully defined terrorist campaigns where proportionality could be satisfied. Terrorism is, as it were, the other end of the spectrum from nuclear war: in both cases the innocent are intentionally killed, so both fall outside the bounds of traditional just war theory. Nuclear war is unthinkable; terrorism is not. Terrorists surely exaggerate the good they seek by killing innocent people, whether the ends they seek can be obtained only by violence, or even whether their ends are good; they are undoubtedly mistaken about much of what they do. But this is not necessarily so.

Imagine an occupying force that has long suppressed an indigenous people, who now lead demeaning lives as second-class citizens in their own land. The country is administered by occupiers who exploit the people for their own gain; many occupier civilians now live there, too, enjoying lives of privilege and ease at the expense of the local people, who lack freedoms that afford any sense of the dignity that comes from political self-determination. And suppose that by acts of terrorism a handful of fighters can awaken their brethren to the humiliation they have suffered and as a people they arise against their oppressors, who finally acquiesce.

This is a fairy tale, to be sure, but real situations can approximate it. Are we to say that even if proportional and effective, innocent occupier civilians should never be killed, even if doing so liberates an oppressed political community, the "highest value of international society"? Absolutists cannot abide it, and there are good prudential reasons to worry about any such appeal, but such cases can exist, as vividly depicted in the classic war movie *The Battle of Algiers*. Irrespective of what precisely would justify a supreme opportunity, non-absolutists seem committed to its possibility, and depending on how we interpret some armed struggles, perhaps to its actuality as well.

Defenders of the supreme emergency exemption will surely object to a positive version of the doctrine, but this is an inevitable result of a threshold view; it is just a threshold in the "other direction." Perhaps some will see this implication as a good reason to maintain a traditional just war categorical opposition to intentionally targeting innocent people. But the reasons that justify moving away from that position still hold. I suggest that non-absolutists are committed to revising just war theory even further to include a supreme opportunity exemption.

NOTES

1. Michael Walzer's *Just and Unjust Wars*, third ed. (New York: Basic Books, 2000), is the contemporary exemplar of just war thinking. In distinguishing combatants from noncombatants, Walzer claims that "simply by fighting . . . they [the combatants] have lost their title to life and liberty" (136). He goes on to claim that "everyone else retains his rights...these bystanders [the innocent] do not forfeit their rights . . . they [the innocent] are men and women with rights . . ." (137).

2. See "Some Ruminations on Rights," reprinted in *Rights, Restitution, and Risk*, ed. William Parent (Cambridge: Harvard University Press, 1986). Thomson writes: "Suppose that someone has a right that such and such shall not be the case. I shall say that we infringe a right of his if and only if we bring it about that it is the case. I shall say that we violate a right of his if and only if *both* we bring about that it is the case *and* we act wrongly in so doing" (51).

3. In *Just and Unjust Wars*, Walzer writes: "The immediate problem is that the soldiers who do the fighting . . . lose the rights they are supposedly defending. They gain war rights as combatants and potential prisoners, but

they can now be attacked and killed at will by their enemies. Simply by fighting, whatever their private hopes and intentions, they have lost their title to life and liberty, and they have lost it even though, unlike aggressor states, they have committed no crime" (136).

4. See Jeff McMahan, "The Ethics of Killing in War," *Ethics* 114 (July 2004): 693–733, for a sophisticated and compelling argument for why unjust combatants have no legitimate targets.

5. National Conference of Catholic Bishops, *The Challenge of Peace* (Washington, DC: The U.S. Catholic Conference, 1983), iv and 46. Similar categorical claims about intentionally killing civilians can be found throughout the document.

6. Paul Ramsey, *The Just War* (New York: Charles Scribner's Sons, 1968), 144 (emphasis added).

7. In *Morality and Contemporary Warfare* (New Haven: Yale University Press, 1999), James Turner Johnson writes: "In short, the denial of the distinction between combatants and noncombatants is wrong" (124). See also Johnson, *Can Contemporary War Be Just?* (New Haven: Yale University Press, 1984), 28 and 63. In *Innocent Civilians: The Morality of Killing in War* (New York: Palgrave, 2002), Colm McKeogh states: "Civilians may not be targeted in war whatever the consequences" (165). In "Discrimination," chapter 8 of *Moral Constraints on War*, ed. Bruno Coppieters and Nick Fotion (Lanham, MD: Lexington Books, 2002), Anthony Hartle writes: "The Principle of Discrimination provides clear and specific guidance: combatants are never to target noncombatants directly" (148).

8. Walzer, *Just and Unjust Wars*, 259.

9. Ibid, 254.

10. Thomas Nagel, "War and Massacre," in *Mortal Questions* (Cambridge: Cambridge University Press, 1979), 62.

11. John Rawls, *The Law of Peoples* (Cambridge: Harvard University Press, 1999), 105.

12. Walzer, *Just and Unjust Wars*, 259.

13. See, for example, Henry Shue, "The Impossibility of Justifying Weapons of Mass Destruction," in *Ethics and Weapons of Mass Destruction*, ed. Sohail H. Hashmi and P. Steven Lee (Cambridge: Cambridge University Press, 2004). Shue writes: "And that, I have insisted, is the real rub for the notion of supreme emergency: If it is formulated narrowly enough not to threaten to undermine the entire edifice of just war, will it ever again apply, as it did to the Nazis? . . . would [a supreme emergency] actually be militarily useful by contributing significantly to *victory?*" (154; emphasis added).

14. Walzer, *Just and Unjust Wars*, 254.

15. Rawls, *The Law of Peoples*, 98.

16. Walzer, *Just and Unjust Wars*, 254. In his "Terrorism: A Critique of Excuses," in *Arguing About War* (New Haven: Yale University Press, 2004),

Walzer is more explicit about the defensibility of killing the innocent in a supreme emergency: "Against the imminent threat of political and physical extinction, extreme measures can be defended, assuming that they have some chance of success" (54).

17. Walzer, "Emergency Ethics," in *Arguing About War*, states: "political and military leaders may sometimes find themselves in situations where they cannot avoid acting immorally, even when that means deliberately killing the innocent" (46). Nagel, in "War and Massacre," makes a similar point: "We must face the pessimistic alternative that . . . the world can present us with situations in which there is no honorable or moral course for a man to take, no course free of guilt and responsibility for evil" (74).

18. I disagree here with Elizabeth Anscombe, who claims in her celebrated essay "War and Murder": "For murder is the deliberate killing of the innocent, whether for its own sake or as a means to some further end" (45). Reprinted in *War and Morality*, ed. Richard Wasserstrom (Belmont, CA: Wadsworth, 1970).

19. In *Michael Walzer on War and Justice* (Montreal: McGill-Queen's University Press, 2000), Brian Orend states: "Thus, in a supreme emergency we are not truly confronted with options that are both right and wrong; rather, we are confronted with options all of which are wrong. It is a moral blind alley: there is nowhere to turn and still be morally justified. In other words, I suggest we understand supreme emergency as a case where we exit the moral realm and enter the harsh Hobbesian realm of pure survival" (133).

20. Walzer, *Just and Unjust Wars*, 135.

21. Walzer, "Emergency Ethics," in *Arguing About War*, 39.

22. Ibid., 40.

23. Walzer, *Just and Unjust Wars*, 268.

24. Ibid., 254.

CHAPTER 6

When Less Is Not *More:* *Expanding the* *Combatant/Noncombatant Distinction*

Pauline Kaurin

I

Consider the following scenario:

Approaching a military checkpoint, a car with three Arab males dressed in civilian clothes slows down and then speeds up. The car has its lights on (a local practice for identification at checkpoints), but the military personnel open fire. When questioned, the lone survivor claims no warning was given, the tank simply opened fire. The military personnel claim that the car failed to slow down, and that the occupants failed to respond to shouted instructions and hand signals. The military personnel believed the car was filled with insurgent suicide bombers; the lone survivor claims to be a freelance journalist traveling with a bodyguard and translator.

In these circumstances, how were the military personnel to make the classical moral distinction between combatants and noncombatants? Such confusion is a common one in complicated counterinsurgencies as in Iraq, as well as in the range of peacekeeping, nation-building, and humanitarian interventions that characterize much of contemporary warfare. This confusion also reflects the practical, "boots on the ground" ramifications of the most basic aspects of this moral distinction: When is killing murder and when is it a legitimate act of war? Whom can one legitimately kill in war?

The clarity of the combatant/noncombatant distinction is crucial since it preserves the essential moral difference between a soldier and a murderer; the difference between doing one's duty and committing a war crime; the difference between coming home in honor or coming home in shame, with the attendant effects for both the soldier and society. If this distinction cannot be rendered in a way that is practical in the field, soldiers become murderers, committers of war crimes and bearers of individual and collective shame. If the most basic of moral distinctions cannot be preserved, if the just war tradition cannot don its combat boots, this brings into question the very possibility of moral warfare itself. To deal with these and other similar scenarios, this chapter will argue that the traditional combatant/ noncombatant distinction must be expanded into a five-part distinction with three categories of combatants and two categories of noncombatants. The aim is to strengthen the case for maintaining the combatant/noncombatant distinction (resisting calls for the abandonment of the distinction), by addressing and providing remedies for the difficult practical issues involved in applying the distinction in contemporary warfare.

II

Much has been made of the difficulties of maintaining the distinction between combatant and noncombatant in the unconventional warfare of conflicts like Vietnam, where there were few standard battle lines and frequent engagements between small units—often in situations of surprise attack and/or ambush—where one could not easily identify the enemy. Given such experiences of warfare, debate ensued as to whether this distinction was (1) outdated, since it did not reflect the current moral realities of warfare; (2) unfair since it put those who observed the distinction at combat disadvantage and greater risk of death and injury; and (3) practically speaking, impossible to enact, even if one thought it should be maintained. Most of the controversy centered on the failure of the traditional binary distinction to recognize different varieties of combatants, as well as various levels of threat that neutrals and noncombatants can pose without being clearly identifiable combatants. This distinction, it is charged, does not allow an adequate response to unconventional belligerents and persons who are usually protected under the conventions of war.

On the other hand, complete abandonment of the distinction seemed morally repugnant and somehow "uncivilized" as evidenced by the controversy, ill will, and distrust in the wake of the My Lai "massacre" and the subsequent court-martial trials of Lieutenant Calley and Captain Medina. While it is true that a great deal of consternation came from the home front, there was also plenty coming from inside Vietnam—even from those who participated in such actions.[1] While recognizing the inherent difficulties of applying rules of war (which are oriented toward conventional battlefield tactics) to guerilla warfare, there was reluctance in both military and the civilian circles to abandon the distinction altogether.

This difficulty of applying the rules of war to nontraditional "war" situations was also a problem with the humanitarian intervention in Somalia in 1992. Fighting in a chaotic urban situation, where one is under attack from all sides and where many of the attackers are children or other "traditional" noncombatants, crystallizes the difficulties associated with distinguishing combatants from noncombatants. This is especially challenging when multiple hostile factions, without clearly identifiable uniforms with insignia, are present alongside of "innocent," uninvolved noncombatants.

In the Balkan conflicts the formula of trying to enforce peace and carry out humanitarian missions in the midst of competing hostile forces, while trying to protect one's own forces, was repeated.[2] This problem was compounded by the opposing forces' use of civilians as human shields in order to protect military targets from NATO bombardment, and/or as hostages to protect military forces or to forestall military attack. As in Somalia, there was the challenge of being able to quickly and accurately distinguish the enemy combatant from the noncombatant entitled to protection. However, there was an additional problem: combatants using noncombatants as weapons and to problematize the battlefield, knowing that the opposing forces were bound to avoid harming and even protect noncombatants.

These situations raise several important concerns. First, it is exceedingly difficult to distinguish the combatants from the noncombatants because they are often located in the same physical locations, often by enemy design. Moreover, opposing forces try to hinder or prevent the other side from making this distinction, through intentional deception or by taking advantage of a lack of local/cultural information or knowledge. Second, even if it were possible to eliminate deception or to acquire the necessary local intelligence, the constraints of the contemporary battlefield (including the nature of modern weaponry) make it impractical. Combatants, it is argued, do not have the time and judgment required to make such distinctions, some of which are complex and subtle, take time, and require local intelligence or information. How might invading combatants be expected to distinguish among the various degrees of cooperation that the population might give? What information might one need to make the determination? How is that information to be acquired?

III

Before laying out the details of the five-part distinction, let us examine the basic line of argument in favor of a multipart distinction, rather than simply a binary distinction.[3] What is it about combatants that justifies their being the object of violence? What is it about noncombatants that does *not* justify the use of violence? The most accessible fact about warfare is the power differential between combatants and noncombatants: combatants are armed and can be a threat to others; noncombatants are not armed and are vulnerable to those who are. Following Michael Walzer's view, combatants are dangerous individuals; they carry weapons, they can/will inflict this harm on others.[4] They are dangerous because they can inflict harm and put others in dangerous situations; they can cause others to have their rights violated, especially their right to life, but also the right to autonomy or noninterference with their livelihood. In short, combatants have a kind of power—a more imminent ability to be a threat, to be dangerous. This core intuition lies at the heart of both the moral and practical arguments for an expanded combatant/noncombatant distinction. The different actions and abilities of the persons in each category justify different treatment; these are not just different administrative categories, but different categories of actions and different levels of force—multiple ways to be/act like a combatant and multiple ways to be/act like a noncombatant.

First, this core intuition can be understood in terms of the requirements of both reason and justice. Reason requires that one treat like cases alike for the sake of logical consistency. If there are persons who by virtue of their gender, age, or social function would normally be considered noncombatants, yet who are acting in a hostile, threatening manner or causing harm, it would be illogical to argue that they should be treated in the same fashion as others who are not evincing threats or hostility. On the other hand, it also seems illogical to lump those hostile or threatening noncombatants as being worthy of the same treatment as those who are clearly identified as combatants, who threaten openly by visible signs (carrying a weapon, wearing a uniform with fixed visible signs, and so forth) and have the advantages and protections of a military or paramilitary structure. The same holds true for noncombatants. Some noncombatants are entirely vulnerable and require protection because they cannot protect themselves; whereas other noncombatants are less vulnerable, may be able to protect themselves, but cannot be legitimately targeted by combatants. If there are fine-grained differences between how these individuals act and the effect that they can have on others, then it would be a category mistake not to make more fine-grained distinction as to how these individuals are to be treated.

Further, it is a requirement of *justice* to treat like cases in a like manner, and morally or legally speaking it is unjust to treat like cases differently, unless there is a compelling reason to do so. In the law, one recognizes different classifications of what would seem to be the same crime (killing another human being) differentiated by different circumstances and levels of threat. A criminal who has been charged with first-degree murder is taken much more seriously than one who has been charged with involuntary manslaughter. However, not all first-degree murderers are treated the same, especially in the sentencing phase. One might look at the circumstances of the crime, a prior record, evidence of remorse, and possible danger to the community, which can affect the length and type of sentence. Therefore, to accommodate both of these considerations, we will clearly need more than the two traditional categories. At a minimum the two traditional categories will be necessary, but also additional categories for unconventional belligerents and a category for noncombatants who might pose a threat. Such an expanded distinction would allow for the greater flexibility required for logical consistency and justice, and flexibility which is neither ad hoc nor unduly partial.

Second, a multipart distinction accords better with just war theory, in particular the *jus in bello* considerations of discrimination and proportionality. The principle of discrimination (noncombatant immunity) calls for soldiers to distinguish legitimate targets and to refrain from attacking illegitimate targets. A multipart distinction maintains that there are crucial differences between combatants and noncombatants, and also recognizes that there are important differences—largely in terms of power and vulnerability—*within* these categories as well. If there are these differences within the categories, then it also follows that there could be different types of *rights within* these categories that ought to be taken seriously. Failure to recognize and accommodate this fact could mean that the traditional two-part distinction (even in its attempt to preserve the rights of the corresponding two groups) violates the rights of the subgroups, that is, hostile noncombatants or unconventional belligerents.

It follows that an expanded distinction also accords better with the principle of proportionality. If one uses more force than is necessary to achieve the end, one is inflicting unnecessary, and therefore unjustified, suffering and destruction that could endanger the possibility of restoring a lasting peace after the conflict has ended. The traditional distinction generally recognizes two categories of force as legitimate: against combatants lethal force is justified, but against noncombatants lethal force is unjustified. Therefore, it is possible that having only two categories may either inflict more harm than necessary or prevent the adequate force needed to achieve the end.

An expanded distinction is able to recognize gradations of power and threat within the categories of combatant and noncombatant, and can require that one use only enough force to stop or deal with that threat, thereby avoiding the infliction of unnecessary suffering. If unconventional belligerents are more vulnerable than traditional combatants, treating them the same makes a category mistake or violates an intuition about justice, but also violates the principle of proportionality. If neutral noncombatants are less vulnerable than traditional noncombatants, treating them in the same manner as the traditional noncombatants also could violate proportionality since more force could be required, and therefore justified, to defend oneself. With an expanded distinction the question becomes, How much force is necessary to deal with this threat? rather than the question, Is the use of force (usually lethal) justified or does this situation preclude any use of force?

In addition to the moral arguments for a multipart distinction, there is also an important practical consideration. Actual field practice in recent conflicts suggests that multiple distinctions within the traditional distinctions are already, albeit informally, in effect. Arguments that the distinction ought to be preserved in its present form ignore the fact that many of these conversations are *already happening*, and that the distinction is *already* being subtly altered as students, teachers, and military professionals grapple with the difficulty of applying and main-

taining the binary distinction. In the face of these practices and complexities in war, if we insist on keeping a distinction with only these
two parts, soldiers may abandon the distinction altogether since the
binary distinction does not reflect the realities of war or at least their
experiences of war in the field. Additionally, they may decide to implement their own version of the distinction, which could produce situations where soldiers in the field are implementing different versions of
the distinction without any formal consistency, guidelines, or oversight.
In that case, the traditional distinction would essentially have been
abandoned in favor of individual and subjective judgments about who
deserves protection and who does not.

IV

What exactly would this multipart distinction look like? How might it
work in the field? To begin with, this scale is designed to be adaptable
and flexible. Clearly, there are areas of ambiguity that the traditional
combatant/noncombatant distinction cannot accommodate, but it is
important not to give up assignations of responsibility, nor to deny the
moral difference between those who threaten and harm and those who
do not. Rather, I suggest a pragmatic way in which an expanded version of the traditional distinction can be quickly understood, adapted,
and applied in the complex and fluid situations that are characteristic
of contemporary war. If taught and trained with, this scale would especially help those in the field determine the potential threat involved in
a given situation and respond with actions that are *consistent* with
International Law and the rules of war without using more force than
necessary.

This way of laying out the distinction between combatants and
noncombatants incorporates the necessity of threat assessment with
the flexibility of the "use of force models" that are commonly used in
police work.[5] These models generally take a look at what kind of threat
the assailant poses and then use the level of force (nonlethal, verbal
control, physical restraint, lethal force) that is necessary to neutralize or
control the threat. In applying this model to warfare, the first determination that needs to be made is whether the person in question is, or is
likely to be, a combatant or noncombatant. Once this determination is
made, then the question of how to treat this person, precisely what
force is to be used and how, can be made by looking at *what kind* of

combatant or noncombatant she might be. This is where, even in dealing with a combatant, one might modify the kind and extent of force that one is using depending on the circumstance. To begin, let us look at each step in the model from the standpoint of assessing threat: What are the intentions of the subject? What are capabilities of that person to carry out any intentions?

The first and highest level of threat (the first category of combatant) would be that of the uniformed combat personnel. This would be an individual with a standardized (at least to his own military context) uniform with discernable symbols and identification announcing him as a soldier. This person carries a weapon openly, often travels in structured groups and has access to the resources of a larger military organization. It can be ascertained from a distance that his intentions are likely to be hostile, that he has the ability to carry out these intentions, and, therefore, poses the highest level of threat to a possible enemy. This category is how the combatant in conventional warfare has usually been defined and includes *anyone* who both carries arms openly and has such identifiable signs, including military chaplains and medical personnel who are armed. This category would also include insurgent fighters or revolutionaries who carry arms openly and who have a distinctive dress or visible sign—the black pajamas of the Viet Cong or even a blue or red bandana worn by certain U.S. inner city gangs. In a conventional combat situation, encountering this kind of combatant is a normal expectation. Since this type of individual clearly poses the largest threat on the scale (since they are not only a threat on their own, but have access to the resources of a military organization and their colleagues), the level of responsibility he must meet should also be high.

The second level of threat (the second category of combatant) would be an unconventional belligerent, not obviously in a standard uniform that clearly announces her intentions. Since this person is armed, it is likely that her intentions are hostile and since her intentions are not evident, but a weapon is, this comprises a fairly serious threat. It may turn out that she has no hostile intention at all—she may simply be afraid or be defending her property or family—but the presence of a weapon at least raises concern and potential threat. The fact that her intentions are not announced also points to the potential threat and, therefore, she should be viewed as a threat—at least until such time as she announces her intentions. One might encounter this kind of combatant in a conventional combat situation, raising questions about whether she is also to be treated with the same force that one would use against a conventional combatant. It is more likely this is the category of combatant that one would encounter in peacekeeping and humanitarian missions. Unconventional belligerents are common in contemporary warfare, but one also encounters armed child soldiers, civilians who are armed and trying to protect their homes and families, as well as civilian contractors who carry arms, particularly those who are engaged in security work (acting as bodyguards or protecting convoys, for example). The presence of clearly discernable arms is the relevant consideration here; one who is armed is a potential threat.

The third level of threat (the third category of combatant) would be classified as provisionally hostile. In this level the intentions of the individuals are not made clear by a uniform or other symbol declaring their intentions and it is also not clear whether or not they have weapons or easy access to them. However, these individuals may meet a certain description that fits potentially hostile forces, be present in an area where such individuals are suspected of operating or in some other way persuade the onlooker that they are neither neutral nor vulnerable (levels four and five noncombatants). This category might include suspected insurgents, suicide bombers, or children in an area where the use of child soldiers is common. In all of these cases it may not be clear whether or not the persons are armed; they may meet certain descriptions common to insurgents or suicide bombers in an area or generally be acting in what one might consider suspicious or threatening *given the context*. It is because of this probability of threat that persons in this category are to be considered provisionally hostile, at least until the facts of the matter become clearer.

While there is a fair amount of ambiguity in this category, it is necessary in order to accommodate differences between combat missions and those that are humanitarian or peacekeeping in nature. Clearly, what looks hostile in a combat situation may differ from other situations, or vice versa. In the less volatile situations one may be able to gather intelligence or use verbal skills to question the person or group, whereas in a combat situation one may have to assume they are hostile until nonverbal cues or behavior indicates otherwise. Another important component here is the fluidity of the situation, such that events and situations are highly volatile and subject to change, which makes the ambiguity of intentions and weapon possession dangerous.

Consider a security checkpoint near the Green Zone in Baghdad. A speeding car might not, *in another context*, be seen as threatening, but a speeding car approaching the checkpoint without slowing down—displaying no arms or indication of whether the occupants are combatants or noncombatants—is hostile, especially given a history of using car bombs to attack targets in the Green Zone. A group of angry young men, dressed in loose clothing that could conceal weapons, shouting religious epithets, and approaching soldiers might not be threatening in another context, but *in this context* is clearly hostile and could be a threat. A young woman, also dressed in loose clothing, approaches the checkpoint alone and with a calm demeanor, but does not respond to verbal questions or commands. In this context (where the possibility of female suicide bombers exists), she, too, could be categorized as hostile—at least for the time being. In all of these cases there is a potential threat, that must be responded to with force that is appropriate, but not excessive. These are examples of precisely the kinds of gray areas that those trying to apply the traditional binary distinction have difficulty in sorting out. Having this category allows recognition that there is a threat without necessarily resorting to lethal force, if it should turn out the threat can be dealt with another way.

At this point, it is essential to stress that these first three categories are different variations on the traditional combatant category; these individuals are to be treated more or less as one would treat a combatant, understanding that different levels of force may be appropriate. This also means that there is a clear conceptual distinction between levels three and four/five (even though individuals might move from the combatant categories to the noncombatant categories or vice versa.) Levels four and five are noncombatants and are entitled to the protections associated with those groups under International Law and the rules/customs of war.

The fourth level of threat (the first category of noncombatant) would be classified as one who is neutral or nonhostile. In this case the individual appears to announce no hostile intentions (symbolically by dress or insignia, by the presence of a weapon, or by verbal or nonverbal communication), but neither has she announced friendly intentions or evinced open cooperation with military forces. In terms of capability, she may have indicated (or opposing soldiers may have discerned) that she has no weapon, nor has she made an immediate attempt to gain one, but she may have potential (not immediate) access to some form of violent self-defense. As long as she maintains her neutrality/nonhostility, she could be considered to be a fairly minimal threat, but clearly if the neutrality appears to change then her status would move to either the third or final category. If the neutral stance is maintained then this person is not a threat, but care should be taken.

This category could include a wide range of individuals. On one hand, persons in this category could include enemy civilians who are sympathetic to or not openly opposing the enemy military forces. On the other hand, it could include military chaplains and medical personnel who would be in uniform, but are not armed. In addition, there are embedded reporters who may be wearing a version of a military uniform (or some kind of apparel with a fixed, visible sign to identify who they are), but are not armed or immediately escorted by an armed guard. The same might be true for civilian contractors who are attached to the military or work in military installations (administrative functions, interpreters, food service, other service-oriented functions), but who do not themselves carry weapons.

The final, lowest level of threat (the second category on noncombatant) would be one who is classified as vulnerable. Any hostile intentions that may be exhibited (i.e., a prisoner in uniform, angry speech) are counteracted by a clear inability or lack of desire to act on them. This individual poses a very minimal threat and, in fact, may require positive protection from other hostile forces. Many of the people who have been traditionally classified as noncombatants would fall into this category—most children, most women, the elderly, prisoners of war, and the infirm or injured—and should be accorded the usual protections because they pose little threat and may be threatened themselves. Persons in this category have no recourse to defend themselves; they will require protection from another. In addition, this class might include civilian contractors who do not have access to the protection of a military unit, freelance reporters, humanitarian workers—especially those connected with the United Nations, nongovernmental organizations (NGOs), or members of religious or other charitable groups (clergy, missionaries, civilian teachers, nurses, or orphanage workers) who may be in areas where conflict is occurring.

V

How might one implement this scale in the field? What difference will the five-part distinction make in identifying combatants and protecting noncombatants? To see how this expanded distinction might work, we need to look at conventional combat, counterinsurgency warfare, as well as peacekeeping and humanitarian missions. In each of the following scenarios, there are two important considerations; first, the fluidity of each situation and second, the flexibility of force that the additional categories bring to the analysis.

First, let us look at a conventional combat situation (e.g., the ground invasion of Iraq). Consider one of two variations on the Road to Basra scenario in which a convoy of Iraqi troops is leaving Kuwait City.[6] In the first version of the scenario, American troops encounter Iraqi regular troops and some paramilitary units who are still in rough military formations, but some of whom are displaying the white flag of surrender. A difficulty here is a past history of Iraqi troops misusing the white flag of surrender as an ambush ruse, not to mention the fact that it is not clear whether it is individuals or units who are trying to surrender. This scenario seems fairly straightforward, so the main determination to be made is whether a force differential between level one combatants (regular Iraqi army) and level two (if the paramilitary groups are not in some type of uniform, but clearly armed) is appropriate. It may also be the case that lethal force is appropriate to both levels, but that one uses different kinds of lethal force or different strategies in dealing with conventional belligerents as unconventional ones. In addition, the possibility of surrender raises the possibility of having level five noncombatants, who when they surrender are vulnerable and entitled to protection.

In a modified version of this scenario, we might have a convoy of people trying to escape the fighting in Kuwait. This convoy includes paramilitary units, but also includes various kinds of civilians, mostly unarmed. In such a situation it is likely that one will encounter persons in the second and third levels, as well the fourth and fifth categories. One must immediately ascertain whether the individual in question is a combatant or noncombatant. If the other turns out to be a noncombatant, then one can immediately lower the force used to be adequate to deal with level four (controlling the situation) while one ascertains what kind of noncombatant is involved. If one decides that the other is in fact level five, then one can further modify tactics.

On the other hand, if one ascertains that the other is a combatant (either through obvious signs or by a suspicion of hostility) then the soldier should start with force in accordance with level one or two, probably lethal force. If the other is a conventional belligerent, one would start with that scale of force and if not, one starts with level two force and moves down the scale if it becomes clear that less force is necessary. It should be pointed out that in many combat situations (both conventional and asymmetrical) level three persons could actually be more dangerous simply by virtue of what is not known, so that the force differential between levels two and three may be minimal if there is any difference at all. In all three of these levels, the other is or is regarded as a combatant and so lethal force could be legitimate, but it should be stressed that lower levels of force *may* be appropriate if they allow for the disarming of the combatant without resort to lethal force. It may be here that there are possibilities for using force to disable the combatant—shooting to injure rather than to kill—or using nonlethal weaponry to neutralize the combatant's ability to be a threat.

Second, let us look at counterinsurgency warfare in an urban setting that could be part of conventional combat or adjunct to peacekeeping or humanitarian type missions. We have a house-to-house search by troops looking for suspected insurgents, in particular the leaders of the insurgent group, as well as weapons caches or other material that would be relevant for intelligence purposes. In this case, it is very likely that one will encounter level two and three combatants and likely will encounter level four and five noncombatants living in these homes—whether or not there are insurgents or weapons present. In this case, the first order of business is to ascertain whether or not there are any combatants, especially of level three, who might be concealing weapons. While the soldiers would have to be prepared with lethal force in the event there are armed combatants, it is highly likely there are noncombatants so the level of force would likely need to be moderated quite quickly—using just enough force to control the situation and disarm any combatants who are armed and resistant.

Third, let us look at how this scale might work in the case of a peacekeeping operation (e.g., recent military interventions in Somalia or Haiti) where U.S. forces are charged with keeping opposing forces in check and/or keeping civil order, usually in an urban setting. In such a situation it is likely that one will be dealing with level two and three combatants, as well as level four and five noncombatants. In any case, as in the aforementioned combat scenarios one will still need to be able to discern combatants from noncombatants, typically a difficult task in settings where all of these individuals will be present in fairly large crowds. Unlike the last scenario where one is encountering small groups or individuals, in this scenario one also has to contend with the crowd dynamic where (1) it is harder to separate the combatants from the noncombatants and (2) because of the sheer numbers involved the situation will be harder to control, which may make it more tempting to use lethal force.

If it is determined that one is dealing with combatants, then one would start with the highest level of force applicable (likely to be level two and three) and modify in descending order as it becomes appropriate. For example, it may turn out that these are provisionally hostile forces who could turn out to be nonhostile noncombatants, but for now it seems likely that they are hostile and not clear whether or not they are armed. In this situation, one might be able to use less force than one would in a similar combat situation (because the individuals in question could be noncombatants, and also it is likely that there are noncombatants in the area), but because of the *potential* danger (level three is still a combatant category) one may still need to keep ready lethal force. Once it is determined that one is dealing with noncombatants or after one has isolated and dealt with the combatants, then the level of force would need to be reduced to the minimum amount necessary for crowd control and protection of any vulnerable (level five) noncombatants who are in danger.

Fourth, there is the case of a humanitarian intervention: protecting a civilian convoy in Rwanda when it is attacked by a local militia with orders to kill all Tutsis or protecting a civilian population in a UN-declared safe zone that suffers from nightly militia attacks and incursions. In these scenarios, it is likely that one has even more noncombatants in the area and is probably dealing with the level three combatants, although level two combatants could likely show up to disrupt the situation. One probably has to assume level three combatants with a force appropriate to dealing with level of threat, but also not unduly endangering the surrounding noncombatants. To further complicate matters, it may turn out that the level three combatants are level two combatants in disguise. The soldier must be prepared, but keep the higher level of force in check until the presence of weapons is ascertained. In peacekeeping and humanitarian missions, the force differential between levels two and three could be significant and so the difference between these two levels is important to establish. With a level two combatant, the first order of business is to disarm the combatant, whereas in level three one has to ascertain whether or not the person is armed. This may be one area where nonlethal weapons, designed to immobilize but not permanently harm, may be called for. Having the individual in question temporarily immobilized makes it simpler to ascertain the presence of a weapon and may aid in crowd control in situations (especially urban combat) where that is a complicating factor. In these two kinds of operations, individuals could easily move from level three to level four (you ascertain they do not have a weapon) or vice versa (they begin exhibiting hostile behaviors or gain access to a weapon as a situation escalates); one must quickly modify the kind of force that is appropriate in level three accordingly.

VI

To sum up, in each military operation, the first matter of business is to ascertain whether the individuals are combatants or noncombatants since that will determine which end of the scale one begins in determining the level of force. If they are noncombatants, then one starts with a lower (less lethal) level of force; if they are combatants, then one starts with the highest (most lethal) level of force appropriate to the likely kind of combatants—modifying (usually reducing) the level of force necessary as finer determinations are made about the kind of combatants involved and the threat posed. Clearly the differences in how one treats a hostile combatant versus a nonconventional belligerent in a combat situation may not always be obvious or drastic, but those differences will be much more significant in peacekeeping and humanitarian missions where verbal negotiation, nonlethal weapons, or other peacemaking strategies may be more appropriate and effective than lethal force.

What I want to suggest is that we can still maintain the traditional combatant/noncombatant distinction with its moral considerations, but also recognize that there are various levels within the parameters of that distinction—especially in how one might present as a combatant—that call for different levels of force and require some fluidity in how one applies that force. Rather than undermining the intentions of the traditional binary distinction, this expanded model potentially reduces unfortunate incidents of "collateral damage": soldiers have more options about how, when, and the extent of force they employ. The original distinction took seriously that at the core of fighting a war justly there are moral and practical differences between combatants and noncombatants; this model more clearly articulates what each of these categories might look like—taking into account the complexities and ambiguities of contemporary combat, peacekeeping, and humanitarian operations. The hope is that teaching, training, and using in the field a distinction that maintains the moral difference but also has some flexibility as to how force is to be applied—especially in different kinds of military situations—will enable soldiers to uphold and implement the distinction, despite the complexities, ambiguities, and fluidity of the contemporary battlefield.

NOTES

1. See Michael Bilton and Kevin Sim, *Four Hours in My Lai* (New York: Viking Books, 1992), 60, 74 ff.

2. See Organization for Security and Cooperation in Europe (OSCE), *Kosovo/Kosava As Seen, As Told,* part III, "The Violation of Human Rights in Kosovo." Online at http://www.osce.org/documents/mik/1999/11/1620_en. pdf.

3. For a more complete version of this argument, see my "Innocence Lost," presented at the Joint Service Conference on Professional Ethics (JSCOPE), 2002. Online at http://atlas.usafa.af.mil/jscope/JSCOPE02/Kaurin02.html.

4. Michael Walzer, *Just and Unjust Wars,* second ed. (New York: Basic Books, 1991), 145.

5. There is a great deal of debate about whether police models are appropriate and effective in military work. However, as the military becomes engaged in more peacekeeping and humanitarian work that seems to have more in common with police work than with "traditional" combat, some commentators are examining the similarities and looking for models that could apply to both. For an in-depth discussion of police models, see Lieutenant Colonel Robert Cassidy, "Back to the Street without Joy: Counterinsurgency Lessons from Vietnam and Other Small Wars," *Parameters* (Summer 2004), and Thomas D. Petrowski, "Use of Force Policies and Training: A Reasoned Approach," part II, *The FBI Law Enforcement Bulletin* (November 2002): 1–2.

6. For a complete discussion of this case, see Martin Cook and Major Phillip A. Hamann, "The Road to Basra," in *Case Studies in Military Ethics*, ed. Captain W. Rubel and George R. Lucas Jr. (Boston: Pearson Education, 2004), 65–74.

CHAPTER 7

Just War Theory and Child Soldiers

Reuben E. Brigety II and Rachel Stohl

"My life is dedicated to killing the Taliban. I will spend the rest
of my life finding the people who killed my family."
> —Mukhtar, age 15, soldier in the
> Northern Alliance for four years[1]

"There has been a revolution in our country for the last 20 years.
Because of the times, we have to take the young people and send
them to war."
> —Sarballan, Northern Alliance commander[2]

I. INTRODUCTION

Just as new kinds of technology (such as nuclear weapons and aerial
bombardment) have been examined with relationship to just war theory, new kinds of combatants also need to be taken into consideration.
One of the most disturbing trends of modern warfare has been the
increased use of children as combatants, largely by irregular forces but
also on occasion by the militaries of sovereign states. Given the special
status that children have historically been accorded as among the most
vulnerable members of society, their use as soldiers poses compelling
ethical problems with profound legal and policy implications. For
example, when children are armed with modern weapons that make
them every bit as lethal as adult combatants, how should this affect their
ability to enjoy their traditionally protected status as noncombatants?
What are the implications of this *jus in bello* question for the entire concept of noncombatant immunity? In addressing these questions, this

131

chapter will explore the challenge that the use of child soldiers presents to the continued development of military ethics and the ramifications it implies for international humanitarian law, military doctrine, and foreign policy.

II. CHILD SOLDIERS AND JUST WAR THEORY

The principle underlying the "discrimination" criterion of *jus in bello* is the notion that some people may be legitimate targets of attack during armed conflict while others, generally speaking, should not be. Richard Regan argues that innocence, characterized by the absence of "wrongdoing," can be the arbiter of who should fall into each of these categories. He writes:

> [J]ust warriors may directly target personnel participating in the enemy nation's wrongdoing but should not directly target other enemy nationals. The reasoning behind the principle is twofold: On the one hand, the enemy nation's wrongdoing justifies the victim nation's use of military force to prevent or rectify wrongdoing. On the other hand, enemy nationals not engaged in the war or contributing to waging it are committing no wrong against the victim nations, and so the victim nation has no just cause to target such nationals.[3]

Regan's argument is rooted in the concept of forfeiture, suggesting that the actions of some people in warfare can cause them to lose their "innocence" and make it morally permissible to kill them. Combatants typically fall in this group. Conversely, other people retain their innocence by not participating in combat and there should be a moral presumption against killing them. Noncombatants, wounded soldiers, and prisoners of war have traditionally fallen into this category.

Another way of thinking about innocence, however, has less to do with actions and more to do with identity. Many societies throughout history have believed that, in war, there are certain people who should be presumed to be innocent by virtue of their inherent vulnerability and, thus, should not be attacked. Traditionally, these people have included the elderly, the infirm, and children. Paul Ramsey writes: "[we] have only to know that there *are* noncombatants—even only the children, the sick, and the aged—in order to know the basic moral difference between limited and total war."[4] Children are of particular concern. Their vulnerability lies not only in their physical weakness relative to adults, but also in their impressionable emotional state as well as in their immaturity. For these reasons, it is a basic human instinct to protect children from the dangers of the world even in times of peace, and especially during times of war.

A profound ethical dilemma exists, then, when children participate in war. If a person can lose his "innocence" by participating in warfare and become a legitimate object of attack, then a child who engages in armed violence during war can be killed without moral consequence— or at least with no more moral consequence than killing an adult combatant. Yet such an implication grates against our most basic moral instincts to protect children from harm, even when they engage in behavior that may be dangerous to themselves or others.

III. USE OF CHILD SOLDIERS— GENERAL TRENDS AND DATA

Armed conflict has always had deleterious effects on children around the world. In countries plagued by war, children suffer from poverty, malnutrition, disease, lack of educational and economic opportunities, and the absence of reliable healthcare. But in the last ten years, in countries where the adult population, including parents and community leaders, has been diminished by these conditions, children have been forced to undertake adult responsibilities. One of the most horrific phenomena of modern warfare has been the use of and reliance on child soldiers. While the use of child soldiers is certainly not new to battlefield strategy (one must only think back to little drummer boys of the U.S. Civil War or their utility in World War II), the use of child soldiers has become increasingly more systematic and widespread in the intrastate wars of the last decade. In these wars, small arms have become the primary tools of violence, as they are low in cost, widely available, extremely lethal, simple to use, durable, easily portable, able to be concealed, and have legitimate military, police, and civilian uses.[5]

Hundreds of thousands of children are used as soldiers in virtually every current conflict waged around the world. The Coalition to Stop the Use of Child Soldiers estimates that twenty countries and territories had child soldiers used in their conflicts[6] and sixty countries recruited tens of thousands of child soldiers in the period between April 2001 and March 2004 alone.[7] Among the most egregious cases of the use of child soldiers are conflicts in Burma, Uganda, and Colombia.

Rebel groups, guerilla armies, militias, and armed gangs utilize child soldiers in their violent conflicts against each other, against the state, or to gain control of resources and power. Many of these armed groups would be unable to wage war without the added troop strength provided by child soldiers. Eighty percent of the Lord's Resistance Army in Uganda, for example, is believed to be made up of child soldiers.[8] Even though governments are bound by international law, child soldiering is not just a phenomenon among nonstate actors. Indeed, the coalition found that ten government forces have used child soldiers in direct combat[9] and continue to utilize children in combat support roles. Even when governments do not directly use children themselves, they may support paramilitaries and militias that use child soldiers, such as in Colombia and Sudan.[10]

There is no universally accepted definition of child soldiers, but most experts agree that child soldiers are "any person under the age of 18 who is a member of or attached to government armed forces or any other regular or irregular armed force or armed group, whether or not an armed conflict exists."[11] Not all child soldiers are direct combatants, and while some children wield assault rifles on the front lines, others are used in combat support roles as messengers, spies, porters, or cooks. Both boys and girls serve as child soldiers, with both genders suffering from sexual abuse. Girls face additional hardships, as they may serve as sex slaves as well as fulfill their soldiering responsibilities.

While child soldiers serve alongside adult soldiers, they often face dissimilar treatment on the battlefield. Child soldiers are seen as expendable and are forced to do the most dangerous tasks, such as walking across fields to clear the area of landmines or serving as human shields. In addition to rape, child combatants may also face dehumanizing treatment, such as torture and various forms of psychological abuse, at the hands of their adult commanders or other child soldiers. Child soldiers may become addicted to drugs and alcohol as they are often plied with these substances to make it easier for them to undertake combat activities.

IV. CHILDREN'S SPECIAL STATUS IN INTERNATIONAL LAW[12]

The 1949 Geneva Conventions and the additional Protocols I and II (1977) protect children from use in war. Protocol II, in particular, prevents children under the age of 15 from being recruited for or used in armed hostilities.[13] In 1989 these same standards were reinforced in the UN Convention on the Rights of the Child (CRC). While the CRC defined a child as any person under the age of 18, Article 38 established 15 as the minimum age for allowing children to serve as combatants, consistent with the standards set out in the additional protocols to the Geneva Convention.

In 1994 a working group was established in order to pursue developing a higher standard for the protection of children in conflict. The working group faced years of impasse as countries that use children under 18 in their armed forces (the United States and the United Kingdom, for example) were unwilling to allow a higher standard to be enshrined in international law. In the meantime, the July 1998 statute of the International Criminal Court (ICC) established, under Article 8, that it was a war crime to conscript or enlist children below the age of 15 into the armed forces or groups or use them to participate actively in hostilities. In addition, the June 1999 International Labor Organization (ILO) Convention 182 included child soldiers among the worst forms of child labor banned by the Treaty, prohibiting forced or compulsory recruitment of children under the age of 18 for use in armed conflict.

In 2000 the working group was finally able to reach agreement on developing a new standard concerning the use of children in armed conflict. In May 2000 the UN General Assembly adopted this agreement, known as the Optional Protocol to the Convention on the Rights of the Child on the Involvement of Children in Armed Conflict. The Protocol requires states to "take all feasible measures" to ensure that members of their armed forces under the age of 18 years do not participate in hostilities; prohibits the conscription of anyone under the age of 18 into the armed forces; requires states to raise the age of voluntary recruitment from the existing age of 15 and to deposit a binding declaration of the minimum age for that country's recruitment into its armed forces; and prohibits the recruitment or use in hostilities of children under the age of 18 by rebel or other nongovernmental armed groups and requires states to criminalize such practices.[14] The Protocol entered into force on 12 February 2002 and as of 26 July 2005 had been signed by 117 countries and ratified by 100.[15]

Regional agreements, including the African Charter on the Rights and Welfare of the Child (1990), encourage states to "take all necessary measures" to avoid the recruitment or use of children under 18 in combat. The United Nations has also become an important forum for addressing the issue of child soldiers and developing measures to high-light and tackle the use of child soldiers worldwide. Since 1999, the Security Council has adopted five resolutions that concern the protection of children in armed conflict; incorporate child protection into operational mandates; provide special provisions for the disarmament, demobilization, and reintegration of former child combatants; and encourage ratification of the Optional Protocol.[16] Moreover, in July 2005 the Security Council adopted a resolution that develops a mechanism "to collect and provide timely, objective, accurate and reliable information on the recruitment and use of child soldiers in violation of applicable international law and on other violations and abuses committed against children affected by armed conflict."[17] Monitoring will first commence in Burundi, Cote d'Ivoire, Congo Republic, Democratic Republic of the Congo, Somalia, and Sudan and will expand to examine practices in Colombia, Myanmar, Nepal, the Philippines, Sri Lanka, and Uganda in 2006.

V. CHILD SOLDIERS—THE IMPACT OF SMALL ARMS

Children suffer disproportionately from the privations of war. The misuse of small arms, however, increases the negative impact of war on children and contributes to their utility as soldiers. These weapons can become tools of human rights abuses, psychosocial trauma, and internal displacement. Their misuse also facilitates the weakening of the family structure, and contributes to limited access to healthcare, education, and economic opportunities, prevention of the delivery of humanitarian assistance, and undermining of food security. Moreover, small arms proliferation is a factor in the cultures of violence that influence the behavior and judgment systems of children.[18]

In the hands of children, small arms can become tools of horrific violence. Indeed, researchers have found that "small arms have made child combatants just as effective as adults, and have to a large extent erased distinctions between child and adult combatants."[19] For many children in conflict, the use of small arms is an integral part of their experiences as soldiers.[20] Children's use of small arms can be vicious. Because children do not have a fully developed sense of right or wrong, they can become brutal warriors, terrorizing populations and finding power in the barrel of a gun. Child soldiers may receive little or no training, but may be given assault rifles, machine guns, grenades, mortars, and rocket-propelled grenade launchers to wage war. Child soldiers may view their weapons as their primary tool for survival and be less than willing to turn in their weapons or participate in demobilization programs at the conclusion of conflicts.

VI. CHILDREN AS SOLDIERS— THE LOSS OF SPECIAL STATUS

The *jus in bello* criterion of discrimination presupposes the ability of actors to be categorized as combatants and noncombatants. As noted previously, such categorization can be based on the actions of an individual or on the individual's inherent identity as one who is in need of protection and thus should not be targeted.

Child soldiers present a morally complex problem because they cross this action/identity divide with regard to the discrimination criterion. On the one hand, their actions—particularly with small arms— can make them deadly adversaries on the battlefield and classify them as combatants who may be targeted. On the other hand, their identity as children suggests that they are individuals in need of special care who should not be the object of attack.

The action/identity dichotomy, however, must be seen as a hierarchy rather than a juxtaposition of equally important criteria. That is, individuals who are protected in warfare by virtue of their identity will retain their special status until their actions characterize them as combatants, when they will accordingly lose their protection. The wounded solider is morally entitled to succor until he fires on the enemy. The civilian shopkeeper should not be targeted unless he takes up arms against an invader. And the innocent child should be protected from the violence of combat, until he participates in combat himself.

The modern law of war reflects this hierarchical approach to the discrimination criterion. Article 50 of the 1977 Additional Protocol I (AP I) to the 1949 Geneva Conventions essentially says that any person who is not a combatant, as defined by portions of Article 4 of the Third Geneva Convention and by Article 43 of AP I, "shall be considered to be a civilian."[21] Article 51 of AP I goes on to say:

1. The civilian population and individual civilians shall enjoy general protection against dangers arising from military operations. . . .
2. The civilian population as such, as well as individual civilians, shall not be the object of attack. . . .

3. Civilians shall enjoy the protection afforded by this Section, *unless and for such time as they take a direct part in hostilities.* [Emphasis added].

Even though the killing of child soldiers who pose a threat to other combatants may be morally and legally permissible, it nevertheless presents a tactical and psychological problem to conventional military forces. In his acclaimed book *On Killing*, Lieutenant Colonel Dave Grossman writes:

> Being able to identify your victim as a combatant is important to the rationalization that occurs after the kill. If a soldier kills a child, a woman, or anyone who does not represent a potential threat, then he has entered the realm of murder (as opposed to a legitimate, sanctioned combat kill), and the rationalization process becomes quite difficult. Even if he kills in self-defense, there is enormous resistance associated with killing an individual who is not normally associated with [presenting tactical] relevance or payoff [through his or her death].[22]

Hence, while the actions of child soldiers may make them combatants who may be legitimately killed, their presumed identity as people who should be protected creates a powerful psychological barrier for the "moral" warrior who must confront them on the battlefield. This psychological barrier can have significant tactical consequences as soldiers try to decide when, and how, to engage this unique group of combatants.

VII. CHILD SOLDIERS— A CHALLENGE FOR MILITARY FORCES[23]

During the lead-up to the 2003 war in Iraq, experts debated the effects of the potential use of children by Iraqi forces. While experts agreed that the use of child soldiers would not impact the outcome of the war in Iraq, there was consensus that the use of child soldiers "could create considerable problems for coalition forces . . . and could slow the progress of U.S. forces, particularly when operating in an urban environment, and needlessly add to casualty totals on both sides."[24]

While child soldiering may not turn the tide of a war between militaries such as the United States and Iraqi, child soldiers do have the ability to impact a conflict's length, brutality, and tactics. Therefore, conventional militaries must undertake five categories of initiatives to deal with the reality of facing child soldiers on the battlefield: prepare before battle, consider all possibilities, think strategically, deal with the aftermath, and prepare for the future.[25]

First, in terms of preparation before battle, soldiers must familiarize with the threat posed by child soldiers in the area to which they are deploying. Militaries must focus on effective intelligence collection to determine whether or not child soldiers are present in an area and in what capacity they are used. Militaries must understand the impact child soldiers will have upon their own forces, as there may be significant psychological trauma that results from encountering and engaging child soldiers. Lastly, militaries must harmonize their doctrine, training, and rules of engagement for dealing with child soldiers before they enter the battlefield, to avoid confusion and casualties.

Second, militaries must consider all tactical possibilities for encountering child soldiers on the battlefield. Some strategies seem to be more effective in reducing the casualties of both child soldiers and conventional military forces when the two groups engage each other. For example, some military experts have found the value of firing for "shock," even though such actions are counter to traditional doctrine. Moreover, if possible, troops can learn to hold the threat of child soldiers at a distance, break up the threat by utilizing unconventional tactics, and try to shape the battlefield and create avenues for escape for those child soldiers eager to leave their fighting forces.[26] Lastly, if possible, militaries should exploit nonlethal weapons possibilities[27] to limit the casualties of child soldiers and prevent additional psychological hardships for forces.

Third, military forces must think strategically and utilize the intelligence gathered concerning the use and recruitment of child soldiers in the given area. When possible, military forces should target adult leadership and try to break up existing groups with which child soldiers fight. If the leaders of the units are gone, child soldiers may turn to avenues of escape. Military forces must eliminate recruitment zones, areas where children are vulnerable to conscription, and protect at-risk groups of children from recruitment (or re-recruitment). Military forces can employ tools already at their disposal, such as psychological operations (to convince child soldiers to stop fighting) and public affairs units (to explain that they are not there to harm children and to provide children with escape possibilities). Furthermore, military forces should be prepared to welcome and process prisoners and escapees who have been captured or chosen to leave their units. Child soldiers have needs that transcend those of their adult counterparts and require separate and specialized processing and demobilization. Such needs must be considered before the operation begins.

Fourth, military forces must prepare for the aftermath of the battlefield with regard to child soldiers. The military's engagement with child soldiers does not end once the fighting ends. Militaries must familiarize themselves with demobilization and reintegration programs in the area. Military forces themselves should not be responsible for disarmament, demobilization, and reintegration (DDR) programs but should look to identify which nongovernmental organizations and intergovernmental agencies are undertaking this work in the area in question. Child soldiers should be turned over to these groups as quickly as possible. And, just as importantly, the psychological needs of conventional forces must also be taken into consideration. The trauma of encountering and engaging child soldiers in battle can severely impact soldiers for years to come and those effects must be dealt with by trained professionals in a timely manner.

Fifth, militaries and their civilian colleagues can undertake efforts now to prepare for the continued reality of facing child soldiers in the future. For example, educating forces on a regular basis on the issue of child soldiers must become a regular aspect of training. Such preparation could include classes for students at home bases and units preparing to deploy to specific countries and regions; seminars, panels, and other forums that provide continuing education for enlisted soldiers and officers; the incorporation of child soldiers into exercises and war game scenarios; and foreign military training and joint exercises, where nations train with or for each other on battlefield tactics and strategies. These training sessions would allow troops to familiarize themselves with the child soldier issue; examine possible regions of future deployment where the issue of child soldiers is relevant; discuss possible tactics, techniques, and procedures; highlight international law and standards; and develop rules of engagement. Such training could save the lives of both conventional forces and child soldiers.

VIII. CHILD SOLDIERS—A CHALLENGE FOR MILITARY ETHICS AND FOREIGN POLICY

In some senses, the ethical challenge posed by child soldiers is no different from that of other ethical conundrums created by the nature of modern warfare. At its core, the problem is about innocence. If resort to warfare is justified (and if its moral conduct is defined) by protecting those who are innocent and attacking those who are not, then there must be some moral implication for the deliberate or accidental taking of innocent life in combat. Traditional approaches to just war theory deal with these problems through the *jus in bello* criterion of proportionality and through the natural law doctrine of double effect. They do so, however, by simultaneously recognizing the innocence of noncombatants who may be killed and reconciling it with the greater importance of the military objective sought (in the case of proportionality) or with intent of the one who takes such life (in the case of double effect). The fact that a child is killed in a bombing raid may be morally justified not because the child is any less innocent than she was previously, but because she may be in close proximity to the enemy's headquarters, whose destruction might bring great military advantage, or because her death was unintended by the bombardier.

The problem of child soldiers is unique, however, because the presumed and inherent innocence of children is made ambiguous by their martial conduct in war. Unlike adult noncombatants who take up arms and thus immediately lose their legal and moral protected status, virtually every cultural norm suggests that children require special protection. Yet there is nothing in *jus in bello* that explicitly suggests taking particular care toward a certain group of combatants. The discrimination criterion presumes a combatant/noncombatant distinction, which lays the foundation for the combatant's privilege to kill other combatants at will during war. The criterion does not require that soldiers only kill other soldiers who pose an imminent and direct threat, but allows them to kill any of the enemy at any time.[28] By this logic combatants could kill child soldiers at any time, so long as it was clear that they were combatants. This, however, is a less than satisfying result. The proportionality criterion is of little help as well. It has traditionally only applied to cases of complete innocence on the part of the noncombatants affected when trying to balance the harm done to them against the military necessity of the situation. Proportionality, strictly speaking, need not be applied to the killing of combatants by other combatants.[29] Finally, the doctrine of double effect is not of much help with regard to child soldiers because, presumably, a regular combatant intends to do harm in such cases, however regrettable they may be.

Therefore, the principal question that child soldiers create for military ethicists is the problem of providing special protections for a particular group of combatants. In other words, can the combatant's privilege be circumscribed in order to prevent unnecessary harm to child soldiers? If so, what are the criteria that would comprise such constraints and what are the implications for the conduct of warfare?

Central to these questions is the problem of risk. Even if one accepts that child soldiers still require extra protection given their status as children, this almost necessarily means that adult combatants may have to take additional risks to their own lives in order to protect a child that is also a potentially lethal adversary. What, then, should be the limits of those risks? Must child soldiers pose a clear and imminent danger to the life of an adult combatant before the latter is morally justified in killing the former? Or is it enough for a child soldier to be armed and identified with an enemy force during times of hostilities for their killing to be morally justified? Should such judgments be prudential considerations on the part of an adult combatant or should they be morally required? There is no other category of combatants with whom other combatants are morally *expected* to take similar risks. Such questions represent a departure from the breadth of ethical questions with which soldiers and ethicist have had to contend. The continued use of child soldiers in conflicts around the world, however, demands that these questions be studied and answered.

One potential framework for addressing these questions might be the following. First, for reasons outlined earlier, children are in need of special protections, even when they take up arms in the context of warfare. Furthermore, their immaturity and vulnerability to manipulation make them fundamentally different from adults who would normally be protected (such as civilians who engage in combat against an invader or wounded soldiers who fire upon an adversary) but whose considered and (presumably) mature decisions to enter combat strip them of their special status. Hence, child soldiers constitute a sui generis category of "protected combatants" who should be treated with particular care for their well-being.

Though they are of a special category, however, the protection afforded to child soldiers must not be absolute. Their potential lethality means that they can be just as dangerous as adult soldiers to an adversary. Since soldiers must be able to defend themselves against threats on the battlefield, it follows that child soldiers must not have an uncontested ability to kill other soldiers in combat by virtue of their special status. Neither should commanders be able to employ children in combat with a reasonable assurance that they will not be engaged.

Such a situation would only encourage the recruitment and use of minors, creating a perverse moral hazard for those who try to treat child soldiers in an ethical manner.

Hence, as difficult as it is to contemplate, adult combatants can justify the application of lethal force against child soldiers, but only under conditions that account for their immaturity and exploitation. Two principles should guide this action: self-defense and proportionality.

In the context of warfare, soldiers need not determine that regular adult combatants pose an imminent threat to their lives in order to be morally and legally justified in killing them. Their very identity as soldiers implies that they are a threat to an enemy force, regardless of whether they are supply clerks or snipers. The same assumption, however, should not be made for child soldiers. This is not because their age makes them any less lethal than regular soldiers, but because applying the same logic that is applied to adults about why they pose a threat would necessarily permit a much wider scope of hostile action toward children than would seem to be morally appropriate. Thus, rather than *assuming* that children pose a threat, adult combatants should apply a three-part test to determine if a child soldier is a threat in the circumstances prevailing at the time, and thus may be killed in self-defense under the principle of forfeiture. The three-part test is:

- Capability: Does the child posses the means to mount a lethal attack against a combatant?
- Intent: Does the child demonstrate through his actions a lethal intent toward an adversary?
- Immediacy: Do the child's capability and demonstrated hostile intent create a circumstance in which there is no time for any other reasonable action for self-defense other than engaging the child with hostile force?

The second general principle that should be considered regarding child soldiers is proportionality. As noted earlier, proportionality is not applied to combatants, but rather to noncombatants who may be subject to harm in the course of combat operations aimed at the enemy. It is not legally necessary that an attacking force refrain from killing soldiers who are in retreat but not surrendering (though one could make a moral case that one should spare the lives of an enemy force that is not actively resisting). It is, however, both legally and morally required that an attacking force weigh the military advantage that will likely come from an attack against the anticipated harm that it will cause to noncombatants. To improve the protections of child soldiers, the concept of proportionality should be applied to them as well. For example, an attacking force should consider whether the military advantage from assaulting an ammunition dump is worth the deaths that will result from the child soldiers who are guarding it. It may very well be that the answer to such a question, tragically, would be yes. By adhering to this criterion, however, two results would follow. First, it would minimize unnecessary loss of life among children in an enemy force. Second, by permitting an attack to occur if the advantage was great, it would prevent an enemy from gaining special protection for an objective by guarding it or surrounding it with child soldiers, thus discouraging their use in such circumstances.

Finally, rather than being prudential in nature, consideration of such a moral framework should be incumbent upon every adult combatant who encounters a child soldier on the battlefield. This would make the application of these principles less arbitrary and more likely to save the lives of children forced to engage in war.

Precisely because the use and engagement of child soldiers is such a vexing moral problem, it has implications for foreign policy as well. One of the most remarkable characteristics of the post–Cold War era, and indeed of international relations since the end of World War II, is the increased importance of normative considerations in the development of foreign policy. From the drafting of the Geneva Conventions and the Universal Declaration of Human Rights to the debate surrounding humanitarian intervention and the "responsibility to protect," governments are increasingly affected by the role of normative concerns as both means and ends in foreign policy. During Operation Enduring Freedom in 2001–2002, for example, United States government officials took great pains to assure a global audience that it was doing everything it possibly could to avoid civilian deaths as it prosecuted its war against Taliban and Al Qaeda elements in Afghanistan. They did this, arguably, not only because of a humanitarian impulse to avoid unnecessary human suffering, but also because they understood that the death of large numbers of innocent civilians could undermine the strategic objectives for which they were using force in the first place—namely, to eliminate terrorist threats against the United States.

Similarly, the deaths of child soldiers in a war zone where a state is conducting military operations could also undermine the strategic objectives that are the basis of the use of force. This may be especially true if the stated political purpose for action is humanitarian in nature. Television images of young children dead on a battlefield, killed by a state's military, could have profound repercussions for the direction of a particular set of foreign policy initiatives, even if those children had been combatants. Avoiding such circumstances will require not only skillful "message management" but also rules of engagement based on an ethical framework that takes into account both the requirement to protect children and the necessity of engaging them in combat.

NOTES

1. Quoted in Hannah Beech Farkhar, "The Child Soldiers," Time.com, 4 November 2001 at http://www.time.com/time/asia/news/magazine/0,9754, 182805,00.html.

2. Quoted in David Rhode, "12–Year-Olds Take Up Arms Against Taliban," *New York Times*, 2 October 2001.

3. Richard J. Regan, *Just War: Principles and Cases* (Washington, DC: The Catholic University of America Press, 1996), 87.

4. Paul Ramsey, *War and the Christian Conscience* (Durham, NC: Duke University Press, 1961), 444.

5. Jeffery Boutwell and Michael Klare, "Special Report: A Scourge of Small Arms," *Scientific American* (June 2000): 30–35.

6. Coalition to Stop the Use of Child Soldiers, *Global Report 2004* (2004), 13.

7. Ibid., 14.

8. World Vision, "Pawns of Politics: Children, Conflict and Peace in Northern Uganda" (2004), 18.

9. Coalition to Stop the Use of Child Soldiers, *Global Report 2004*, 13.

10. Ibid.

11. Ibid., 15.

12. For more detail on the agreements discussed in this section, see Rachel Stohl, "Children in Conflict: Assessing the Optional Protocol," *Journal of Conflict, Security and Development* 2:2 (2002): 135–140.

13. NGO committee on UNICEF's Sub-Working Group on Children in Armed Conflict, "Summary of International Treaties to Protect Children in Armed Conflict" (May 1999).

14. Protocol, Articles 1–4. General Assembly Resolution 54/263, adopted 25 May 2000.

15. The United States has ratified both ILO Convention 182 and the Optional Protocol, but neither the Convention on the Rights of the Child nor the ICC Statute.

16. Specific resolutions dealing with the issue of children and armed conflict include UNSC Resolutions 1261 (1999), 1314 (2000) 1379 (2001), 1460 (2003), and 1539 (2004). The text of the resolutions are posted at http://www.un.org/Docs/sc/unsc_resolutions.html.

17. United Nations Security Council, Resolution 1612, par. 2(a), 26 July 2005.

18. For more information on the impact of small arms on children see Rachel Stohl et al., "Putting Children First—Background Report," Biting the Bullet Project (December 2001); Stohl, "Under the Gun: Children and Small Arms," *African Security Review* 11:3 (2002); and Stohl, "Targeting Children: Small Arms and Children in Conflict," *Brown Journal of World Affairs* 9 (Spring 2002).

19. Stohl et al., "Putting Children First—Background Report," 10.

20. However, while small arms may make the use of children more feasible and attractive, the relationship is not causal, nor does small arms proliferation serve as an indicator for the use of children as soldiers. Around the world, there are many examples of child soldiers being used in areas without excessive supplies of small arms, and child soldiers may not be used in areas saturated with small arms. See Stohl et al., "Putting Children First—Background Report"; Stohl, "Under the Gun: Children and Small Arms"; and Stohl, "Targeting Children: Small Arms and Children in Conflict."

21. It must be noted that while Article 4 of the Third Geneva Convention and Article 43 of AP I present the criteria for being a combatant as someone who is a member of the armed forces of a party to the conflict, of other militias, or of the regular armed forces of another government not recognized by the detaining power, it is reasonable to assume that the drafters of the Convention did not foresee the use of children as members of these forces. This can be deduced from the fact that elsewhere in the conventions, especially the Fourth Convention, the drafters took care to note that children were to be accorded special protection in times of belligerent occupation. Thus, we can infer that the intent of the drafters was to assume that children are noncombatants by virtue of their inherent vulnerability and traditional position in society, and that they should be accorded the protection of Article 51 unless, as stated in paragraph 3, they take a direct part in hostilities.

22. Lieutenant Colonel Dave Grossman, *On Killing: The Psychological Cost of Learning to Kill in War and Society* (Boston: Little, Brown and Company, 1995), 174–175.

23. For additional analysis on tactics for fighting child soldiers, see P. W. Singer, *Children at War* (New York: Pantheon Books, 2005), chapter 9.

24. P. W. Singer, "Iraq Memo—Fighting Saddam's Child Soldiers," Brookings Institution, January 14, 2003, Memo #8.

25. These five initiatives utilize information presented by Rachel Stohl and Colonel Charlie Borchini, USA (ret.), Research Fellow, Center for

Emerging Threats and Opportunities, as part of a seminar on child soldiers delivered to noncommissioned officers assigned to the Marine Corps Combat Development Command on 31 January 2003; officer faculty of The Basic School, 7 March 2003; the House International Relations Committee on 25 June 2003; the 11th Marine Expeditionary Unit on 5 January 2004; the Potomac Institute for Policy Studies on 20 April 2004; and the NEH Summer Institute "War and Morality" at the United States Naval Academy, 2 June 2004.

26. P. W. Singer, "Iraq Memo—Fighting Saddam's Child Soldiers."

27. Ibid.

28. This, of course, presumes that a combatant is not *hors d'combat*. Should a soldier become wounded or if he surrenders, then the modern law of war as well as certain martial traditions throughout history dictate humane treatment.

29. While this interpretation of micro-proportionality may be controversial in an ethical sense, the law is clear. An attacking force, for example, need not refrain from killing an enemy that is in retreat but is not surrendering, even if ceasing such an attack would spare further enemy lives.

CHAPTER 8

Dehumanization of the Enemy and the Moral Equality of Soldiers

Michael W. Brough

> Looking another human being in the eye, making an independent decision to kill him, and watching as he dies due to your action combine to form the single most basic, important, primal, and potentially traumatic occurrence of war. If we understand this, then we understand the magnitude of the horror of killing in combat.
>
> —Lieutenant Colonel Dave Grossman[1]

I. INTRODUCTION

In the book that ignited contemporary just war discourse, Michael Walzer posits the moral equality of soldiers, holding all combatants are blameless for the *jus ad bellum* crimes of their countries:

> In our judgments of the fighting, we abstract from all consideration . . . the justice of the cause. We do this because the moral status of individual soldiers on both sides is very much the same: they are led to fight by their loyalty to their own states and by their lawful obedience. They are most likely to believe that their wars are just, and while the basis of that belief is not necessarily rational inquiry but, more often, a kind of unquestioning acceptance of official propaganda, nevertheless they are not criminals; they face one another as moral equals.[2]

Walzer's conception of moral equality is a thick one, more specific than conceptions of moral equality considered by rigid Kantianism or

149

utilitarianism, but it is one I accept. Thinner, or more general, conceptions argue for the moral equality of soldiers on the basis of principles that regard all soldiers (including enemy combatants) as ends in themselves, or as sentient beings whose happiness counts as much as any other's in a selection of options. In accordance with such thin conceptions, soldiers on all sides of a conflict are morally equal in the sense that they all possess some moral value to be considered, but soldiers may also be blamed for the wrongness of their cause: soldiers are potentially responsible here (through conscious participation in an unjust war, or through mere negligence) for furthering an injustice, and soldiers may be moral equals, even while they are criminals due to complicity.

David Rodin's recent criticism of the moral equality of soldiers runs along this line.[3] He argues that soldiers (like executioners, who mete out sentences but do not decide them) might be exculpated for fighting *if* they had good reason to trust the government's decision for war. The context of a fair judicial system and a difficult case would fulfill the conditions for considering the executioner unblameworthy, even for a wrongful execution. Rodin does not consider most soldiers to be in a similar circumstance, though: if, as Grotius tells us, only less than half the states that fight in wars are fighting justly (according to *jus ad bellum*), then odds are that any randomly chosen war is wrong. Knowing this, soldiers who are not capable of independently judging a war's *jus ad bellum* justness would be morally reckless to fight simply on the state's assurance that the war is just.[4]

Walzer's conception, and the one to which I am drawn, takes account of the circumstance of common soldiers worldwide. They are uneducated, lacking in refined reasoning abilities, and unprepared to navigate the complexities of foreign policy. One of war's tragedies is that a large portion of the fighters in most wars are immature—physically so, as well as mentally and morally. The claim is not true always, of course, as many soldiers are fully developed and well-educated; statistically speaking, though, the overwhelming majority are not. And far more often than not, soldiers (and populations as a whole) are led into war by a campaign of misinformation and propaganda against which they have little defense. When confronted with the combination of a staggeringly complex moral problems (requiring intricate understandings of law, ethics, history, international relations, and the all-too-hard-to-get contextual facts), the realization that one's state and people may be in grave danger, and the state's forceful assurances that *this* war is as just as any war ever has been, it is easy to see that the common soldier's decision to fight is understandable. That does *not*, of course, mean it is the right decision. But because most soldiers lack both the ability to understand the moral issues involved in going to war and the faculties to discern between truth and government-propagated lie, we usually cannot hold a soldier blameworthy for his participation in an unjust war.[5]

The notion is not a new one in the development of just war thought; rather, it has remained a measure to prevent wholesale slaughter of the enemy, a constant (though, history shows us, not always successful) reason for returning defeated foes back to their lives, a step toward a return to normalcy and peace—for how can one punish in the enemy what one would have done oneself, if in the same situation? It has also provided a check on a wartime inclination that I will argue is dangerous both pragmatically and morally: to dehumanize one's wartime opponent.

Dehumanization is something of a universal wartime tradition, and it found willing participants in its perceptual viewpoint throughout the twentieth century.[6] Consider the following letter from the war zone: "Dreadful, dreadful race; the more we see them from close up, the more we loathe them. The bands of prisoners are revolting to see, vile, trying too hard to be liked, delighted to be caught. . . . It is annoying to get killed behind the parapet by such animals. They have a peculiar, powerful odour."[7] Although Augustin Cochin, the author of the letter, aims his vitriol toward the Germans, his enemy in the First World War, one could easily imagine the same words penned by any Serb about Croats (and vice versa), by Hutus and Tutsis, by Americans, Iraqis, Koreans, Afghans, Russians, Chechens . . . and by Germans about Frenchmen like Cochin. The idea that the enemy is subhuman is powerful, and it strikes me that the idea is both a catalyst for and a result of the environment of killing. Whether the killing in war causally precedes the dehumanization of the enemy (such that a soldier learns that the enemy must be subhuman from actions taken on the battle-field—"after all, if he were a person possessing inherent worth, why would we be shooting him?") or the killing committed within the context of war can be psychologically permitted only after a soldier already perceives his enemy as something other than a fellow human is a fascinating psychological question—one that, while important, I will sidestep in my evaluation of the moral universe of war. Although the answer to this "chicken-or-the-egg" question is beyond the scope of this essay, I suspect most will agree that these two aspects of war—the dehumanization of the enemy and the collective killing of "it"—become mutually reinforcing, and to some degree inseparable.

Dehumanization might seem morally unconscionable in the modern context, but it still possesses its contemporary exponents and practitioners. Writing during World War II, Columbia University psychiatrist Leonard Sillman explained that the common (nonintellectual) soldier needed more than mere facts to motivate him to kill other humans: "all the technics [sic] of mass suggestion and pressure need to be employed. The approach, of necessity, must stir deep emotions of hate and revulsion against the enemy, inasmuch as it is impossible for most men to embrace passionately an ideal or a concept without passionately hating its antithesis. . . . This can be accomplished only by a highly condensed dramatization of the virtues and the immortal greatness of the Allied countries and the loathsome, revolting and degenerate qualities of the Axis countries."[8] According to Sillman, equipping the fighter with dehumanized conceptions of the enemy is tantamount to outfitting him with "a steel helmet prior to going into battle to protect his brain from external trauma."[9] The practice of dehumanization has in some ways continued: soldiers fought "gooks" in Vietnam, and they fight "ragheads" or "hajis" in Iraq. Although most professional militaries would officially frown upon the practice, it is unknown how often this kind of immunization against killing is self-prescribed by troops and lower-level leaders. But the mindset is extant today. According to a veteran of Operation Iraqi Freedom, "You just sort of try to block out the fact that they're human beings and see them as enemies. . . . You call them hajis, you know? You do all the things that make it easier to deal with killing them and mistreating them."[10]

Seeing the enemy as monstrous is only one form of dehumanization, and it need not take this particularly repugnant form. The practice may instead paint all the members of one group with a common moral stain. According to psychologist Lawrence LeShan, wartime changes perception, so that in wartime, "'We' and 'they' are qualitatively different, so different that the same actions are 'good' when we do them, and 'evil' when the enemy does them. There is doubt that we and they really belong to the same species."[11] Common contemporary use of the term *terrorist* provides examples of this, when so often the action considered valiant taken by one's own forces (say, a suicide mission against a legitimate military target) becomes terrorist activity when undertaken by enemy forces.[12]

As Sillman and others have explained, there is a variety of reasons to dehumanize in combat: dehumanizing removes psychological barriers from the killing that combat requires, and it provides the soldier a bulwark against psychological damage. In this essay, I will argue against that somewhat intuitive strain, reasserting the importance of the just war tradition's moral equality of soldiers for both moral and prudential reasons.

II. CONFUSING ENEMY AND ETHNICITY

For some people (perhaps the practitioners—the soldiers and state officials whose decisions involve life-and-death repercussions), ethical arguments may take a back seat to the pragmatic ones. So my first argument is one that appeals on both levels. The dehumanization of the enemy, as frequent as it seems in war, has historically resulted in going too far—in erasing all distinctions except for that of friendly/enemy, rendering anyone who does not wear *my* uniform or does not look like *me* (racially, for example) into a legitimate target. We have seen in the past century the results of this psychological tool: the Nazis characterized Jews as vermin, and this rationalization cleared the moral path for the genocide that followed. Later genocides in Europe and Africa have followed the same kind of logic: when other races are characterized as subhuman, they no longer retain a dignity that is uniquely human. When they are seen as animals (and animals are seen as expendable), they can be butchered as pigs or sheep.

The atrocities that result are not limited to totalitarian regimes. The American-perpetrated massacre at My Lai during the U.S. intervention in Vietnam is a classic, horrific example of dehumanization of an enemy that became the dehumanization of an entire race: "Americans fighting [the war in Vietnam] . . . become profoundly confused by their inability to distinguish the enemy from the people. Their anger at allies who do not fight, and who seem to be part of an environment of general deterioration, becomes readily converted into racist perceptions of the Vietnamese as nonpeople."[13]

In that case, a number of American troops committed a fundamental error (and one that resulted in moral, psychological, and political disaster). It is important to see what the error is comprised of, at least in terms of what ignites moral repugnance. The soldiers at My Lai

were culpable of a moral glissando, one eliding the Vietnamese Viet
Cong and North Vietnamese Army with the Vietnamese civilians
(and, one wonders, perhaps their South Vietnamese allies). According
to Robert W. Rieber and Robert J. Kelly, "what was immediately pal-
pable to people back home—that the victims of My Lai were women
and children—was exactly what was absent from the point of view of
the soldiers involved. From their point of view, they were merely
enacting a due measure of revenge against the gooks."[14] Richard
Swain, an American Vietnam veteran and current Olin Professor of
Officership at West Point, takes issue with Rieber and Kelly's description, writing that "what was absent from the point of view of the soldiers was not the gender and age of the victims but the notion that
gender and age entitled the victims to protection."[15] Swain's correction
reinforces my point: it is easy to see that the tactic of dehumanization
of the enemy possesses the potential to undermine an operation's
political and moral coherence. The danger enters even in offhand
comments, like the occasionally heard "the only good [Krasnovian] is
a dead [Krasnovian],"[16] and even when dehumanization does not
impair the effort as a whole, it can leave an indelible moral taint. The
World War II internment of Japanese-Americans did not significantly
besmirch the overarching justice of the Allied cause, but left its own
blot in America's ethical history.[17]

As I write, similar attempts at dehumanization threaten American
efforts in Iraq and Afghanistan. The U.S. soldier's conception of the
enemy spills over, seemingly ineluctably, into his conception, and con-
comitant treatment of, other groups of persons—prisoners of war
(POWs), for example, and even common citizens. Though these
groups share with Iraqi combatants such features as a common culture,
common language, common ethnicity, and common religion, they are
dissimilar in important ways from Iraqi combatants who are engaged
in battle. As at least some soldiers find themselves blurring the moral
status distinctions between different groups of people in Iraq, they find
themselves endangering or mistreating the groups they should protect
and respect.[18] Perhaps as a result of dehumanization, some U.S. Army
personnel have been charged with murders (that is to say, extra-com-
bat killings) and prisoner abuse. The mistreatment of prisoners by
Army police personnel in the Abu Ghraib prison continues to grab
headlines many months after its initial revelation. In a telling interview, an American soldier remarks that the way Iraqi prisoners were
described made a significant difference in how they were treated: "We

were pretty much told that they were nobodies, that they were just enemy combatants. . . . I think that giving them the distinction of soldier would have changed our attitudes toward them."[19]

III. THE PSYCHOLOGICAL COST OF DEHUMANIZATION

The objects of dehumanizing treatment are its most obvious, but not its only, victims. When a soldier dehumanizes the enemy, he makes himself more psychologically apt to violate *jus in bello* prohibitions. While those who suffer at his hands suffer the first-order effects of war crimes, he himself (perhaps the only survivor) must endure the higher-order effects. These can include punishment or censure by his military unit. They may also involve a psychological torment very few of us can understand—a torment that, according to psychologist Jonathan Shay, is not psychopathic, but rather that of "good people who will be seared by knowing themselves to be murderers."[20]

But even when dehumanization does not result in war crimes, it can still take a psychological toll. Acts that comply with the war convention but are committed in an unfavorable frame of mind can become incredibly damaging for the soldier decades after the war's terminus. I use the word *unfavorable* to avoid the issue of moral wrongness, though I will confront that issue in a later section of this chapter. My present idea, like that of the previous section, takes account of the consequences: the torment that results from a policy of dehumanization can be crippling; if we can reasonably avoid it, we ought to.

So crucial is the practice of dehumanization to some combat veterans' psychological debilitation that their treatment requires a sort of reversal: "Restoring honor to the enemy is an essential step in recovery from combat PTSD [post-traumatic stress disorder]. While other things are obviously needed as well, the veteran's self-respect never fully recovers so long as he is unable to see the enemy as worthy. In the words of one of our patients, a war against subhuman vermin 'has no honor.'"[21] Although Shay does not make the assessment explicitly, he implies that much of the psychological devastation he has treated in U.S. veterans from the Vietnam War might be precluded in future conflicts if soldiers can avoid seeing their enemies as monstrous or inhuman. Perhaps even better for them would be to accord a certain amount of honor to their enemies.[22] Dave Grossman agrees: killing an enemy while respecting him is a "noble kill," an event that "place[s] the minimum possible burden on the conscience of the killer. And thus the soldier is able to further rationalize his kill by honoring his fallen foes, thereby gaining stature and peace by virtue of the nobility of those he has slain."[23]

An important aspect of this conversation is the state's obligation to its soldiers. In time of war, the state claims absolute authority over the soldier's life, available to use and sometimes discard. But this absolute authority over the soldier lasts only for a time, and the state must continue to respect its soldiers as human beings even as it uses them as tools for waging war. Kant's dictum is relevant here: states, like humans, ought not treat their soldiers as a means only, but as ends in themselves, as well. If states do this, they will not simply refrain from squandering lives, but they will also bear in mind their soldiers' psychological well-being. During the fighting, the state will look not just to winning the war, but to the post-conflict welfare of its fighters. If a state values the latter, it will choose against a policy of dehumanization; in doing so, it simultaneously improves its chances of attaining the former.

IV. THE REALITY OF MORAL EQUALITY

A final reason against dehumanizing the enemy is that there is no moral basis for the practice. In his essay "The Narcissism of Minor Difference," Michael Ignatieff portrays the mirror image of dehumanization—nationalism—as a particularly dangerous perspective from which to view the surrounding world.[24] Nationalism within war (or, ostensibly, outside it) distorts reality, making the rightness of one's people dwarf the rightness of others, and requiring the characterization of enemies as inferior. A first irony, of course, is that all sides of a conflict feel this way—each views itself as obviously superior vis-à-vis its competitor. A second is that both sides are so often completely wrong: it is agonizingly common for all belligerent parties to have made atrocity commonplace, so that the common claims of unique purity all ring simon-pure.

For Ignatieff, nationalism "takes 'minor differences' [such as custom, language, culture, tradition, and history]—indifferent in themselves—and transforms them into major differences."[25] Ignatieff's experience from recent conflict in Croatia informs his writing here, but the point is widely relevant: notice how much conflict in the past century shares this common trait with the fighting in the Balkans, that it involves peoples which, though they vehemently hate each other's members on the single criterion of nationality, are otherwise relatively indistinguishable to the larger world. I suspect I am not alone in being unable to differentiate between a Tutsi and a Hutu.

We must admit that even when they do exist, racial and ethnic differences are minor ones. Physical attributes are extremely poor criteria for winnowing out the inferior—morally or otherwise.[26] As far as moral judgments go, a nation's history, or a people's custom, or a state's economic system is equally lacking. That an individual shares these aspects with others probably says very little about him as a moral being—doubtless, it says nothing *conclusive* about him, and it therefore cannot be a credible basis for dehumanizing the enemy soldiers one must face in combat. In his philosophical account of World War II fighting, J. Glenn Gray characterizes the image of the enemy held by "reasonable men": "the opposing enemy as an essentially decent man who is either temporarily misguided by false doctrines or forced to make war against his better will and desire. The foe is a human being like yourself, the victim of forces above him over which he has no control . . . people are much alike all over the world, and only an accident of history has made the soldier across the front into a foe rather than an ally."[27]

It is for this reason that Richard Holmes remarks that the "concept of a hateful and inhuman enemy rarely survives contact with him as an individual."[28] When a soldier gets to know the enemy, the enemy transforms from a demonic creature to a person much like me—with a spouse, children, memories, dreams. This realization is one reason that surrendering soldiers often hold up pictures of their families as they capitulate: they count not so much on their enemy's human decency or willingness to adhere to international law as on the recognition of persons much like themselves. They hope for a visceral and immediate reaction to the family pictures, as anything slower can be deadly. I suppose that, for most, glancing at the photos will be unintentional—certainly unbidden, perhaps undesired, as they return humanity to the enemy and thereby make the act of killing him (their single-minded purpose only a moment before) seem repugnant again. It would seem that a soldier would have to be either extremely driven or extremely callous to kill a surrendering enemy with the prospective widow and orphans clearly in mind.

Grossman describes what accepting surrender entails: "In order to fight at close range one must deny the humanity of one's enemy. Surrender requires the opposite—that one recognizes and takes pity on the humanity of the enemy. Surrender in the heat of battle requires a complete, and very difficult, emotional turnaround."[29] And yet, the immediate reversal of perception is possible, we know, as fighters *are* taken prisoner in war. When this happens, the captors accept a vision of the enemy much closer to the truth than the dehumanizing caricature they had possessed: a creature who is, as Grossman notes, both human and pitiful. In this way, perhaps, the soldier notices how very much alike he and his foe are.

It seems one of war's ironies that adversaries on the battlefield commonly have more in common with each other than they do with their own countrymen, at least in the moment they are fighting. They share with their people the most superficial characteristics (race, language, custom), but are really isolated from them by the experience of combat. Encountering killing close-up does (or can do) something to humans, separating them from the larger society; killing another human being, it is often said, "changes you forever." During one of Grossman's interviews, a Vietnam veteran described simply what the "worst of it" was for him: the fact that he had killed accounted for only half of the pain. "The other half was that when we got home, nobody understood."[30] In some ways, though perhaps not the commonly understood ones, wartime foes are something like brothers in arms, for they have experienced the same horrors and bear the same psychological scars. If they could move across battle lines and breach the language barrier, they would no doubt find war-born commonalities that overwhelm similarities to "the folks back home."

Another irony (which serves to reinforce the positional, though not actual, kinship between wartime enemies) is that even while dehumanizing the other, they commonly dehumanize themselves, as well. Soldiers become aware that their own lives, though valuable, are also disposable. The understanding that one's life is, in the big scheme, insignificant within the context of war is another aspect of armed conflict that places mortal enemies in the same camp, opposed to those who lack the experience. Opponents on both sides use cadences and other tricks to accustom themselves to the possibility of their own deaths, understanding full well that the state may easily forfeit their futures in its pursuit of other goals. In the end, the dehumanization of the enemy or of oneself traduces the truth of the matter: that human life, whether instantiated as a foe, a comrade, or oneself, possesses value.

V. COMMON HUMANITY

There is the very real possibility that the moral high road—compassion for one's enemy even while killing him—is out of the question for psychological reasons. Perhaps for one (normal) human being to kill another in combat *does* require a special mechanism that perceptually removes the latter from the realm of common humanity. According to Grossman, "In order to fight at close range one must deny the humanity of one's enemy."[31]

Sun Tzu made a similar, though not identical, point over two millennia ago: "The reason troops slay the enemy is because they are enraged."[32] Sun Tzu's illustration of this principle deals with retribution by the Ch'i army for war atrocities including defiling corpses of the war dead and disfiguring prisoners. Recognize, though, that with Sun Tzu, foes become the objects of rage caused by acts they (each one) did not personally commit. There may be arguments in support of justified anger or righteous indignation—ire in the face of a gross injustice—but these arguments cannot often be leveled at soldiers taken individually. If it is the case that anger is to be reserved for targets that warrant it, then the generic enemy soldier will not be considered less than human for moral reasons.

The injunction for soldiers to love their enemies, derived from Christ's own command to love one's enemy in biblical passages such as Luke 6:27, is a part of the just war tradition that seems forgotten in recent years (and perhaps neglected in all times). Augustine portrays dehumanization as condemnable: "The passion for inflicting harm, the cruel thirst for vengeance, an unpacific and relentless spirit, the fever of revolt, the lust of power, and such like things, all these are rightly condemned in war."[33] These human traits are prima facie reprehensible, both within and without the context of war.

How, then, should soldiers view the killings they commit in war, and how should nations teach their soldiers to view them? Dehumanization is too costly. Is it possible, though, to simultaneously kill and love one's enemy? The warrior, in Vitoria's day and now, should heed the radical friar's advice to the prince: "remember that other men are his neighbours, whom we are all enjoined to love as ourselves (Matt. 22:39); and that we all have a single Lord, before whose tribunal we must each render account for our actions on the day of judgment. It is a mark of utter monstrousness to seek out and rejoice in causes which lead to nothing but death and persecution of our fellow-men, whom God created, and for whom Christ suffered death."[34] The religious and non-religious alike should apprehend the signal point here: that we are more like our enemies than we sometimes want to imagine. If states and their soldiers can learn to see the enemy as someone fully human and individually morally equal, they will discern the moral landscape more clearly and avert moral disaster for both sides of the war.

Is not revulsion the natural reaction to suffering and death exacted upon one who does not deserve it, and perhaps regret the appropriate feeling if I myself have knowingly caused it? It seems that the notion of ennobling the enemy, seeing him as a moral equal (or at least recognizing his potential in this regard), requires that one feels a degree of sorrow at his death, or perhaps recognizes a loss. When one kills a human, it seems that the action demands something of that sort, and that such a demand unmet is another of the injustices of war, with (as Grossman and Shay tell us) damaging psychological repercussions.

Psychological repercussions notwithstanding, Grossman admits the importance of Stanley Milgram's idea of "total distance from the victim" in making killing easier for a moral agent. Grossman's application of Milgram to explain killing in war indicates that the act of killing becomes easier as physical distance and emotional distance increase. The first category of distance is both self-descriptive and intuitive: stabbing a foe is more difficult than shooting soldiers at a distance, which is still more difficult than killing soldiers one cannot even see unaided. The second category includes social distance (which emphasizes differences in social caste), cultural distance (which accentuates racial and ethnic differences), and moral distance (which envisions the enemy's moral inferiority).[35] This second category is the most familiar method of dehumanization: portrayal of the enemy as something approaching the *sub*human: either base, as an animal or insect, or evil, as a monster or demon. I will call this brand of dehumanization *subhumanization* in order to distinguish it from a different form.

There is, as I have argued, strong moral impetus for political and military leaders to deny subhumanization a foothold in the military. For reasons of prudence and ethics, they should suppress the practice of identifying the enemy as demonic or monstrous. What is the best way to do this in a time of combat? There are a number of solutions available to heads of state, officers, and noncommissioned officers, some more coercive than others. Perhaps the best initial method to change the culture of subhumanization is by personal example. From leaders of squads to leaders of nations, those who recognizably refuse to subhumanize, and instead accord respect to an unknown foe, can change the perceptions of troops.

Milgram's second category also contains a more recent technique that seems morally different from the others: mechanical distance (which involves viewing the enemy through a "mechanical buffer" such as a thermal sight or radar screen).[36] This enabler of dehumanization allows perception of the enemy not as a *sub*human creature, but as something *non*human. The age of *nonhumanization* began with the invention of indirect trajectory artillery, when enemy soldiers became pushpins or pencil dots on maps, or shouted coordinates to a gun section. In the past few centuries, artillery batteries often have never seen the results of their actions, and the feel of artillery combat is therefore different than that of frontline infantry combat. Through improved technology, the scale of nonhumanization has expanded, as enemies are with increasing frequency fought and destroyed as blips on a computer screen. There is an acceleration, perhaps unstoppable, toward soldiers in today's technologically sophisticated militaries becoming able to see their enemies only as dots—things neither base nor evil, but also things devoid of inherent worth.[37]

Nonhumanization, too, presents problems for the just war tradition's common understanding that soldiers on all sides of a conflict are moral equals. If it is important, as Shay and Grossman have argued, for combat veterans to honor their slain enemies, then nonhumanization might rob combat soldiers of this opportunity. Firing a cruise missile from a ship-based platform prevents the naval crew from coming to terms with the deaths they have caused. The question becomes: Is something lost here? If so, do those who kill this way share in the loss—though not equally—with the killed, since they are deprived the opportunity to honor the fallen? And, offered no other weapons, do they inevitably disregard the humanity of the enemy?

The answers to these questions are similar in many respects to the replies given for subhumanization. But there may be something freeing in nonhumanization, as well—freeing in the sense of making killing easier. The previous sentence's idea is abhorrent to me, and no doubt it should seem so to any who read it. Making killing easier is not what we all, seeing the enemy as a being with worth, should embrace; we should instead seek to retard those things that make killing easy.

This is, naturally, the paradox of just war thinking. For its inadequacies, the just war tradition has got at least one thing unequivocally right: that war is hell and ought to be avoided. Augustine states it forcefully: "And so everyone who reflects with sorrow on such grievous evils, in all their horror and cruelty, must acknowledge the misery of them. And yet a man who experiences such evils, or even thinks about them, without heartfelt grief, is assuredly in a far more pitiable condition, if he thinks himself happy simply because he has lost all human feeling."[38] Of course, whether we ought to avoid the terrors of war at all costs or not remains the key contentious issue that separates inheritors of the just war tradition from pacifists. But assuming non-pacifism—that is, assuming that war for *some* causes and motivations, and by *some* means, *can be* just—requires accepting that killing can be morally defensible. If killing can be morally defensible, even morally obligatory sometimes, should we always seek to "retard those things that make killing easy"? In the *jus ad bellum* sense, perhaps: the easier it is for a state's soldiers to kill, the greater the effortlessness with which it can vanquish an enemy. The greater the effortlessness of war, the greater the motive to conduct it, and the weaker the inhibitions against using organized violence as a substitute for diplomacy.

And the relative effortlessness of war counts in the decisions for or against war in obvious ways. The body of just war thought is a moral goulash, filled with references to Christ, Kant, and consequences, but the practical decision about going to war seems almost always one of pure cost and benefit.[39] Costs and benefits can be construed a number of ways, to be sure, and human goods can be calculated in spiritual, moral, or material terms, using considerations of rights, desires, and other metrics.[40] However a state's legitimate authority calculates the likely outcomes of military restraint, a recourse to war in accordance with the just war tradition must outweigh the enormously high costs that have never failed to accompany war; it seems that while they may disagree with particular methods for calculating the costs of war and restraint, all just war theorists would agree with this simplification of the central decision of *jus ad bellum*. The fulfillment of the *jus ad bellum* principles of just cause, right intention, and right authority must be combined with a satisfactory proportionality of ends: if the foreseen outcome is tragic, and the just cause, while just, is also slight, war is unwarranted and therefore unjust. This principle is what, generally speaking, can allow (or perhaps even mandate) intervention against mass atrocity or genocide when the moral repercussions for doing nothing are unconscionable, and prohibit armed interference in the face of limited violations of human rights, as repugnant as they may be, considered individually.

This consequences-focus carries over into the conduct of war in this way: if the war is justified (that is to say, if its expected horrific effects are sufficiently less than the expected horrific effects absent military action[41]), then soldiers must be allowed to kill. States must be allowed to direct that killing, and (if acting rightly) they will attempt to make the killing increasingly efficient. One aspect of this is making the killing increasingly easy for the fighters. Distancing those who kill from their targets seems intuitively to diminish the psychological burden on the killers. If we regard their actions as at the least morally neutral, thereby acquitting them of wrongdoing, then we should applaud the (ceteris paribus) reduced chance for psychological disaster. Whether the intuitive is the actual in this case is a question for psychology to investigate.

In such a case, though, it appears there is something lost. Standoff technology now allows weapons crews to receive and execute fire missions for missiles targeting unseen objectives—at very little risk to themselves, so that the killing of enemy soldiers can become a mere interruption from a movie or card game, two favorite distractions from modern wartime's boredom. Can not noticing the death of the enemy be as harmful as hating him? If we feel uneasy about such a scene, perhaps it is because we recognize that an intangible aspect is missing. In refusing to "retard those things that make killing easy," we have attained our goal, and made killing easy. But easy killing does not preclude honoring the dead after the battle. A prayer, a thought, a muttered farewell might suffice as a sign of respect for the fallen. Perhaps there is something not simply beneficial, but inexplicably appropriate about honoring one's enemy in war, even while killing him.[42]

V. CONCLUSION

If my description of dehumanization is reasonably accurate, then it should influence both how soldiers do battle and how they think about their enemy. Even more so, it should influence the military leaders and the states for which they fight. The leaders, for their part, should make positive steps to prevent subhumanization within their units, not hesitating to address the comments and actions that demonstrate it. And, while training soldiers to nonhumanize, they should train them to honor their enemies after a kill.

States have a double responsibility. The first mirrors that of their military leaders: to set in policy the unambiguous disapproval of subhumanization of the enemy—to affirm the moral equality of soldiers—and to live this in speech and deed. The second concerns the state's unique *jus ad bellum* role: that state governments that choose war should do so with a lucid appreciation of war's psychological prerequisites and results, both for the individual fighter and for the larger state populace, and that the leaders of such states should enter into war cautiously, hesitantly. A choice for war not only engenders bloodshed, but risks turning its perpetrators into moral monsters, with the entire civil society facing the burden of moral culpability.[43]

NOTES

1. *On Killing* (New York: Little, Brown and Company, 1995), 31.

2. *Just and Unjust Wars*, third ed. (New York: Basic Books, 2000), 127.

3. *War and Self-Defense* (Oxford: Oxford University Press, 2002), 165–173.

4. Ibid., 169–170.

5. I am sympathetic to the view that in some cases, cognizant soldiers may be morally responsible, but as a general and overarching statement of the moral relation between soldiers of different sides (as well as a rule directing soldiers' guilt for unjust wars), it seems to me Walzer's description is more morally accurate. For an example of an argument attacking the idea that all combatants are free from blame with regard to the wrongness of their cause, see Richard Schoonhoven, "Invincible Ignorance," in *Moral Theory and Military Action: New Essays on the Just War Tradition*, ed. Roger Wertheimer and George R. Lucas Jr. (Albany: State University of New York Press, forthcoming).

6. I have found especially valuable the following two studies of accounts of dehumanization taken from memoirs, literature, and interviews: Richard Holmes, *Acts of War: The Behavior of Men in Battle* (New York: The Free Press, 1985), 360–393; and Peter S. Kindsvatter, *American Soldiers: Ground Combat in the World Wars, Korea, and Vietnam* (Lawrence: University Press of Kansas, 2003), 192–228.

7. Augustin Cochin, quoted in Stéphane Audoin-Rouzeau and Annette Becker, *14–18: Understanding the Great War*, trans. Catherine Temerson (New

York: Hill and Wang, 2002), 146. I wish to thank Edmund Santurri for recommending this history to me.

8. "Morale," *War Medicine* 3 (1943): 500.

9. Ibid. A helpful review of the sparse psychological literature on dehumanization of the enemy is John A. Ballard and Aliecia J. McDowell, "Hate and Combat Behavior," *Armed Forces and Society* 17 (1991): 229–241.

10. Quoted in Bob Herbert, "'Gooks' to 'Hajis,'" *New York Times*, 21 May 2004, late edition, A23.

11. *The Psychology of War: Comprehending Its Mystique and Its Madness* (Chicago: The Noble Press, 1992), 36.

12. To what extent the just war tradition applies to a "war against terror" is itself vigorously debated, of course.

13. Robert Jay Lifton (interview) in Erwin Knoll and Judith Nies McFadden, *War Crimes and the American Conscience* (New York: Holt, Rinehart, and Winston, 1970), 105.

14. "Substance and Shadow: Images of the Enemy," in *The Psychology of War and Peace: The Image of the Enemy*, ed. Robert W. Rieber (New York: Plenum Press, 1991), 17.

15. Email communication with author, 8 January 2005. Swain continues: "That is a very different thing entirely and it matters because stated that way the deviance is amenable to treatment and punishment."

16. For a number of years, Krasnovians have been the enemy at the U.S. Army's National Training Center in California. The name, of course, is a substitute for any current or future enemy of the United States.

17. For a disturbing examination of reciprocal dehumanization within World War II's Pacific theater, see John W. Dower, *War without Mercy: Race and Power in the Pacific War* (New York: Pantheon, 1986).

18. A U.S. Army commander made this commonsense comment about the difficulties of appraising a civilian populace that is indistinguishable from the enemy: "The soldiers have been asked to go from killing the enemy to protecting and interacting, and back to killing again. . . . Soldiers who have just conducted combat against dark-skinned personnel wearing civilian clothes have difficulty trusting dark-skinned personnel wearing civilian clothes." Human Rights Watch, *Hearts and Minds: Post-war Civilian Deaths in Baghdad Caused by U.S. Forces*, available at http://hrw.org/reports/2003/iraq1003/.

19. Douglas Jehl and Andrea Elliott, "Cuba Base Sent Its Interrogators to Iraqi Prison," *New York Times*, 29 May 2004. To some, the terms *combatant* and *soldier* are interchangeable. It is obvious from the statement, however, that *enemy combatants* meant something different in this context. *Enemy combatants* were nobodies, whereas *soldiers* were (I presume) people more honorable, more worthy, perhaps more like us?

20. *Odysseus in America: Combat Trauma and the Trials of Homecoming* (New York: Scribner, 2002), 224–225.

21. Jonathan Shay, *Achilles in Vietnam: Combat Trauma and the Undoing of Character* (New York: Touchstone, 1994), 115.

22. Shay makes his case for the latter specific: based in part on his reading of the Iliad, he believes it possible (and preferred) to kill one's enemy while simultaneously honoring him; see *Achilles in Vietnam*, 103–119.

23. Grossman, *On Killing*, 196.

24. "The Narcissism of Minor Difference," in *The Warrior's Honor: Ethnic War and the Modern Conscience* (New York: Metropolitan, 1997), 34–71.

25. Ibid., 51.

26. Ignatieff writes, "Genetic research shows that there are no significant variations in the distribution of intelligence, of cognitive or moral ability, among racial, ethnic, or gender groups. The significant variations are among individuals *within* these groups. The paradox of intolerance is that it customarily fixes on the group differences as salient and ignores individual difference." Ibid., 62–63.

27. *The Warriors: Reflections on Men in Battle* (Lincoln: University of Nebraska Press, 1970), 158–159.

28. Holmes, *Acts of War*, 368.

29. Grossman, *On Killing*, 199.

30. Quoted in ibid., 250.

31. Ibid., 199.

32. *The Art of War*, trans. Samuel B. Griffith (New York: Oxford University Press, 1971), 75 (II: 16).

33. *Contra Faustum*, xxii: 74. Cited in Thomas Aquinas, *The Summa Theologica* (New York: Benziger Bros., 1947), II–II, question 40.

34. Francisco de Vitoria, "On the Law of War," in *Vitoria: Political Writings*, ed. Anthony Pagden and Jeremy Lawrance (New York: Cambridge University Press, 1991), 327.

35. Grossman, *On Killing*, 188–189.

36. Ibid.

37. The ability to deliver precision munitions brings with it other moral complications I will ignore here; see Michael Ignatieff, *Virtual War: Kosovo and Beyond* (New York: Metropolitan, 2000), 161–215; and Paul W. Kahn, "War and Sacrifice in Kosovo," *Philosophy and Public Policy* 19 (Spring/Summer 1999), also available at http://www.puaf.umd.edu/IPPP/spring_summer99/kosovo.htm.

38. *The City of God*, trans. Henry Bettenson (New York: Penguin, 1984), 19:7; see Herbert A. Deane, *The Political and Social Ideas of St. Augustine* (New York: Columbia University Press, 1963), 157.

39. This is not to say that the discourse of the JWT is conducted in these terms, but that the decisions heads of state make typically are. And so the lofty requirements of justice vie with budgetary considerations, for example. Of course, there is more than a consequentialist tinge inherent in the JWT: prin-

ciples of macro- and micro-proportionality highlight it. I argue the criterion of last resort does, as well: many have rightly noted that the last resort is never really the last option available (see Michael Walzer, *Arguing About War* [New Haven: Yale University Press, 2004], 88). One thing that makes the last resort a final attempt is a look to the consequences, an attempt to balance (1) the probability of "just one more" diplomatic effort's success with (2) the probable strategic costs of waiting for this next diplomatic effort to work.

40. There is also the question of whose costs and benefits count, and how much.

41. Precisely how we define the *jus ad bellum* threshold for military action is problematic, and I will not touch upon it here. It appears the consequential analysis that just *barely* supports military actions cannot be regarded as sufficient reason to war, but the threshold's precise location is a subject I am not at all sure about.

42. I am not prepared, therefore, to agree with Sam Keen, author of the fascinating exploration *Faces of the Enemy: Reflections of the Hostile Imagination* (New York: Harper and Row, 1986). In his catalogue of methods of dehumanization, he lists what I have called nonhumanization as the foulest of the list, worse than equating the enemy with monsters, animals, or death itself. In his words, nonhumanization reduces the foe "even to the point of not dignifying him with an image we can hate" (86).

43. The views expressed in this chapter are those of the author and do not reflect the official policy or position of the U.S. Department of the Army, the U.S. Department of Defense, or the U.S. government. I would like to acknowledge the help of the following individuals, who include scholars, military personnel, and combat veterans; my thanks to Richard Anderson, Nancy Brough, Rex Hall, Anthony Hartle, John Lango, Rob Sayre, Richard Swain, and Harry van der Linden.

PART 3

Intervention and Law

CHAPTER 9

Rethinking the Ban on Assassination: Just War Principles in the Age of Terror

Whitley R. P. Kaufman

The September 11, 2001, terrorist attacks appear to have undermined, at least in the United States, what had previously been a firm moral and legal consensus against the use of political assassination. Though it is banned under international law[1] and has been prohibited as a matter of U.S. policy since 1976 when President Ford signed an executive order banning assassination, U.S. policy appears to have reversed course in response to the increase in terrorist attacks. President Clinton revealed at a news conference in 2001 following the Trade Center attacks that his administration in 1998, following the bombing of U.S. embassies, had authorized the "arrest and, if necessary, the killing of Osama bin Laden," though a lack of intelligence prevented the successful completion of the mission. In October 2001 George Bush authorized the CIA to carry out missions to assassinate Osama bin Laden and his supporters (and indeed publicly declared that bin Laden "was wanted, dead or alive"). In addition, Israel has increasingly resorted to the use of assassination of terrorist leaders among the Palestinians to prevent suicide bombing attacks. Vigorous debates have also arisen over the question of the potential assassination of political leaders such as Saddam Hussein or Muammar Qaddafi. More fundamentally, these actions have taken place in a shifting moral environment, in which the earlier assumption that assassination is morally impermissible no longer seems convincing in an age of terrorism.

In this essay I will analyze the ethics of political assassination from within the context of the just war tradition. Just war doctrine involves a strong presumption against the use of violence or killing (in peace-

171

time or in war) outside of certain limited contexts, specifically the punishment of the guilty, defense against an unjust attacker, and the enforcement of natural justice or law. Even in those contexts, the use of violence is subject to the just war requirements including last resort (aka necessity), proportionality, noncombatant immunity, and right motive. Crucially, just war doctrine rejects the Realist/consequentialist position that an action can be justified merely because it leads to good overall results (though of course consequences are morally relevant in just war doctrine). Given that the most commonly stated rationale for assassination is consequentialist in nature—that is, that assassination would be the most efficient means of achieving one's goals—the practice of assassination would then seem to be ruled out in just war doctrine. But is this in fact the case, and even if it is, does the rise of terrorism and weapons of mass destruction require a modification of the tradition? On one extreme is the view that assassination is never morally permissible, no matter the circumstances; at the other extreme is the position that the conditions of the present day are so dangerous that traditional moral constraints must be sacrificed where necessary. I will argue here that neither position is correct; assassination is not automatically prohibited by just war doctrine, though it will be morally permissible only under very limited circumstances.

A first issue is, of course, the problem of defining *assassination*, a concept which is very difficult to pin down. Traditionally, the term *assassination* was held to refer to killing by means of treachery, betrayal, or perfidy. Some commentators have argued that this prohibition reflected a concern for honor or chivalry, and that it was not meant to prohibit targeting military or political leaders per se. Thus Caspar Weinberger has argued that when assassination is forbidden in the law of armed conflict, what is meant is "murder by treacherous means,"[2] and that therefore there is nothing wrong with assassination per se, so long as it does not involve "treachery." This argument however is a red herring. Whatever the concerns about the use of treachery in war, the central moral issue at stake is not the betrayal of trust, but rather the morality of premeditated, extrajudicial killing of specific individuals (i.e., those in leadership positions). Such an action would seem far removed from the paradigmatic case of justified killing: the soldier on the battlefield with a weapon in hand. Alberico Gentili, for example, allowed for seeking out the leader on the battlefield, but disapproved of the killing of the leader if he were "remote from arms and happened to be swimming in the Tiber," for this is killing an "unarmed man remote from war.">³ Such actions would ordinarily be considered simply murder, and the question is whether there is sufficient moral basis for permitting such a prima facie wrongful act. Some commentators have adopted the term *targeted killing* so as to avoid any connotations of treachery associated with the term *assassination*.⁴ However, in this essay I will use the terms *assassination* and *targeted killing* interchangeably, whether or not "treachery" is involved. The moral question is then whether assassinations—the premeditated, extrajudicial killings of a named individual—are permissible or not under just war doctrine.

A second issue we will have to examine is whether there is an essential difference between military and political leaders as regards the legitimacy of assassination. It is often assumed that military leaders, as they are obviously combatants under just war principles, are legitimate targets in wartime, and therefore it is permissible to assassinate them. Political leaders such as Saddam Hussein or Fidel Castro, some have argued, are different: they are not obviously combatants, even where they have ultimate control over the military. Similar difficult questions concern countries where the commander of the military is a civilian, as in the United States. The question is of course further complicated by the problem of assigning combatant status at all when there is not a state of war, especially as regards the problem of terrorism, which takes place in what William Banks calls the "twilight zone between war and peace."⁵ But even within terrorist groups one can distinguish between political and military leaders. Israel's policy to date has been to accept just such a distinction within terrorist organizations such as Hamas, so that it does not try to kill political leaders who do not direct suicide bombers. This Israeli policy may however be breaking down currently, and many advocates of assassination reject the political/military distinction as artificial.

The question to be faced then is the following: is there a moral basis for a policy of premeditated, extrajudicial killing, and does it depend on whether the target is a military or merely political leader? Discussion of this question is often muddled by a failure to clearly distinguish the punishment rationale from the self-defense rationale for assassination. Indeed, the idea of justifying a policy of assassination under the rubric of punishment would seem to run into intractable moral problems, for a policy of summary execution without trial or any significant procedural constraints would not ordinarily be considered a legitimate form of punishment. Consider for example Caspar Weinberger's discussion: he begins with a just war defensive rationale for targeting leaders on the grounds that they are combatants), then switches to a punishment argument ("there is every reason to punish the leaders for the acts that brought on the war"), and ends with a consequentialist rationale for assassination ("killing leaders may end a war with a big saving of soldiers' lives").[6] He concludes that if killing the leaders would not violate the laws of armed conflict, "then clearly the taking of any enemy commander (without any treachery) and holding him for trial conducted under normal national rules would not violate any moral or legal prohibition."[7] But the confusions in this argument are legion. The just war tradition, as I have said, does not obviously dictate that heads of state are combatants, and in any case Weinberger's invocation of consequentialist justifications are clearly ruled out under just war doctrine. More importantly, the syllogism with which Weinberger concludes his essay—that if killing the leader is permissible, then trying him is permissible—is not to the point. What is clear is that capturing an enemy commander and placing him on trial is morally and legally permissible. What is not clear is whether intentionally killing him—without benefit of trial—is permissible.

Given that the punishment rationale for extrajudicial assassination seems so obviously inapt, and given that most commentators do not want to resort to the Realist/consequentialist reasoning that Weinberger invokes, it is no surprise that most defenders of the assassination policy invoke a self-defense rationale. Thus, for example, Secretary of Defense Donald Rumsfeld reportedly told CNN that "the US would be acting in self-defense" in carrying out missions to assassinate bin Laden and other terrorists.[8] Yet even this line of argument is repeatedly conflated with nondefensive justifications. Brenda Godfrey, for example, defends Rumsfeld's position, and correctly distinguishes self-defense from backward-looking motives of reprisal or retaliation.[9] Yet she too fails to clearly distinguish defense from forward-looking consequentialist or punishment motives. When there is an imminent threat of a terrorist attack, she argues, force is justified "in order to prevent the attack or to deter further attacks."[10] But the deterrence rationale is not obviously part of the doctrine of self-defense. Rather, deterrence belongs to the sphere of punishment and of consequentialist reasoning. Godfrey also appears to conflate the preventive use of force with the consequentialist justification that whatever leads to the best results is thereby morally permissible, as evidenced by her claim that "use of force should include the covert killing of the terrorist because it is the most efficient means of averting future harm."[11] Thomas

Wingfield similarly invokes deterrence, consequentialist, and punishment rationales for assassination: "The proportionality doctrine of international law supports a conclusion that it is wrong to allow the slaughter of 10,000 relatively innocent soldiers and civilians if the underlying aggression can be brought to an end by the elimination of one guilty individual."[12] So, too, does Louis Beres confuse self-defense with consequentialism, arguing that the right of self-defense in Article 51 of the United Nations Charter authorizes assassination, given that a "utilitarian or balance-of-harms criterion could surely favor assassination" over large-scale uses of defensive force.[13]

Beres further asserts that in certain circumstances, the resort to assassination would be "decidedly rational and humane."[14] It is important to acknowledge just how tempting the idea of assassination is even from a moral standpoint. It offers a trade of a single death to avoid the death of millions, and as former White House press secretary Ari Fleischer put it, "The cost of one bullet, if the Iraqi people take it on themselves, is substantially less" than going to war.[15] The televangelist Pat Robertson recently on his television program called for the assassination of Venezuelan President Hugo Chavez, on the grounds that assassination is "a whole lot cheaper than starting a war."[16] Perhaps more pertinently, it appears to vindicate our moral sense, in that assassination goes directly after the responsible, indeed morally guilty, parties rather than after the "innocent" soldiers who in most cases are merely following orders, often under duress (as for instance in the Iraqi army). Jeff McMahan, for example, far too quickly assumes that morality favors targeting the guilty in war rather than those presenting a direct threat: "morality concedes that certain morally noninnocent noncombatants, like the political leader who initiates an unjust war, may be attacked."[17]

However, as tempting as these arguments sound, they do not in fact provide a moral basis for killing in war. Under just war doctrine, the primary justification for killing in war is defensive; it follows that neither of the aforementioned factors is morally relevant. The rationale of self-defense, as we have said, is distinct from the consequentialist or Realist rationale that aims to minimize overall costs and permits adopting any means so long as the ultimate end is permissible. Equally important, moral guilt, while it is the basis for the justification of punishment, is not the rationale for the use of defensive force. Defensive force in general is justified by the fact of aggression, not by the guilt of the aggressor. Hence soldiers may be killed even if they are not morally guilty of any wrong. "Innocence" in just war doctrine (and in self-defense doctrine generally) is a term of art, meaning one who is not presently threatening harm (from the Latin *nocere* = to harm). Thus it is crucial to understand the nature of the justification for killing and avoid conflating incompatible moral theories.

Thus we may conclude that the just war rationale for killing enemies in conflict is that the enemy poses a direct, unjust threat that can be countered by no other means than violence. While this rationale is often described as *defensive*, this term must be understood in a broad sense. That is, it is not necessarily limited to imminent or immediate threats, but can include preventive force against potential future threats. Thus the just war tradition has long recognized the legitimacy of *preventive* force against a potential future threat (assuming one has also satisfied the conditions of last resort, proportionality, and other requirements for going to war).[18] One is legitimately entitled to act so as to protect oneself against an unjust threat, even if that threat is in the future and not yet imminent. However, it is crucial to note the distinction between the preventive rationale and the consequentialist justification. For the consequentialist, any use of force is justified so long as it leads to a net balance of good results. The just war preventive rationale, in contrast, insists that one is also constrained by a moral duty only to use harm against unjust threats. It is this distinction that accounts for why terrorism (intentionally targeting civilians for political or military purposes) is prohibited under just war doctrine, whereas terrorism in principle would be morally permissible for consequentialism. For just war doctrine, the preventive or defensive use of force must be targeted only against an unjust attacker.

Hence the question facing us, in order to determine whether assassination is permissible, is whether political or military leaders are legitimate military targets, that is, whether they are unjust attackers. It is often taken as uncontroversial and unproblematic that military leaders are legitimate military targets, given their presence in the chain of command—and sometimes this is extended to political leaders, too, so long as they direct the military. Thomas Wingfield, for instance, approvingly cites Schmitt: "lawful targeting in wartime has never required that the individual actually be engaged in combat. Rather, it depends on combatant status. The general directing operations miles from battle is as valid a target as the commander leading his troops in combat. The same applies to Saddam Hussein. Once he became a combatant, the law of war clearly permitted targeting him."[19] But, even apart from the logical leap between military commanders and heads of state, the chief error in this passage is what we might call the *formalist fallacy*. Just war doctrine indeed is often accused of formalism (sometimes called *essentialism*), of making combatancy simply determined by one's formal role, as if one can simply read off one's combatant status by identifying the essence of one's role. But this is I think a mischaracterization of just war doctrine.

Stephen Kershnar, for example, accuses the just war doctrine of holding that certain roles have "essences" that in turn determine one's status as combatant or noncombatant.[20] A doctor's essential role is to heal, a farmer's essential role to grow food; hence they are not combatants. But a soldier's—and a military leader's—essential role is to fight, thus making him a combatant. The question of whether a political leader is a legitimate target then comes down to the question of whether his role is essentially one connected to aggression. Kershnar rightfully criticizes this view as clumsy and unconvincing. Indeed, it is not even clear on this view whether the political leader is a combatant or not. Is the nature of his role political leadership or military leadership? The formalist doctrine is also unhelpful in its application to terrorism, where there is no war and thus no combatancy in the technical sense. But it is also wrong, I would argue, because it mischaracterizes just war doctrine.

In the just war doctrine, combatancy is not determined by one's formal status, but rather by one's current and ongoing actions: that is, whether they constitute aggression or not. A soldier who lays down his weapons, or is no longer a threat, is no longer a combatant for purposes of exercising one's right to use deadly force. He may be captured, but he may not be shot. Correspondingly, a civilian who takes up arms and attempts aggressive action is a legitimate target, despite not being a combatant in the formal or essential sense. In other words, there is no avoiding a substantive analysis of the notion of combatancy. One is a combatant to the extent one is engaging in unjustified aggression; one is a noncombatant to the extent one is not a present or imminent threat. The paradigm of the combatant, then, is the soldier with the weapon pointed at you. On this view, it is not automatically true that a military leader is a combatant in the strict sense, and it is even more difficult to say whether a political leader—who is typically unarmed and not a fighter, nor himself an imminent threat—constitutes a combatant. Thus law professor Abram Chayes, appearing on *Nightline*, argued that "if Saddam was out leading his troops and he got killed in the midst of an engagement, well, that's one thing. But if he is deliberately and selectively targeted, I think that's another."[21] Chayes goes too far, for surely actual presence on the battlefield is not the only way one can constitute a direct threat. The problem, of course, is to say just under what circumstances a leader is himself a direct threat sufficient to justify making him a legitimate military target.

But how can we answer such a question? What I would suggest is that we must resort to the substantive criteria for aggression. Jeffrie Murphy's definition of aggression provides a good starting point: "What I mean by this [i.e., aggression] is that the links of the chain (like the links between motives and actions) are held together logically and not merely causally, i.e., all held together, in this case, under the notion of who it is that is engaged in an attempt to destroy you."[22] The idea here is that the criteria are more than merely causal (or else doctors and farmers would be aggressors), but have to do with the nature of one's agency. Is one a direct agent in the unjustified aggression? Thomas Wingfield concedes that merely being a "regime elite" does not render one a legitimate target; this only applies to those members "participating in or taking an active role in directing military operations."[23] But even this is too weak. The further away we get from this paradigm case of the soldier wielding a weapon, the more suspect must be the use of force against someone. With those in a supervisory role, the presumption must be against killing them, unless their role is immediate and direct in the act of aggression. It is more plausible to consider them aggressors where it is they who are actually initiating the acts, that is, issuing orders to subordinates to carry out specific acts of violence. (It should be noted that *aggression* can refer either to external and internal violence: attacks on other countries, or unjustified attacks on one's own people, as say Hitler's policy of genocide or Hussein's use of chemical weapons on the Kurds.)

Clearly, military leaders will be far more likely to qualify as part of the direct chain of aggression than will political leaders. On this analysis, there can be no simple answer as to whether a given political leader is an aggressor, and hence a legitimate target in war. The answer will depend on the extent of involvement with the waging and oversight of the aggression, including, importantly, the extent to which he provides the initiative for the war itself, or for particular acts of aggression within it. The political structure of the society will obviously be relevant; in a dictatorship, there is far more centralized control of state functions, and thus a much stronger presumption of direct responsibility on the part of the ruler. In a democracy, in contrast, the leader may be acting as the agent of the legislature or the people in general. Even having the ultimate responsibility for giving the green light to war does not necessarily constitute the leader as an aggressor—this will depend on such factors as whether he is the initiator of the aggression or merely a figurehead. But it seems that in general political leaders are sufficiently different from military leaders such that the ordinary presumption of combatancy does not apply to the former category. Arguably Saddam Hussein was a legitimate target in that he appeared to maintain "operational control over military action"[24] and was himself directly responsible for the immediate or future potential harm. This would be even more justifiable where a leader is on the verge of ordering a nuclear strike, or authorizing an act of terrorism—assuming that he is genuinely the initiator and motivating force of the action, not merely a bureaucrat providing formal approval. It is true that in the age of modern warfare, the traditional paradigm of the target as one who is on the battlefield or even wielding a weapon is less useful, given the capacity of a political leader to order the launching of weapons of mass destruction from behind the lines (though this is not so much due to terrorism, but to the development of high technology, especially WMD). But of course the standard must be set very high here; the further removed a person is from direct control over the attack, the stronger the presumption must be against treating him as a direct threat and therefore a legitimate target.

Nonetheless, there remain serious concerns about the idea of assassination even if we decide that the leader is a legitimate target; these concerns apply to the assassination of military leaders as well as political leaders. The fact of premeditation is troublesome; in any case of homicide, premeditation often indicates a motive to kill whether or not such killing is strictly necessary. A primary moral duty with respect to any use of force is to use the minimum necessary harm. An assassination order, or a bounty offered for the target "dead or alive," is in itself not morally permissible, because it violates this duty. Any planned assassination must be one in which killing is only a last resort; the order must be to capture alive if at all possible. (Some questions were raised, for example, about the killing of Hussein's sons: was every reasonable effort made to capture them alive?) This is to say, a premeditated killing is always suspect; the aim must be to capture if at all possible, and to kill only to prevent the target from escaping and carrying out further harm.[25]

A second concern is the danger of the slippery slope: if assassinations are permitted, will this undermine the just war limits on killing? The worry here is about breaking down the barrier between legitimate killing in self-defense or prevention of future harm (or, more controversially, punishment in the context of war crimes tribunals) versus the sort of illegitimate killing of which terrorism is a prime example, and which can simply be called *murder*. Assassination, given its premeditated character, is uncomfortably close to the side of illegitimacy. This is not necessarily a reason to reject the legitimacy of all assassinations, but it is a reason to reiterate the strict limitations on the policy. To the extent a person is in a role distant from the actual aggression itself (i.e., a supervisory role), there must be a direct connection between him and the acts of violence. A mere figurehead leader, as Wingfield suggests, is not a legitimate target, nor ordinarily is a civilian commander in a democratic state. The ordinary assumption must be that one may use defensive force only against those who are the agents threatening unjust violence. In just war doctrine, targeting of political leaders should be especially avoided. The Israeli policy of assassination of Hamas terrorist leaders has been defended on the grounds that it is designed to prevent imminent unjust attacks on civilians, that these leaders are directly responsible for planning and authorizing attacks, and that all reasonable alternatives have been exhausted (including issuing arrest warrants to Palestinian authorities, requesting extradition, etc.). To the extent these claims are true, they would seem to constitute a legitimate case of justifiable assassination.

In conclusion, it appears that the policy of assassination or targeted killing, though it raises serious moral concerns, can in some circumstances be a legitimate tool of war. However, the justification for such acts cannot be consequentialist in nature, aiming at a more "efficient" victory or at waging war "on the cheap." Much of the recent shift in opinion in favor of the use of assassination can be revealed for what it is: a newly emboldened effort of the Realists and the consequentialists to make inroads into the just war doctrine.[26] Nonetheless, the targeting of military or political leaders can in certain circumstances be a morally legitimate tool of war, justified as a preventive use of force against the initiator or controlling force of unjust aggression (even where there is not an imminent threat). Indeed, a murderous tyrant such as Hussein would seem to provide just such a case: where the political leader exerts near-total control over military and political decisions, where he is clearly the initiator of the unjust aggression, and where his capture or prevention is not possible other than by killing him. While we must reject the Realist idea that assassination is simply another tool of war to be used wherever effective, we must also reject the view that assassination is wholly prohibited under just war doctrine. It is only under very limited circumstances that the assassination of a political leader will be morally permissible.

NOTES

1. Article 23b, Annex to the Hague Convention IV (1907), prohibits "assassination, proscription, or outlawry of an enemy, or putting a price upon an enemy's head, as well as offering a reward for an enemy 'dead or alive.'"

2. Weinberger, "When Can We Target the Leaders?" *Strategic Review* (Spring 2001): 21–24, p. 23. See also Thomas Wingfield, "Taking Aim at Regime Elites," *Maryland Journal of International Law and Trade* 22 (1999): 287–317, p. 287.

3. *De Jure Belli Libri Tres* (1612), Book II Chapter VIII, in *The Classics of International Law,* trans. J. Rolfe (Oxford: Oxford University Press, 1950), 171.

4. See, e.g., Williams Banks, "Targeted Killing and Assassination: The U.S. Legal Framework," *University of Richmond Law Review* 37 (March 2003): 667–749, p. 671.

5. Ibid.

6. Weinberger, "When Can We Target the Leaders?" 22.

7. Ibid., 24.

8. Quoted in Brenda Godfrey, "Authorization to Kill Terrorist Leaders," *San Diego International Law Journal* 4 (2003): 491–512, p. 491.

9. Ibid., 501.

10. Ibid., 504.

11. Ibid.

12. Wingfield, "Taking Aim at Regime Elites," 312. Note the two distinct errors in this claim: (1) a conflation of self-defense with the punishment-based notions of guilt and innocence, and (2) a misunderstanding of the proportionality constraint as a consequentialist provision.

13. Beres, "On International Law and Nuclear Terrorism," *Georgia Journal of International and Comparative Law* 24 (1994): 1–36, p. 33.

14. Ibid.

15. See http://www.whitehouse.gov/news/releases/2002/10/20021001-4.html.

16. See, e.g., "A Call for Assassination Brings a Cry of Outrage," *Los Angeles Times*, 24 August 2005, 1.

17. McMahan, "Realism, Morality, and War," in *The Ethics of War and Peace,* ed. Terry Nardin (Princeton: Princeton University Press, 1996), 90.

18. See my "What's Wrong with Defensive War?" *Ethics and International Affairs* 19:3 (2005), for a discussion on the legitimacy of the use of preventive force in war.

19. Wingfield, "Taking Aim at Regime Elites," 314.

20. "The Moral Argument for a Policy of Assassination," paper delivered at APA Central Division Meeting, 2003. This paper has since been published in *Reason Papers* 27 (Fall 2004): 45–67.

21. Program on 4 February 1991. Wingfield dismisses Chayes's example too quickly (see Wingfield, "Taking Aim at Regime Elites," 314).

22. Murphy, "The Killing of the Innocent," in *War, Morality, and the Military Profession*, ed. Malham Wakin (Boulder: Westview Press, 1986), 346.

23. Wingfield, "Taking Aim at Regime Elites," 311.

24. Sebastien Jodoin, "The Legality of Saddam Hussein's Assassination," Part II, 3 (available at http://www.law.mcgill.ca/quid/archive/2003/03040805.html).

25. One might argue that the "dead or alive" idea means that the ultimate goal is to get the target, however necessary. Still, it implies indifference as between the two, even a veiled preference for "dead." Clearly, the moral rule requires the aim of capturing alive if at all possible.

26. See, for example, John Yoo's assertion that "a nation at war may use force against members of the enemy at any time, regardless of their proximity to hostilities or their activity at the time of attack." Yoo is believed to have authorized a Justice Department opinion justifying the use of assassinations in wartime. See Paul Barrett, "Opinion Maker: A Young Lawyer Helps Chart Shift in Foreign Policy," *Wall Street Journal*, 12 September 2005, A1.

CHAPTER 10

Preventive War and Lawful Constraints on the Use of Force: An Argument against International Vigilantism

Jordy Rocheleau

I. IRAQ, JUST CAUSE, AND PROPER AUTHORITY

While many empirical questions remain regarding the effects of and motives for the 2003 U.S. invasion of Iraq, the war highlights two central issues in just war theory: those of just cause and legitimate authority. First, the Iraq war raises the question whether prevention of gathering threats constitutes a just cause for war. Recent just war thinking, following Michael Walzer's *Just and Unjust Wars*, has argued that only defensive wars, preemptions of imminent attacks, and humanitarian interventions can be justified. Yet many argue that in the face of threats of the proliferation of weapons of mass destruction and global terrorism, the stricture against preventive war should be rethought. Although it appears that Iraq did not even pose a gathering threat, the question remains whether preventive strikes should be used in response to clearer and more imminent dangers in the future.

The Iraq war also raises questions about the proper authority for determining when to use force. One strain of just war thinking argues that wars should be authorized by state governments, while a second argues that the legitimate authority for authorizing disturbances of international peace is the international community, as embodied in international law.

Although the two debates are analytically separable—one's position on preventive war need not determine one's position on unilateralism and vice versa—I suggest that the cause is relevant to the determination of proper authority, so that the two issues are interdependent. While there is a basis for some preventive wars, such wars are only legitimate if authorized by the international community through lawful procedures.

II. THE "LEGALIST PARADIGM"

Walzer argues that most reflection on just cause starts with what he calls the "legalist paradigm": the idea that states ought to refrain from forcibly intervening in each others' affairs except in defense. The world can be thought of as composed of distinct political entities, like individuals in domestic society. States, like individuals, ought to respect each other's freedom and physical integrity.[1] To assault another state, as to assault another individual, is to commit the crime of aggression. Neither State A's national interest, nor the greater good, as A sees it, can justify A's going to war against State B, which has not committed a prior act of aggression. Since our most developed moral and political language regards the relationships of individuals, it is not surprising that just war theory conceives of the relationship of states in similar terms. However, since states are not individuals, with distinct conscious subjectivity and moral agency, the moral intuitions that flow from the domestic analogy need additional argument.

There are two sorts of arguments against aggression. The first, deontological, argument has to do with states' rights of sovereignty. States, like individuals, have the right to self-determination. State sovereignty is itself valuable because it promotes the political autonomy of individuals. This is particularly true of democratic states that represent public opinion. However, even undemocratic states tend to reflect and preserve local culture, supporting citizens' identities and well-being. If a liberal democratic state could somehow engineer a bloodless takeover of an undemocratic state (say China or Algeria) and replace the authoritarian government with its own form of liberal democracy, our intuitions tell us that it ought not.[2] What is lost is the value of local sovereignty. To use an actual example, if the 1991 Iraqi invasion of the kingdom of Kuwait violated the latter's right of independence, as most believe, then state sovereignty exists independently of democratic representation. Furthermore, as Walzer argues, even if liberal democracy is desirable everywhere, it is more likely to be sustainable if it is implemented through internal rather than external pressure.[3]

The prohibition of intervention is also supported by a second, consequentialist, argument. The norm of non-aggression maintains overall utility by securing peace and preventing the death and destruction that war brings. Even a flawed state is likely to defend itself from attack, resulting in casualties to both attacker and defender. War almost inevitably kills large numbers of noncombatants; sacrificing or risking nonconsenting individuals is not usually thought justified even by expected gains in utility.[4] War also disrupts the local economies, environments, and services that even bad governments provide. The uncertain benefits of any war are generally outweighed by its enormous and certain costs.

The norm against aggression is central to existing international law as a system of stable cooperation between states. Article 2 (4) of the United Nations Charter states that "all members shall refrain in their international relations from the threat or use of force against the territorial integrity or political independence of any state." The presumption against war, particularly for self-interest or expected utility, is supported by a combination of principled arguments, intuitions, and customary rules. Although any of these are questionable in themselves, their confluence gives reason to think that a Rawlsian reflective equilibrium has been achieved and that the ethical conclusions under consideration are justified.

To say that there is a presumption against war is not to say that war is never justified. Indeed it is widely agreed that force may be justly used to *defend* against international aggression. Defense of a state preserves the value of national self-determination. Furthermore, since attacking parties are at fault, they, unlike the defenders, have waived their right not to be attacked. Acceptance of state self-defense can be argued to maximize utility by discouraging aggression and reducing the number of wars. The right of self-defense is embodied in international law, which makes exceptions to the prohibition of war in cases of "individual or collective self-defense."[5]

Walzer has called the theory that war is only justified by defense against aggression the "legalist paradigm." This phrase is misleading, however, for Walzer's case against aggression ultimately rests on moral arguments rather than positive law. Furthermore, both domestic and international law allow the use of force in situations that are not strictly defensive. Indeed, Walzer and most other just war theorists argue that there are at least two sorts of exceptions to the legalist paradigm. First, it is widely agreed that *humanitarian interventions* to prevent catastrophic violations of human rights are justified. If the norm of non-aggression is justified by its furtherance of individual rights to life and liberty, then the system must allow exceptions for interventions to prevent massive rights violations. The second exception to the legalist paradigm, the *anticipatory strike*, is the focus of this chapter.

III. PREVENTIVE WAR

Walzer calls the anticipation of relatively certain, imminent attacks "preemptive" strikes and anticipatory strikes against gathering, distant, and uncertain threats "preventive" wars.[6] Preemptive strikes are essentially a form of early self-defense. State A's waiting to receive an aggressive strike by State B may reduce A's chance of successful defense and result in greater damage than if A could attack B preemptively. If there is a right to defend against attacks after they have occurred, it seems there should also be a right to defend preemptively against attacks that are reasonably certainly forthcoming. If the United States had intercepted intelligence to the effect that Japan was about to attack Pearl Harbor, the United States would have been justified in attacking the Japanese fleet as it was en route without waiting to suffer an enemy strike.

Preemption of imminent, clearly intended attacks gains support from their domestic analogy. Legal scholars maintain that individual self-defense is justified if a person has a reasonable belief that he or she is under attack, the attack is imminent, and defense is necessary to avoid the attack.[7] If in an argument a disputant angrily reaches for a weapon, both intent and ability to attack are clear enough to satisfy the reasonable belief requirement, and the act is a legitimate form of self-defense.

By contrast, *preventive* wars have generally been condemned by just war theory. Because the target state is not clearly planning to attack and may well never attack, preventive wars cannot be justified by the logic of self-defense. Reasonable belief in an attack, the necessity of defense, and imminence are all lacking. The target of a preventive strike, for its part, has not yet committed a wrong that would abrogate its right not to be attacked. Preventive wars are designed not to defend against a forthcoming attack so much as to reduce the risks of an attack in the future. The ability of State A to attack State B may generate fear in B that an attack is forthcoming, and make it in B's interest to strike A first. But neither fear nor risk of a potential attack justify using force to deprive others of their sovereignty and lives.

The wrongness of preventive wars is suggested by domestic analogies. If one has a personal enemy who could harm one, one may rationally or irrationally fear attack, but one is not justified in striking first until one knows one will be attacked and that violence is the only means of avoiding serious injury. If the enemy orders a gun or takes up kickboxing, one may fear that future conflicts will go badly, but one is not justified in attacking today.[8]

In addition to these deontological considerations against preventive strikes, there is a strong consequentialist argument against preventive war. The logic of prevention replaces the possibility of a future war with a certain war in the present. As Walzer argues, over time the policy of preventive strikes multiplies wars, many of which need never have been fought.[9] Most states face some risk from other states and their weapons programs, such that if preventive war were justified, any state could justly attack any other state with which it had conflict. Take the conflicts between India and Pakistan, Israel and its Arab neighbors, and the United States and North Korea, Iran, and China; the logic of preventive war justifies an anticipatory strike by each side, a counterintuitive and dangerous consequence. If prevention of gathering threats gained acceptance as a legitimate reason for initiating the use of force, just cause would cease to be a meaningful criterion for waging war. No state would desire a general policy of preventive war, and therefore no state can justify wars by this rationale.

At times it may be difficult to determine whether a foreign party has a clear intention to attack and aggression is imminent, making it impossible to distinguish between preemption and prevention. While Walzer's discussion of the 1967 Israeli strike against Arab forces in the Six-Day War is treated as the paradigm case of a preemptive strike, recent scholarship has questioned the imminence of an Arab attack.[10] Though there may be difficult cases, it will be rare that a state can know in advance that it will be attacked. Most anticipatory strikes will be clearly preventive, not preemptive.

The U.S. invasion of Iraq was unquestionably preventive. The Bush administration did not even allege, much less attempt to provide evidence, that an Iraqi attack on the United States was imminent. The United States' stated intent was to seize suspected Iraqi chemical and biological weapons and prevent the Hussein regime from developing nuclear weapons. Insofar as the war was an anticipatory strike, founded on U.S. national security concerns, it was done to lessen the chance that Iraq would carry out or enable an attack on the United States or its allies in the indefinite future. The subsequent failure to find a weapons program in Iraq, much less an Iraqi plan to attack the United States, in addition to the ongoing strife in the U.S. occupation, provides a paradigm example of why preventive war is unjust and unwise.

IV. A JUSTIFICATION OF LIMITED PREVENTIVE WAR

However, the blanket rejection of preventive war involves serious problems. In light of the dangers of weapons of mass destruction and global terrorism, it has become more dangerous to wait for clear signs of an imminent attack before disarming a potential threat. Weapons of mass destruction (WMD), particularly nuclear, but also biological, weapons, have the potential for causing immense damage in a short time. The harm of a single use seems too great to wait to endure a first strike. The speed of WMD makes them difficult to preempt. Although nuclear weapons have not been used since the United States' bombing of Japan in 1945, continuing proliferation and international terrorist organizations make their use more likely.[11] To this point, WMD use has been prevented, in part, by the deterrent threat of massive nuclear counterattack. However, terrorist organizations, which, unlike state powers, are difficult to locate and have no particular region for whose well-being they are accountable, may be undeterrable.

A strict prohibition of preventive war would have ruled out the use of force against Iraq even if the Hussein regime was openly developing nuclear and biological weapons. The intolerability of doing nothing in the face of such gathering threats leads to skepticism about the constraints of traditional just war theory. A blanket rejection of preventive war would involve grave risks to human rights and could invite arms proliferation more deadly than preventive strikes. If defensive, preemptive and humanitarian wars are justified because they reduce human rights violations and preserve long-term international stability, then it seems that some preventive wars should be justified as well.

Since the categorical approval of preventive war is untenable, the question becomes how anticipatory strikes can be rationally restricted. Criteria are needed that would specify states against whom preventive force is morally warranted but not permit "innumerable and fruitless wars."[12] A common move in recent arguments for preventive war, adopted by the Bush administration in its National Security Strategy (NSS), holds that preventive war is justified against only particularly dangerous "rogue states." David Luban defends this approach, arguing that "the trajectory of the rogue state makes it an 'imminent' attacker provided that we recharacterize imminence in probabilistic rather than temporal terms." For Luban, the risks posed by the rogue's existence and behavior justify preventive defense by "potential victims of a rogue state's aggressive attack." Luban defines rogue states as those characterized by "militarism, an ideology favoring violence, a track-record of violence to back it up, and a build-up in capacity to pose a genuine threat."[13] The NSS defines rogue states as those that do the following:

- brutalize their own people . . .
- display no regard for international law, threaten their neighbors, and callously violate international treaties . . . ;
- are determined to acquire weapons of mass destruction . . . to be used as threats or offensively to achieve the aggressive designs of their regimes;
- sponsor terrorism around the globe; and
- reject basic human values and hate the United States and everything for which it stands.[14]

Both Luban's and the administration's definitions fail the criteria of justice and sufficient practical constraint on preventive war. Determining whether a state is "militaristic," "favors violence," has "no regard for international law," is "determined" to acquire WMD, "rejects basic human values," and "hates" other states (since specifically hating the United States could not serve as general valid universal criterion for preventive war), all require speculative interpretation of the thoughts and intentions of foreign actors. Because this sort of definition of a rogue is ambiguous and subjective, it fails to provide a rational limit and permits too many wars. Many states glorify their own militaries, possess or might like to possess WMD, and have a history of violating just war doctrine. Indeed, the definition could easily be argued to fit the United States, Russia, Israel, and India, as well as Iran and North Korea.

Such conceptions of roguishness also fail to provide a just cause for preventive war. They justify force against states because of political ideology rather than any wrong that they have actually committed. A basic principle of law and morality states that individuals should only be punished for what they have done, not what they might do. Arguments that certain types of states are statistically more likely to commit aggression—say undemocratic states or states with high military expenses—would not justify a first strike against them, since states of this sort do not necessarily wage wars and have done no wrong that waives their right not to be attacked. The NSS criterion of having brutalized its own people is related to the justification of humanitarian intervention but not anticipatory strikes.[15]

A more defensible criterion for preventive war is suggested by international law—that the state must have been found to have engaged in violations of international norms designed to secure peace and preserve human rights. In particular, I argue that preventive armed intervention is justified if states violate norms regarding WMD development, such as the Nuclear Non-Proliferation Treaty and the Biological Weapons Convention. Such weapons are banned because they pose intolerable threats to international peace and undermine the security of states in general. Furthermore, due to the destructive magnitude and indiscriminate nature of WMD, they could not be used without massively violating human rights.

Of course, mere WMD possession does not automatically imply that a state intends to or will use them. Presumably, states may develop WMD for defensive and deterrent purposes. Deterrence by others as well as moral restraint can prevent their use. However, as John Lango argues, the more states that possess WMD the more likely these weapons will be used.[16] A state possessing WMD risks using them accidentally or in response to actual or suspected enemy attacks. WMD could also be sold to, stolen by, or seized by less responsible parties. This is to say that WMD possession endangers the world in a manner that cannot necessarily be controlled either through the good intentions of the owner or deterrence by others. This means that WMD development is negligent in imposing large risks on others.[17] Since most states have signed antiproliferation treaties and all benefit from the safety that these afford, states have an obligation to obey this social contract.

By engaging in actions that recklessly endanger the international community, states illegally developing WMD commit a wrong that waives their own right not to face coercive violence. Though some proponents of just war theory would maintain that merely dangerous WMD development does not constitute a harm that warrants violent response, I argue that reckless actions that pose a significant threat to others constitute harms and thereby justify forceful response.[18] Furthermore, possession and development of WMD, unlike political ideologies, are objective standards for determining cause. Attacks are justified against those states and only those states clearly found to violate international WMD norms, posing a threat to the international community.

This criterion for preventive war is allowed by existing international law. Chapter VII of the United Nations Charter states that "the Security Council shall determine the existence of any threat to the peace . . . and shall make recommendations, or decide what measures shall be taken . . . to maintain or restore international peace and security." Armed intervention is among the measures that the Security Council may employ.[19] As illegal WMD threaten the peace, the Security Council may authorize the use of force to combat them when necessary.

Although the legalist paradigm is understood to rule out preventive wars, domestic law offers support for this type of intervention. There are punishable laws against the possession and manufacture of large-scale weapons, such as bombs. Individuals who engage in such behavior may be arrested, which is to have force used against them. The use of force is considered justified by the combination of the level of threat and the intentional breach of the social contract. Thus preventive force is sometimes justified in instances in which no single individual could claim a right of self-defense. By analogy, force could justifiably be used against states that illegally develop dangerous weapons even if no single state is about to be attacked.

My argument implies that any illegal arms developer is a potential target for the use of force, avoiding the bias of judgments about which states are roguish in their ideologies. However, as in domestic law, past norm violations by states may lead to reduced rights, for example justifying arms inspections or forbidding some states to develop nonmilitary nuclear power.

It might seem that my criterion for preventive wars—illegal WMD possession or development—would once again dangerously justify too many wars. Since numerous states, including the United States, have engaged in illegal weapons development,[20] my legal criterion risks being more broad than the NSS's rogue state conception, with its numerous, if unclear, criteria. It is incumbent on my argument to explain why it does not allow for the multiplication of devastating, fruitless wars.

Preventive wars against illegal weapons development would be subject to criteria of last resort, proportionality, and proper authorization. First, the last resort criterion implies that if negotiations, sanctions, and threats short of war have a reasonable chance of ending illicit weapons possession, they ought to be used instead of armed force. In most cases, as with Iraq in the 1990s, a state could be disarmed without significant military strikes.

Secondly, armed intervention should only be undertaken if the gains in security are expected to be proportional to—in other words, outweigh—the costs of war. Since war tends to lead to unforeseen harms, it is wise to interpret this principle strictly and approve only those interventions in which it is fairly certain that destructive capacity can be reduced without causing greater harms.[21] If WMD development is uncertain or intervention would be likely to lead to prolonged conflict and massive suffering, preventive strikes are not worthwhile. Since states with advanced WMD programs and large conventional forces could be presumed to use them in defense if attacked, the proportionality criterion rules out preventive strikes versus many states against which they would in principle be justified, including the United States, Russia, China, Israel, India, Pakistan, and probably North Korea.

Proportionality also implies that, in wars to prevent WMD proliferation, only as much force as needed for disarmament is justified. Targeted strikes on production or storage facilities would frequently be sufficient. Rarely would it be necessary to overthrow a country. If the location of WMD is unknown, there is probably not enough evidence to use force at all. Of course, lack of knowledge could result from a suspect state refusing to allow mandated weapons inspections. In such cases, other punitive measures, including targeted strikes against the state's leadership, could be employed. The central point is that only as much force as required to restore international security is justified. A rationally limited doctrine of prevention justifies few uses of force and almost never warrants large-scale invasions.

The determination whether a preventive war is appropriate requires context-sensitive judgment about whether (1) a state has violated international law, (2) a serious threat to international security and human rights exists, (3) reasonable alternatives to force have been exhausted, and (4) a war's consequences would be desirable. The justice of interventions will depend on these judgments being made wisely, in good faith, and in a defensible manner. This is to say that the morality of preventive wars will depend on the quality of the decision-making process. This leads us to us to the second issue posed by the Iraq war: the legitimate authority for declaring wars, particularly preventive wars.

V. INDIVIDUAL STATES VERSUS INTERNATIONAL LAW AS LEGITIMATE AUTHORITY

In civil society, private individuals are supposed to leave the legislation, adjudication, and execution of crime punishment and prevention to state authorities. Individual attempts to enforce justice and punish crimes, outside of and in violation of the law, are known as vigilantism. Vigilantism is unjust for two basic reasons. First, the vigilante lacks the restraint, knowledge, impartiality, and deliberation of law enforcement agencies and so is more likely to be biased, make mistakes, and enforce the law unevenly or disproportionately. Second, the vigilante undermines a legal system that is generally more just than the absence of law. While individuals have not explicitly promised to refrain from vigilantism, it is to the benefit of each that others refrain from vigilantism, so reciprocity indicates that each citizen should refrain himself or herself. Since one expects others to give up their rights to vigilantism, one should as well. Vigilantism is not only not universalizable, but also, insofar as it is retaliated against or emulated, tends to foster rather than reduce violence and injustice.

The critique of vigilantism has implications for just war theory. Just war theorists have long argued that only states or political communities, not private individuals, may authorize warfare. The state as a representative body charged with pursuing the common good, and possessed with rational procedures is considered more likely to make a good decision in this regard. The state has greater resources for gathering intelligence and determining when negotiations with foreign powers are no longer feasible. Allowing only state officials, rather than private individuals, to authorize war also reduces the number of conflicting parties and the frequency of war.

However, the argument for a state monopoly on the use of violence in domestic society is not sufficient to justify state discretion in using force internationally. National laws specify who a state recognizes as having authority to declare war and command its military forces, but this local policy cannot justify the state in striking beyond its borders. Since war directly affects other states, it implicates international norms. To say that a war is just is to say that it should be approved, or, minimally, should not be interfered with, by other states. This is to say that war must be justified to the international community. A state cannot authorize itself to enforce norms throughout the world any more than a single individual can authorize himself or herself to punish other individuals. International vigilantism by states, like domestic vigilantism by individuals, should be rejected.

Unlike national law, international law is specifically designed to address the preservation of international security and human rights. It is widely recognized that in their dealings with foreign powers, states tend to be motivated by self-interest rather than justice. International authorities can be expected to represent a wider range of interests and perspectives and come closer to an impartial procedure in adjudicating the claims of various disputants. International law serves as a more rational, nonarbitrary source of decisions regarding international violence than do the actions of individual state actors.

Such reasoning implies that the determination of whether to wage war should be made by international authorities according to international law. National governments are only justified in using force externally when their decisions conform to international procedures, just as state governments within the United States are authorized to make decisions regarding the state's trade policies on the condition that they not violate federal laws.

The division of labor between the state and international community depends upon the cause and circumstance of a war. If a state is under attack, it has the right to defend itself without awaiting international authorization. As with individual self-defense, one need not take time to contact authorities while suffering violence. If states had to wait for UN or Security Council approval to defend themselves, aggressors could have months to inflict damage on and engineer a takeover of a victim state. A state is well positioned to determine whether it is under attack and cannot be reasonably expected to refrain from defending itself.

Since a state's right of self-defense is enshrined in international law there is no conflict between the recognition of international authority and the delegation of self-defense to unilateral state decision making. However, the right of self-defense is conditional upon its reasonable and legitimate use, and is subject to review by outside authorities. Like individuals, states should be able to provide evidence that they were under attack or reasonably believed themselves to be in immediate danger of attack necessitating defensive action. If not subject to reasonability criteria and external review, the right of self-defense would become a general right to aggression.

Similar arguments can be made for defending other states under attack and intervening to prevent humanitarian catastrophes. Time constraints justify acting as a "good Samaritan," aiding victims without waiting for legal authorization. The certain wrong of the ongoing attack means that one can be assured of acting justly and accomplishing more good than harm.

However, preventive wars cannot be justly undertaken unilaterally. Since the state contemplating preventive war has suffered no immediate attack, it can hardly be said that its right of unilateral self-defense is triggered. The mobilization of forces—both of the preventer and the preventee—take time that can be used for an international appeal. It is unlikely that the delay for international consultation will result in failure to preempt aggression by the preventee. Thus, a state suffers no great harm by deferring to international legal procedures.

Furthermore, a state's private decision about whether the potential danger to it from a foreign power warrants a preventive war is especially likely to be mistaken. An individual state is likely to weigh the potential risks to its citizens and national interests more heavily than concern for foreign citizens and global peace and prosperity. Individual states may harbor irrational suspicions of foreign states that have traditionally been perceived as enemies. A state may perceive any augmentation of military power by a traditional foe as a provocation, when an impartial decision maker would decide differently.

I argued earlier that the justification of preventive war hinges on the assessment of whether international law has been breached in a manner that warrants punitive force. The interpretation and application of international law are appropriately done by the international community through its legal procedures. Law enforcement, unlike self-defense, is outside the sphere of decision making normally delegated to individual parties. In domestic law, the right of self-defense does not extend to punishing individuals perceived as potentially dangerous. If one perceives one's neighbor to have a violent temper or to be acquiring illegal weapons, one is expected to contact the police rather than attacking and punishing him oneself.

VI. QUESTIONING INTERNATIONAL
LEGAL OBLIGATIONS

My case that only international law can authorize preventive wars invites several objections. First, detractors of international law argue that law requires procedures for its legislation, adjudication, and execution that the international community lacks. International lawyers counter that even without a legislature, a body of international norms can be discerned. Lawyers generally agree that international treaties and customarily observed international norms constitute law if compliance is understood by parties as obligatory, with breaches rare and widely condemned.[22] Although disputes arise about which norms constitute international law, few deny that it exists.

The lack of an enforcement mechanism remains a threat to international law's legitimacy. Unlike domestic law, in which the police have a monopoly of power and citizens can more or less expect to be secure without enforcing norms themselves, international law gives states no such assurance. Absent an international sovereign to punish norm violators, the world's states could be argued to be in a Hobbesian state of nature. In the face of incentives to cheat and the probability of norms being broken by other parties, it can be questioned whether any individual state can have an obligation to obey international norms. The persistence of violations of international treaties gives empirical support to theoretical skepticism about international law.

While the lack of systematic enforcement reduces the effectiveness of international law, there are sufficient forms of sanction to give international law compelling force. The Security Council can and sometimes does authorize sanctions, making lawbreaking risky. Apart from official sanctions, violations of international law can incur loss of public standing, economic partnerships, and credibility in securing allies for future causes.[23] That international law is of consequence is shown by states' attempts to conceal violations and, when accused, defend themselves as innocent. Although such defenses frequently involve lies and insincere rationalizations, the fact that they are given implies that states fear repercussions. If norms had no teeth, international criminals would simply shrug their shoulders as their transgressions were catalogued.[24] Although observance of international treaties is imperfect, occasional violations do not nullify law; if they did, there would be no law at all, domestic or international. It is only when violation becomes frequent and observation is no longer experienced as obligatory that law loses authority.

A second objection to international authority holds that although there is a legal system, with norms and sanctions, it lacks legitimacy. International law lacks equal standing for states, giving some rights, such as nuclear weapons capability, that are denied to others. Since five states have permanent membership on the Security Council with the ability to veto any proposed sanction, these states can act with impunity. In fact, my own argument for preventive war, in order to place practical limits on war, emphasized that proportionality would rule out strikes against powerful states, even when they refuse to honor disarmament treaties.

Such unequal enforcement of norms violates basic fairness and reifies existing power relationships. It is questionable whether states can be expected to obey a legal system that does not grant them equal standing. Of course, such an argument would only seem to justify disobedience by underprivileged states. States privileged under current rules, such as the United States, would have little reason to find them invalid. However, if weaker states had no reason to comply with law, reciprocity would be lost and powerful states would also lose their reason to comply.

Although existing international law is at odds with ideal conceptions of justice, a workable international law must respond to actual conditions it is intended to regulate if it is to effectively secure compliance. In light of this, unequal rights may be necessary to secure consent to and compliance with security-enhancing norms. In the case of nuclear weapons, a universal and equal right to possess them would have dangerous consequences for the whole world, not just existing powers. While universal prohibition of nuclear weapons would, if effective, achieve both equality and security, it is probably unachievable in the near future. Complete and immediate disarmament poses a threat of losing any deterrent force against a state that secretly retained or sought weapons, making it risk ridden for the international community as well as impossible to force upon powerful states. As long as immediate disarmament is not feasible, agreements to cease the proliferation of weapons are in the interest of all parties. Although each has an incentive to break rules, the social contract remains obligatory.

If practicality rules out the use of force against powerful possessors of illegal WMD, such as the United States, such sanctions remain valid in principle. Proposed sanctions could be brought against even veto-wielding states in order to embarrass them into greater compliance. To those who deny international law's legitimacy because of its unfairness,

I would respond that unconstrained unilateral power politics are still less fair than adherence to the United Nations Charter and international treaties.

If states have a duty to obey international norms, the question becomes whether this obligation is sufficient to override competing considerations. Realists have long argued that a state's supreme obligation is to pursue its national interests. Though this is not the place for a comprehensive critique of realism, I take it that realism is implausible as a theory of international affairs. If just war theory makes any sense, it must be that states can and should sometimes place moral obligations above national interest.

VII. INTERNATIONAL DISOBEDIENCE?

A different kind of objection to deference to international law has recently gained currency in just war theory. On this view, although states have an obligation to obey international law, which supersedes their self-interest, they nonetheless are justified, indeed obligated, to disobey international law for compelling moral reasons. Allen Buchanan has argued that if international law fails to protect human rights, then the law loses its legitimacy and cannot compel obedience.[25] The condemnation of vigilantism assumes that the legal system generally protects life and liberty. However, the United Nations and the Security Council have failed to protect human rights, notably by not authorizing intervention to prevent genocide in Rwanda and intervening late in Bosnia.[26] Because one of five veto-wielding states is likely to have strategic objections, it is difficult to get authorization for any proposed use of force. Successful interventions, such as India's intervention in Pakistan in 1971 and the U.S.-led intervention in Yugoslavia over Kosovo in 1999 have occurred without UN authorization.

Against my contention that international law provides greater rationality and fairness than unilateral action, it can be objected that the international legal system lacks the disinterested pursuit of justice that is expected in domestic law enforcement and adjudication. Representatives at the UN tend to vote according to state interest rather than the demands of truth and justice. Although the recent Iraq vote seems to have been right in refusing to authorize the U.S.-led invasion, the process leading up to the vote demonstrates the flaws of international law. The United States and its French, German, and Russian opponents had economic and political stakes in the outcome and bargained for votes with incentives and threats. This experience supports Walzer's argument that international authorization adds little to the justice of decision making: "If governments have mixed motives, so do coalitions of governments. Some goals perhaps are cancelled out by the political bargaining that constitutes the coalition, but others are superadded; and the resulting mix is as accidental with reference to the moral issue as are the political interests and ideologies of a single state."[27] Theory and experience reveal failures of international law to protect human rights, providing a moral case for international disobedience.

Although failures of action are particularly glaring when they thwart humanitarian intervention, similar arguments could be made for preventive wars. The spread of WMD undermines international security and threatens human rights. When the Security Council fails to act to prevent such dangers, it would seem that individual states could justly act in its stead, as in humanitarian intervention. In 1981 Israel's destruction of Iraq's nuclear power program at Osirak was illegal and widely condemned. But such unilateral vigilante actions could be viewed as the necessary means to preserve international security and human life. George Lucas has classified preventive wars along with humanitarian interventions as "constabulary" interventions for the sake of international lawfulness, which may violate the letter of the law. He writes: "Vigilantes are self-deputized constables, performing police-like functions, in some cases wholly divorced from . . . national interests."[28] For Lucas, vigilante interventions such as the U.S. invasion of Iraq indicate problems with the law rather than the lawbreaker. Although Lucas and other supporters of international disobedience recognize vigilantism as nonideal, they defend it as necessary until international law is improved.

I would argue against any general principle validating state authority to wage preventive wars without international authorization. First, international procedures do test the validity and sincerity of arguments and truthfulness of evidence. Though actors in the United Nations are clearly influenced by national interests, they are more likely to be influenced by a range of practical and moral considerations than are individual states. Even if states have mixed motives, international debate about preventive wars leads to the airing of arguments and objections about evidence of illegal WMD development, the satisfaction of last resort, and the proportionality of proposed interventions. Such arguments must be addressed in their own terms. The publicity of international debate, today aired throughout the world, creates pressure on involved parties to argue sincerely and only invoke principles that they are willing to have all live by. It is odd for just war theorists such as Walzer to question the value of global dialogue and agreement about war in improving judgments, for their own arguments presuppose an international audience possessing a capacity for moral reasoning transcending national interest. On the other hand, if states really are incapable of transcending self-interest when reasoning about the evidence for and morality of war, then unilateral preventive wars are particularly untrustworthy.

It could be objected that individual states, particularly democracies, contain their own deliberative processes that should be adequate to critically evaluate evidence and moral arguments. Unfortunately, the rationality of national public debate about preventive war is limited. Security concerns, real or exaggerated, are cited to justify withholding relevant evidence from the public. The prospect of conflict also excites nationalistic passions. Regardless of their views about the justification of wars in the abstract, citizens have historically enthusiastically supported any war fought by their compatriots. This was illustrated in the Iraq war, which the U.S. public opposed until it was clear that the U.S. government was committed to military action. Against traditional enemies, prejudice, suspicion, and imagination of ill intent on the other side are easily created, sustained by a combination of real and mythological past wrongdoings. In such a climate, opposition to war is rare and politically dangerous. State irrationality may involve either government error about the evidence and moral justifiability of a war or government deception of a citizenry easily swayed to war. In either case, national debate fails to make decisions on the basis of a rigorous assessment of facts and the principles of international law and just war theory.[29]

Even when a state has good reason to believe that the Security Council has failed to act to prevent WMD development, it should defer to the international legal process. Vigilantism establishes a precedent likely to be followed by others, thus undermining the stability of the international system. Actions such as the U.S. invasion of Iraq and the Israeli bombing of Osirak are not only questionable in themselves, but also enable other states to use similar justifications to proliferate war. Subsequent cases may be even more problematic than the originals.

One might question whether norms are significantly undermined by individual violations. After all, others will rarely have the same interest in and ability to undertake a preventive strike. Other states lack the power to copy the U.S. attack on Iraq and the Israeli attack on Osirak. So long as only a few powers—or perhaps today, the one super-power—make exceptions to the rules, no chaos should ensue. Luban notes that a primary justification of U.S. unilateralism is that its exceptional role as a sole superpower allows it to be an effective norm enforcer.[30] It could be argued that the United States, being generally committed to human rights and the spread of democracy, contributes to international security by acting as a self-deputized vigilante.

Whether human rights are better protected by adherence to international law or U.S. vigilantism admittedly involves empirical issues too complex to address here. However, I defend a general presumption in favor of the rule of law. Other states have good reason to distrust and resist U.S. unilateral actions. Even a state generally opposed to human rights abuse and respectful of just war theory is prone to interpret principles in a way that promotes its interests at the expense of the rights of foreign citizens. The United States has a history of supporting rights-violating regimes in order to further geopolitical and economic goals. The prevalence of force protection in U.S. rules of engagement at the expense of noncombatants and the record of inhumane interrogation practices in Iraq, Afghanistan, and Guantanamo Bay provide ongoing illustrations of the risks of U.S. unilateralism to the world community.

Not only is U.S. unilateralism difficult to justify to others, but it is also inadequate to achieve the goals of world peace and prosperity that the United States itself favors. There is much agreement that international security requires the resolution of ethnic conflicts, especially that between the Israelis and the Palestinians, the fostering of sustainable economies in developing states, and world commitment to fighting terrorism and weapons proliferation. All of these conditions for peace require extensive international cooperation and defy solution by unilateral force. If international organization and cooperation are necessary to achieve international security, the formation of a legal system based on reciprocally recognized obligations acquires fundamental importance.

None of what I have said here implies that international law cannot be improved. Its many flaws, such as the paralyzing and unfair Security Council vetoes, can and should be amended. The recommendations of a recent UN report, "A More Secure World: Our Shared Responsibility," show a commitment to balancing power on the Security Council and taking responsibility for preventing humanitarian catastrophes and WMD proliferation.[31] While international law is currently in fledgling form, global security is best served by strengthening its norms through observance. When frontier law begins to emerge, well meaning gunslingers do well to show respect for it, not only for their own integrity but also to win over other parties. Engaging international procedures and forums lends them credibility and fosters reciprocity. When states that could attack unilaterally seek Security Council authorization and defer to its judgments, other members of the international community are pressured to do the same. In instances of the United Nations' failure to act against those developing WMD, bad votes can be noted and censured.[32]

The case for unilateral preventive war draws its plausibility from the dangers of inaction. However, the benefits of prevention are unclear, whereas the harms of violating and undermining international norms and spreading violence are certain. Few deaths in history can be traced to a failure to wage preventive war, whereas preventive wars themselves have taken countless lives. Although some fear the consequences of deference to international authority, the greatest danger to peace and justice today lies in the too-ready abandonment of law.

NOTES

1. Michael Walzer, *Just and Unjust Wars* (New York: Basic Books, 1977), 58.
2. Walzer gives an example of this thought experiment in "The Moral Standing of States: a Response to Four Critics," *Philosophy and Public Affairs* 9 (1980): 225–226.
3. Walzer, *Just and Unjust Wars*, 87–95.
4. Cf. Richard Miller, "Respectable Oppressors, Hypocritical Liberators: Morality, Intervention, and Reality," in *Ethics and Foreign Intervention*, ed. Deen K. Chatterjee and Don E. Scheid (Cambridge: Cambridge University Press, 2003), 223–226.
5. Charter of the United Nations, Article 51.
6. Walzer, *Just and Unjust Wars*, 74–85.
7. David Rodin, *War and Self Defense* (Oxford: Oxford University Press, 2002), 41.
8. One can get a restraining order if one is threatened by an individual. However, the restraining order normally requires a material act of aggression or explicit threat by the restrained individual. Also, the restraining order does not suggest the justification of direct force against potential threats, so much as the specification of conditions under which force would be used. Furthermore, the force justified by violations of a restraining order is third party (state police) force rather than direct self-defense.

9. Walzer, *Just and Unjust Wars*, 77–78.

10. Mary Ellen O'Connell, "The Myth of Preemptive Self-Defense," published by the American Society of International Law Task Force on Terrorism, August 2002, Washington, DC. Online at http://www.asil.org/taskforce/oconnell.pdf.

11. Chris Brown, "Self-Defense in an Imperfect World," *Ethics and International Affairs* 17 (2003): 2–9.

12. This is Walzer's phrase capturing the ill consequences of a doctrine of preventive war. See *Just and Unjust Wars*, 77.

13. David Luban, "Preventive War," *Philosophy and Public Affairs* 32 (2004): 207–248, 228–232.

14. "The National Security Strategy of the United States of America," 2002. Online at http://www.whitehouse.gov/nsc/nss.html.

15. I take it that the humanitarian case for the Iraq invasion was weak. The Hussein regime's admittedly gross violations of human rights were largely past. Humanitarian aims would have been better furthered by interventions elsewhere, such as Darfur, Sudan.

16. John W. Lango, "Preventive Wars, Just War Principles, and the United Nations," *The Journal of Ethics* 9 (2005): 247–268, 254–257.

17. Ibid., 259.

18. For an argument that prevention cannot constitute just cause, see Harry van der Linden, "Would the United States Doctrine of Preventive War Be Justified as a United Nations Doctrine?" forthcoming in *Philosophical Perspectives on the War on Terrorism*, ed. Wendy Hamblet and Gail Presbey (Rodopi Press).

19. Charter of the United Nations, Chapter VII, articles 39–42.

20. Nicole Deller and John Burroughs, "Arms Control Abandoned: The Case of Biological Weapons," *World Policy Journal* (Summer 2003) 2: 37–42.

21. Lango, "Preventive Wars, Just War Principles, and the United Nations," 264.

22. Anthony Arend, *Legal Rules and International Society* (Oxford: Oxford University Press, 1999).

23. For a discussion of the effectiveness of international law, see Michael Byers, ed., *The Role of Law in International Politics* (Oxford: Oxford University Press, 2000).

24. A similar argument is made by Sir Arthur Watts, "The Importance of International Law," in ibid., 7.

25. Allen Buchanan, *Justice, Legitimacy, and Self-Determination* (Oxford: Oxford University Press, 2004).

26. Samantha Power, *"A Problem from Hell": America and the Age of Genocide* (New York: Basic Books, 2002).

27. Walzer, *Just and Unjust Wars*, 107.

28. George R. Lucas Jr., "Methodological Anarchy: Arguing about

Preventive War," forthcoming in *Moral Theory and Military Action*, ed. Roger Wertheimer and George R. Lucas Jr. (Albany: State University of New York Press).

29. That public tendency to support all wars has been recently illustrated by Chris Hedges, *War Is a Force That Gives Us Meaning* (New York: Anchor Books, 2003).

30. Luban, "Preventive War," 236–248.

31. Online at http://www.un.org/secureworld. More radical proposals have called for getting rid of the veto power on the Security Council or creating new regional bodies with authority to declare war bypassing the Security Council. See Allen Buchanan and Robert Keohane, "The Preventive Use of Force: A Cosmopolitan Institutional Proposal," *Ethics and International Affairs* 18 (2004): 1–22.

32. Buchanan and Keohane, "The Preventive Use of Force," 15.

CHAPTER 11

Faith, Force, or Fellowship:
The Future of Right Authority

Hartley S. Spatt

I

The concept of right authority is one of the foundation stones of just war theory. No matter how just the cause, no matter how pure one's intentions, and no matter how much a proposed combat serves the cause of peace, a people considering war must rely on some individual or body to effect the declaration of war, define a strategy that the nation will adhere to, and determine rules of engagement. But for such a system of establishing authority to function effectively there must exist two essential attributes, without which authority is no longer right authority, and obedience to it becomes blind: trust in the reliability of those who are giving orders and a conviction of their moral integrity. A corollary concept, sovereign authority, is traditionally rooted in this demand for right authority; the leader's capability to act depends upon a perception, at least, of the capacity to act well. More and more in today's complex world, unfortunately, the authority being claimed is ambiguous, tenuous, sometimes expired; leaders who hold office on the basis of rigged elections, or military takeovers, claim sovereignty on spurious legalistic grounds, while new leaders holding de facto, but not de jure, authority are denounced as traitors, rebels—enemies of the state. In such circumstances, sovereign authority may lose its claim to right authority; the result may be civil disobedience, mutiny, even revolution. Furthermore, an outside state may become unable to legitimize right authority because it lacks sovereignty or is unwilling to defy a sovereign power even when it is not backed by right authority. Finally, states and organizations must decide whether, if sovereign authority loses right authority, outside intervention becomes justified.

The concept of right authority can be traced back twenty-five hundred years, to Sun Tzu's *The Art of War*: "The Way means . . . the people have the same aim as the leadership, so that they will share death and share life, without fear of danger."[1] A similar precept is voiced by St. Augustine, the founder of just war theory, who declared that "the natural order conducive to human peace, demands that the power to counsel and declare war belongs to those who hold the supreme authority,"[2] and by St. Thomas Aquinas, who noted that "the care of the commonweal is committed to those in authority . . . in lawful defence against domestic disturbance . . . [and] to protect the commonweal from foreign attacks."[3] Separated by thousands of miles and two millennia, these early philosophers shared the conviction that mere authority—power lacking any accompanying moral rightness—alone was not enough to ensure a just war; the citizens of a state must sense that those who claim authority over them represent the "natural order," embody loyalty to the "commonweal"—character traits that Sun Tzu summed up as "intelligence, trustworthiness, humaneness."[4] As Zhang Yu, a Sung dynasty commentator on Sun Tzu, put it: "If the people are treated with benevolence, faithfulness, and justice, then they will be of one mind."[5] One could go so far as to argue that it is precisely the rightness or wrongness of authority that determines the rightness or wrongness of the war: a "right" leader would never declare war in a "wrong" cause; correspondingly, no matter how "right" the cause, one would hesitate to follow a "wrong" leader into violence.

The rise of the nation-state and the resulting need for a strong body of international law led to an unfortunate decoupling of authority, which became linked to de jure state sovereignty, from rightness, which became marginalized as an affair of the Church or of philosophers, not necessarily of the state. When Carl von Clausewitz wrote his magisterial meditation *On War* in the 1820s he listed only three "dominant tendencies" that played a part in warfare: "primordial violence . . . probability . . . [and] policy."[6] As if that dismissal of all moral and ethical concerns were not clear enough, a few pages later he reduced them to the punch line of a joke: "Social conditions being what they are in Europe today, moral forces would not go far."[7] This marginalization continued through the twentieth century, as epitomized by Stalin's famous response to being told that Pope Pius XII disapproved of his actions: "How many divisions does he have?" More recently, Friedrich Kratochwil, a specialist in international law at the European University Institute, has claimed that the ruler of a modern nation-state need demonstrate no morality whatsoever; he could commit almost any crime "as long as he was within his territorially limited domain."[8] For 350 years the world has been dominated by Realpolitik, positivism, and "manifest destiny"; in consequence, the question whether those in power actually deserve the respect and obedience they are accorded has seldom, if ever, arisen.

It took the extremism of the Holocaust and successive twentieth-century revelations that humankind was apparently willing to commit any atrocity in the name of racial, ethnic, religious, and ideological purity—to massacre Armenians, Ukrainians, Hindus, Muslims, Kurds, and Tutsis—to restore a conviction of humankind's unalienable dignity to the people of the world. That conviction was expressed in the preamble to the United Nations Charter:

> We the Peoples of the United Nations determined . . . to reaffirm faith in fundamental human rights, in the dignity and worth of the human person, in the equal rights of men and women and of nations large and small, and to establish conditions under which justice and respect for the obligations arising from treaties and other sources of international law can be maintained, and . . . to practice tolerance and live together in peace with one another as good neighbors . . . have resolved to combine our efforts to accomplish these aims.

The creation of the United Nations established a new sovereign authority in the world, authorized to act in support of "international peace and security"; however, Article 2 of the Charter also specifically acknowledged the continuing sovereignty of "territorial integrity" and "political independence," barring intervention "in matters which are essentially within the domestic jurisdiction of any state." This contradiction has caused continuing controversy over whether the United Nations is allowed to take an active role in world events, particularly for humanitarian reasons. One recent commentator has specifically separated words and practice, arguing that although the Charter severely limits the power of the United Nations to cross the borders of any state that has not first violated the territorial integrity of another, "the practice of the Security Council . . . reveals an increasing recognition that . . . large-scale violations of human rights to life may constitute a threat to the stability, peace, and security of a region and require

208 HARTLEY S. SPATT

enforcement action."[9] This essay attempts a resolution of this schism between definitions of authority founded in questions of mere legal legitimacy and those founded in questions of moral rightness.

There are three distinct roots to political authority. First comes faith: those lower in the hierarchy believe that those above them also serve a higher authority. On this view, we are all agents of a divine power that rules over everything. Second comes force: those lower in the hierarchy obey because disobedience leads to violent retribution. On this view, we are all servants of a totalitarian system of compulsory action generated by an omnipotent leader—who can be benevolent, but who can also be tyrannical—or, perhaps worse, by some faceless bureaucracy. Third comes fellowship: what the UN Charter calls the "combined efforts" of people who reject the hierarchical model of authority in favor of what Kant called "an ethical commonwealth."[10] On this view, we are free peoples who act "as good neighbors." As I will argue, only the last of these offers any hope in our time of transforming affectless power into right authority.

II

The changing view of authority and the growing concern that its use be demonstrably "right" have been articulated by philosophers and students of international relations from widely disparate schools. Michael Walzer, in "The Triumph of Just War Theory (and the Dangers of Success)," put it in terms of the state's responsibility to care not only about its own population but about those of all states: "Political and military leaders . . . [are] responsible, first of all, for the well-being of their own people, but also for the well-being of innocent men and women on the other side."[11] Lori Fisler Damrosch, in *Enforcing Restraint: Collective Intervention in Internal Conflicts*, speaks of the need for those who would be leaders to demonstrate their moral authority before they merit political authority, since "it is, after all, the people's rights, rather than [their] personal rights, that are ultimately at stake." If they succeed in making that demonstration, Damrosch adds, then their moral authority supersedes anyone else's claim to political authority: "authentic leaders [have] a bona fide claim to authority to speak for their people, even if they have never been allowed to run for election or are in exile."[12] This is not, however, the majority view. The majority of commentators on just war theory today connect authority with legality rather than morality, the legal basis of "legitimacy" appearing to make it a more objective criterion than "right."

On the other hand, legitimacy (or sovereignty) in international law can be ambiguous. At its heart, the sovereignty of a state implies little more than a defined territory, a population to inhabit it, and some form of external recognition; Afghanistan remained a sovereign state even when its ruling government, the Taliban, was recognized by only two countries. In consequence, sovereignty in international relations is more a function of perception than of formal recognition. As K. J. Holsti puts it, "States can be inefficient, vulnerable, poorly governed, or highly constrained in their domestic policy choices. . . . But that does not make them less or more sovereign."[13] Thus the supposed objectivity of legitimacy as a standard for authority is put into question.

This divergence between the legal and the functional sense of sovereign authority is important in today's world, where de jure sovereignty offers no guarantee of de facto control. Indeed, half the states in Africa have collapsed into chaos at some point in the forty-five years since they achieved independence, yet none have been denied their sovereign status as a result. As Maryann Cusimano Love declares, "A state is in a process of collapse when its institutions and leaders lose control of political and economic space . . . [and] state authorities can no longer provide security, law and order, an economic infrastructure, or other services for citizens."[14] All too often, in such conditions, popular leadership arises outside formal governmental institutions, leading to de facto revolution.

States have always faced such internal threats to titular authority, created typically when the land-owning class loses control over the production and distribution of food to a rural revolutionary movement. Once the movement can deliver food to the disenfranchised and offer safe haven for the dispossessed in forest or jungle sanctuaries, it is sure to win the battle for hearts and minds; after that, it is only a matter of time before political victory follows. The despised tyrant (who was a short time before the beloved liberator) flees, a triumphal march from the countryside into the city takes place, and the world recognizes a new sovereignty. This process was articulated most clearly by Lin Biao, the tactician of the Chinese Communist revolution, in a speech commemorating the fiftieth anniversary of the Russian Revolution of 1917: "Under the leadership of the political party of the proletariat, to arouse the peasant masses in the countryside to wage guerrilla war, unfold an agrarian revolution, build rural base areas, use the countryside to encircle the cities and finally capture the cities. This is a great new development of the road to the seizure of political power by force of arms indicated by the October Revolution."[15]

Perhaps because of this tendency of states to undergo violent change of leadership, international relations since the Treaty of Westphalia have uniformly granted sovereignty to states, not their rulers; changes of government, no matter how revolutionary and no matter how violent the process, do not threaten legal and territorial continuity. Echoing a century-old classic text, Peter Singer concludes: "The standard view has long been that the recognition of a government as legitimate has nothing to do with how that government came to power, or for that matter how it governs."[16]

But the standard view becomes far less tenable when threatened governments employ wholesale murder as their defense against the rural revolutionary scenario, either inflicted directly, as in Rwanda, or indirectly, as in Sudan. Whether the government inflames the urban masses against the country-dwellers and sends them out with machetes and violent intent, or merely orders its "militiamen" to burn farms and poison wells, the flame of rural revolution is snuffed out before it can spread to the seat of political power. The world has witnessed a succession of such acts in recent decades, and most tragically it has been helpless to intervene. Since it is the sovereign government ordering the massacres, supplying the arms, or bombing the villages, murder can be committed with impunity, in the name of "internal order"; after all, the UN Charter only speaks of "international peace and security." And if the world does try to intervene, with UN peacekeepers as in Rwanda or with food relief as in Somalia, the very fact that airfields and ports are controlled by those in power stifles the efforts at their source. Food intended to feed starving Somali peasants was unable to get through Mogadishu to the drought-stricken areas; Rwandan peacekeepers were permitted to evacuate, but not the Tutsi refugees who truly needed to leave.

In response to these new threats against ethnic, religious, and political minorities, UN Secretary-General Kofi Annan has asserted that "massive and systematic violations of human rights—wherever they take place—should not be allowed to stand."[17] His use of the passive voice, however, reveals a deep-rooted unwillingness to answer the use of violence in the cause of evil with additional violence, even if it is in the cause of good. Recourse to force may assert the ultimate sovereignty of the international community over violations of human rights, even those confined within the borders of a recognized nation-state.

But it also reinforces the greater violation of human and social rights that is inherent in any effort to win over a populace by threatening to annihilate them. One suspects that the Westphalian concept of national sovereignty is too deeply ingrained in our system of international law.[18] The UN Charter speaks of dedication to "the equal rights of men and women and of nations large and small." But when the UN intervenes in order to protect one of those basic rights, men and women's right not to be killed, it violates the "equal rights . . . of nations" deriving from the need for a body of "international law" and international "security." If protecting the rights of men and women means violating the rights of nations large and small, then truly "some are more equal than others." Invoking one set of rights to kill evil rulers and their agents, thereby suppressing their power to commit evil against individuals, the UN threatens an equivalent set of rights: "justice and respect . . . tolerance . . . good neighbors." As I will argue in my conclusion, legalities alone cannot justify the decision to prioritize one set of rights over the other; only the moral authority deriving from fellowship can do so.

III

What use is universal abhorrence of wrongdoing when we are unable to grant sovereignty to those who stand for the right? Whether it is a revolutionary struggling to free the people from oppression, or a UN Secretary-General struggling "to reaffirm faith in fundamental human rights," where is a body of either law or practice that can award the authority to carry on the struggle?

These questions did not arise in ancient times, when the ruler was automatically granted status as an agent of divine power; the presiding deity granted each ruler not merely power, but a portion of divine wisdom. Gilgamesh, king of Uruk, was tutored by Shamash; the Egyptian pharaoh ruled as the living embodiment of Horus; Gaya Maretan, the Persian "King of the Mountain," absorbed and passed down the teachings of Ahura Mazda. Western Europeans follow the model of the Old Testament, in which Jehovah's prophet first chooses, and then advises the king, ensuring that authority will always be wielded rightly. The New Testament offers the same model relationship: "As Paul says, 'He beareth not the sword in vain,'" quotes Aquinas, "'for he is God's minister.'"[19] Halfway around the world, Chinese philosophers articulate the same concept of the ruler's divinely derived authority, by which the emperor is an agent of heaven; as T'ung Chung-shu writes, "Thus the king is but the executor of Heaven. . . . He patterns his actions on its commands and causes the people to follow them. . . . He follows its ways in creating his laws, observes its will, and brings all to rest in humanity."[20]

For more than two thousand years, rulers maintained what came to be called a "divine right," one vested in them in European tradition by the sacramental nature of the coronation ceremony. The crown placed on the head conferred political power: that the rise of state legislatures could lessen. But the holy oil poured onto that head conferred a spiritual power that no secular body succeeded in threatening—until Charles I was beheaded by Cromwell's Parliament in 1642. And even that act of rebellion could not extinguish the ruler's spiritual authority, as witnessed when Charles's son—a man whose only virtue may have been his parentage—regained the throne twenty-four years later.

However, by the time Louis XVI was executed 150 years later, the power of religious authority had declined dramatically, faced with a new power: the power of the people. Throughout the nineteenth century, the power of the ruler as an agent of the divine met the power of the constitutionally selected leader as an agent of the citizenry. This transformation in the seat of authority was, of course, made possible also by a transformation in the technology of social control. European governments could not have put down the revolutions of 1848 without the power of the Chassepot breech-loading rifle, used in the wider streets of the modern urban environment. In its turn, the rise of constitutional authority threatened the perceived legitimacy of divinely inspired authority; consequently, in 1871 the Roman Catholic Church felt the need to affirm a papal infallibility that had been taken for granted since the Church's beginnings.

By 1918 the power of many authority figures had disintegrated along with the authority of their sovereigns. The rulers who went to war were repudiated, but so were the generals who ordered suicidal charges against entrenched defenders, and the lieutenants who pushed their men over the top. Siegfried Sassoon expressed this sense of abandonment in his poem "The General":

"Good-morning; good-morning!" the General said
When we met him last week on our way to the line.
Now the soldiers he smiled at are most of 'em dead,

And we're cursing his staff for incompetent swine.
"He's a cheery old card," grunted Harry to Jack
As they slogged up to Arras with rifle and pack.
But he did for them both by his plan of attack.

The British soldiers maintain a lingering respect, blaming only "his staff"; but the author knows it was the general's "plan of attack" that doomed his company. On the French side, during the battle of Verdun, as many as 40,000 men refused outright to obey their officers until General Nivelle was replaced by General Pétain; nearly 3,500 were charged with mutiny, and about 45 men were executed. But a disturbing pattern of disaffection had been initiated, which would reach its climax fifteen years later when Germany would elect an ex-corporal to replace an ex-field marshal as chancellor.

Such is the vulnerability of modern popular and constitutional authority: in the absence of any appeal to the divine, it must resort to the threat—or the reality—of force in order to retain its power. Subjected to external physical compulsion, rather than free to follow an internal spiritual impulse, the citizen is no longer capable of defining, not to mention recognizing, the "wisdom, sincerity, benevolence" of governmental authority. The subject's original consent to the social contract may have been a product of free will, but his/her subsequent obedience, performed under threat of the strictest penalty, demonstrates that he/she is no longer free. And such a loss of freedom is inevitable. No matter how many times one freely obeys the authority of one's leader, a moment inevitably arrives when one obeys because one must; and at that moment the delicate balance between individual will and governmental command topples over into tyranny. As Thomas Jefferson put it, "Governments are instituted among Men deriving their just powers from the consent of the governed."[21] When citizens lose the power to consent, according to Jefferson's logic, they lose the very possibility of justice, and hence of civil government. Under such conditions, it is no surprise that, as Yeats put it, "The best lack all conviction."[22]

But why must the corollary of this observed failure of the social contract be that "the worst are full of passionate intensity"? Why must the failure of the constitutional ideal lead so swiftly to the usurpation of sovereignty by those who "draw the sword," as Augustine put it?[23] The answer perhaps lies in the very means that constitutional authority employs to protect itself against its vulnerability. Over the past two centuries, popular governments have sought to strengthen themselves against the inevitability of their people's loss of free consent through a resurrection of the once condemned faith-based system of authority. They erect a complex, self-sustaining structure that combines the rhetoric of absolutist faith with the forms of constitutional government, resulting in a "civil religion." Robert N. Bellah cites the 1785 speech of James Madison in the Virginia debate over religious freedom as its locus classicus: "Before any man can be considered a member of Civil Society, he must be considered as a subject of the Governor of the Universe."[24] In the United States, government officials swear their oaths of office on a Bible; coins and bills all declare, "In God We Trust"; the Pledge of Allegiance avows that we are "one Nation, under God." Philip E. Hammond has found evidence for a similar complex of structures in nations as diverse as Bulgaria, Malaysia, the Philippines, and Trinidad.[25] Of course, a civil religion may be used for good ends or for bad. To the extent that it ensures a moral foundation for the state's political, economic, and social policies, civil religion leads to the willing subordination of each citizen's desires through enlightened self-interest. In that way the authority of force is diminished, and the authority of faith is revived.

However, the power of civil religion can also be employed by a cynical authority, to mask its reliance on force. Although the divine right of kings has disappeared as a ruling concept in political theory, there remains a faith—a societywide delusion born of hope and fueled by reaction to repeated political and economic failures—that the head of one's government is not a mediocre human being trying to do an impossible job as well as he/she can, but rather an agent of the deity. Although this tendency is disparaged in some societies as nothing more than a "cult of personality," the people's need to apotheosize their authority figures has been demonstrated in societies from Mao Zedong in China to Idi Amin Dada in Uganda; from Juan Peron in Argentina to Mahatma Gandhi in India. Occasionally, as in the rule of the ayatollahs in contemporary Iran, popular authority overtly resides within religious authority. Whether it is seen as civil religion or as overt theocracy, the return to faith-based authority almost always strengthens the state internally. Nevertheless, it creates a destabilizing force in international relations; one can never be sure whether one is negotiating with an agent of the people, accountable in some way to the electoral process, or with an agent of God, accountable only to some personal deity.

Furthermore, the rise of civil religion as a prop to civil authority has opened a door through which non-state actors, employing religious rhetoric, can enter the political arena. Even though political authority is derived from the "consent of the governed," it must be maintained through a form of quasi-religious faith. If the state's leader is exposed as merely human, or the government ceases to provide the blessings of its alleged divine connections to its people, the reaction can be catastrophic. A new leader will arise, claiming true authority—and that authority will almost inevitably be religious. The parallel to traditional popular revolutions is clear: just as control over food distribution leads ultimately to the legitimizing of national liberation groups, so do allegations of control over the distribution of divine favor lead to the legitimizing of fanatical religious sects. And the very extremity of their exhortations—their "passionate intensity"—is what empowers them; no one who was not intimately in touch with the divine spirit, infer the speaker's audience, would dare to make such claims. So long as the popular authority remains benign, such claims of religious authority can be generally ignored; they lack, after all, any political confirmation. But during times of economic hardship and consequent political weakness, the strident voice claiming "I warned you!" begins to win converts. And because the claim to authority is religious, not popular, it need not persuade a majority; it need only inflame a passionate few, and intimidate the remainder, to wreak havoc. It happened in Florence in 1494, when Savanarola won over a populace depressed by the end of Medici sovereignty; it happened in Salem in early 1692, when a handful of young women, weakened by short rations and a hard winter and egged on by adults with ulterior economic motives, inflamed an entire community.

Today, non-state actors pose the gravest threat to world peace, precisely because they defend no sovereign borders, erect no economic infrastructure to penalize through sanctions or embargoes, present no "top of the pyramid" to target for retribution. Indeed, some non-state actors have rejected the prospect of sovereign authority when offered it, recognizing that the bargains and compromises of political transactions would corrupt the purity of their moral authority. As agents of a divine power, or of economic necessity, these leaders display no reverence for sovereign authority; they have no interest in belonging to the "club" of sovereign states. Hence any state or organization that wishes to address the threat they pose must meet them on a higher ground.

Although the messages of such claimants to religious authority are necessarily extreme, they are not necessarily violent. The victory of the

African National Congress in South Africa was helped immeasurably by the efforts of Bishop Tutu on its behalf, and the popular ratification of his message embodied in the Nobel Peace Prize. In recent decades, however, the most visible non-state religious actors have been Muslim extremists such as the Taliban, Al Qaeda, and Jamaa Islamiyah, for all of whom the need for violence is an integral part of their message. If the violent acts of the extremists evoke a violent response by those in popular authority, the government's dependence on the rule of law to provide moral justification for its own use of power is weakened, perhaps fatally; if those in authority withhold a response in kind, they retain the moral high ground but appear impotent.

IV

So an impasse appears to have been created. On one side, a popular, often constitutional, authority is unable to respond to the violence of religious extremists, precisely because it relies for its continued existence on the same (or a parallel) religious foundation; or, that authority has lost its popular mandate through an undisciplined resort to violence in a vain attempt to counter the threat. On the other side, a group eschewing any claim to political power but claiming absolute authority offers the attraction of moral certainty, but their intolerance of nonbelievers leads to a terrible human cost. Neither of these problems threatens the legitimacy or the sovereignty of the state, but they threaten the moral authority of both the state and its leadership; and in such circumstances the state loses its claim to right authority. Herein lie both the heart of the problem, and the seed of a solution.

In 1970, the United Nations issued a Declaration on Principles of International Law, explicitly rejecting action that threatens a state's legitimacy or sovereignty: "Any attempt aimed at the partial or total disruption of the national unity and territorial integrity of a State or country or at its political independence is incompatible with the purposes and principles of the Charter. . . . Every State has the duty to refrain in its international relations from the threat or use of force against the territorial integrity or political independence of any State." The use of "duty," however, a word repeated ten times in the statement of principles, acknowledges a realm that stands beyond the law, beyond sovereignty: the realm of moral obligation, or right. The Declaration on Principles ends by stressing the duty of individual states "to fulfill in good faith the obligations assumed by it in accordance with the Charter of the United Nations . . . [and] to take joint and separate action in co-operation with the United Nations." Furthermore, it continues, in those cases where the obligations of a state conflict with these duties, "the obligations under the Charter shall prevail."[26]

By basing its argument on "duty" and "obligation," the United Nations seeks an authority that is not based on either force or faith, but on fellowship. Its historic reluctance to employ UN peacekeepers for intervention reflects a refusal to commit to either a faith-based moral code or a force-based pragmatism. The United Nations was founded in part on the principle that offensive violence, even when it is employed in the cause of restoring rightness, is a reflection of arrogance, not obligation. The Declaration of Principles, like the Charter itself, commits the United Nations to the ideals of "justice . . . respect . . . tolerance . . . peace." These are not imposed on people by higher authorities, nor are they delivered to people from some divine power. The four principles singled out by the UN Charter are the immediate results of people choosing to act toward others as they would want others to act toward themselves—and although people within the Christian tradition may say, "This is congruent with the Golden Rule," or people within the Chinese tradition may say, "This Charter reflects the precepts of Sun Tzu," these are not the reasons why people choose such actions. Neither do people choose to act thus because they are desirous of making a social contract, within which justice and tolerance will be defined in legalistic terms and enforced with penalties. Rather, people choose them because they believe that they are themselves just, tolerant, and respectful, and that if they treat others as just, tolerant, and respectful those others will treat them similarly. It is a belief founded in the recognition that, despite the large differences people display in appearance, cultures, religions, and other particular relations, there is an underlying identity that constitutes "humanity."

The principles upon which the United Nations was founded are therefore essentially congruent with the "ethical commonwealth" proposed two centuries ago by Immanuel Kant. Kant foresaw the contradiction between sovereign authority and right authority that threatens to paralyze the community of nations today. "This is precisely the case," he noted, "with separate political states not bound together through a public international law"[27]—an inevitability in a world lacking "a will that is universally valid, under which each can be free."[28] Without voluntary moral laws, entered into on the basis of "tolerance" or "respect," no system of coercive legislative laws, entered into merely on the basis of "prudence," can survive.[29] For this reason, "all the plans of theory for the right of a state, the right of nations, and cosmopolitan right dissolve into ineffectual, impracticable ideals."[30]

Kant also foresaw the ethical limitations of humanitarian intervention. As he wrote in *Toward Perpetual Peace* (1795), "No state shall forcibly interfere in the constitution and government of another state."[31] His reasoning was that, unless a state collapsed into total "anarchy," such as in the failed states discussed in section 2, "such interference of foreign powers would be a violation on the rights of a people dependent upon no other and only struggling with its own inner illness." In his essay, Kant foresaw nothing more coercive than a "federalism" of states, a "pacific league [directed toward] . . . preserving and securing the freedom of a state itself."[32]

Kant's views on the necessity of maintaining sovereign authority rested on his conviction of "the frailty of human nature, the lack of sufficient strength to follow out the principles it has chosen for itself,"[33] a frailty that can be overcome only by "the mutual faith that is required if any enduring peace is to be established."[34] Therefore any process that increased the chance to achieve "the united will of the people" must be pursued, in the hope that "there will arise in the body politic perhaps more charity and less strife in lawsuits, more reliability in keeping one's word . . . and eventually this will also extend to nations in their external relations toward one another."[35]

A century later, those who were winning what was already being called the Great War expressed a similar optimism about the prospect of international fellowship. In January 1918, Woodrow Wilson declared before a joint session of Congress "that the world [must] be made fit and safe to live in . . . for every peace-loving nation which, like our own, wishes to live its own life, determine its own institutions, be assured of justice and fair dealing by the other peoples of the world as against force and selfish aggression."[36] These principles, embodied first in the League of Nations and then in the United Nations, offered a way of combining political authority with moral rightness that brought together Kant's long-term vision of a world at peace and a sense that immoral "trespasses"—incidents where forceful intervention on behalf of right authority was taken, in violation of sovereignty—could be kept short-term. Some contemporary philosophers have also moved in this direction; see, for example, John Rawls' theory of the "overlapping consensus."[37]

So the principles of fellowship allow for, although they do not justify, acts of humanitarian intervention. Prudential acts that "trespass on the rights of an independent people" weaken the moral strength of federalist organizations like the United Nations. Although the preamble to the UN Charter vows "to unite our strength to maintain international peace and security," such acts alienate rather than bind. The prospect of unified action in response to such threats has also diminished as the number of sovereign states has risen. Karen Kovach, in a recent essay, has questioned whether "the United Nations actually does represent the international community." Given the way that "power is distributed unevenly," Kovach asserts, "not all of its member-nations accept the international community's ideas of political legitimacy." She recognizes numerous "people, peoples, and states for whom membership in the international community holds no attraction."[38] If Kovach's observation is accurate, it perhaps is a signal that the United Nations' attempt to create a single set of moral standards acceptable to every nation-state is a failure.

Part of the problem may inhere in the narrowness of Security Council representation. So long as the legal authority for intervention is contained within a small group, dominated by five permanent members, other members of the General Assembly may well resent such a usurpation of their authority, even when they share a sense of its moral necessity. And such a bifurcation of authority within the United Nations may be the reason why the assignment of peacekeepers to Israel in the 1950s, to Cyprus since the 1960s, and to the Balkans in the 1990s failed in each case to lead to any international consensus on a long-term resolution of these conflicts.

Indeed, the UN has failed in its efforts as often as it has succeeded; and the larger problem may be its very vision of humanitarian intervention. Though the legal (sovereign) authority of those who intervene may be readily accepted, and their intervention would be considered just at least by those who are being saved, suspicion about the decision-making process would lead to doubts about the moral (right) authority of the intervention. Intrusions by outsiders into one's personal affairs are necessarily acts of force as well as acts of fellowship. Because such acts parallel the actions of parents with their children, interventions threaten to infantilize rather than to restore one's sense of equality with one's saviors. Only in retrospect can the subjects of humanitarian intervention recognize that, were the situation reversed, they might have acted in the same fashion. As Robert Frost noted nearly a century ago, the same principles that make for "good neighbors" often lead one to erect "good fences."[39]

Unfortunately, the history of the past sixty years strongly suggests that Kant's pessimistic view may have been correct: the principles of fellowship can exist only in antithesis to practices based on faith and force. Where nation-states stand willing to intervene in the affairs of others, to that extent the principles of sovereignty are already degraded. To the extent that the principle of sovereign authority is forcibly threatened, to the same extent the need for a principle of authority by fellowship—by the sovereign power of international consensus—is accordingly increased. Ironically, so long as individual nation-states practice solitary acts of intervention, the appeal to fellowship by the United Nations as right authority is strengthened; every time the United States attempts to be the policeman of the world, the United Nations gains in moral stature. For intervention to have right authority, it must be perceived as an expression of the will of the entire community of nations, not as a prudential result of power brokering by a few powerful states. Thus the United Nations profits from the clear wrongness of forceful unilateral—or as in Iraq, fragmented multilateral—intervention, for such acts underscore the essential "rightness" of its own, openly achieved, right authority. In the absence of any clear articulation of both its reasons for intervening and the basis for its sovereignty, the United Nations' claim of right authority is what will be called into question—and that possibility bodes ill for the Rwandas and Sudans of the future.

And it is right authority that the UN Charter seeks to define—a right authority based in those aspects of humanity that make us alike, rather than the regional, national, even religious aspects that insist we are different. Because intervention, even intervention for humanitarian purposes, implies that those who have chosen to intervene are better (and therefore different) than those whose borders are crossed, it is to be undertaken only in the most extreme circumstances. For it is ultimately not a question of a greater versus a lesser evil; in the world of fellowship there are no such scholastic distinctions. It is rather a question of doing always what the code of fellowship dictates: that which leads to inclusiveness, not sectarianism; that which leads to a turning away from force, not the automatic recourse to it; that which rests on consensus, not compulsion. Such a conclusion is the only one that offers any pathway, no matter how narrow and tortuous, toward an authority that is truly "right."

NOTES

1. *The Illustrated Art of War,* trans. T. Cleary (Boston: Shambhala, 1998), 62 (chapter I, precept 5).

2. *Contra Faustum*, xxii, 75. Quoted by St. Augustine in St. Thomas Aquinas, *Summa Theologiae*, trans. T. R. Heath (New York: McGraw-Hill, 1964), vol. 35, 83 (part II, question 40).

3. Ibid.

4. *The Illustrated Art of War*, 63 (Chapter I, Precept 8).

5. Ibid, 62.

6. *On War*, ed. M. Howard and P. Paret (Princeton: Princeton University Press, 1976), 89.

7. Ibid., 91.

8. "Sovereignty as 'Dominium': Is There a Right of Humanitarian Intervention?" in *National Sovereignty and International Intervention*, ed. M. Mastanudo and G. Lyons (Baltimore: Johns Hopkins University Press, 1995), 26, 33.

9. Richard J. Regan, *Just War: Principles and Cases* (Washington, DC: Catholic University of America Press, 1996), 37.

10. *Religion within the Boundaries of Mere Reason*, Part III, Division I, paragraph 3, in *Religion and Rational Theology*, trans. G. di Giovanni (Cambridge: Cambridge University Press, 1996), 130 (6:94).

11. *Arguing About War* (New Haven: Yale University Press, 2004), 14.

12. Washington: Council on Foreign Relations, 1993, 302–303.

13. *Taming the Sovereigns: Institutional Change in International Politics* (Cambridge: Cambridge University Press, 2004), 138.

14. *Beyond Sovereignty: Issues for a Global Agenda* (Belmont, CA: Wadsworth, 2003), 15.

15. *Advance Along the Road Opened up by the October Socialist Revolution* (Foreign Language Press, 1967), 5. Online at http://www.marxists.org/reference/archive/lin-biao/1967/11/06.htm.

16. Peter Singer, *One World: The Ethics of Globalization* (New Haven: Yale University Press, 2002), 97.

17. Annual Report to the General Assembly for 1999; UN Press Release SG/SM/7136, GA/95/96.

18. As R. J. Vincent, in *Non-Intervention and International Order* (Princeton: Princeton University Press, 1974), puts it, "If a state has a right to sovereignty, this implies that other states have a duty to respect that right by, among other things, refraining from intervention in its domestic affairs" (14).

19. *Summa Theologiae*, 83, referring to Romans 13:4.

20. *Ch'un-ch'iu fan-lu*, sec. 43, 11:5, in *Sources of Chinese Tradition*, trans. Burton Watson (New York: Macmillan, 1960), 179.

21. The Declaration of Independence, paragraph 2.

22. "The Second Coming" (1919), lines 7–8.

23. *Contra Faustum*, xxii, 70; quoted in Aquinas, *Summa Theologiae*, 83.

24. Cited in *Varieties of Civil Religion* (San Francisco: Harper and Row, 1980), 10–11.

25. Ibid., 133–136.

26. Declaration on Principles of International Law Concerning Friendly Relations and Co-operation among States in Accordance with the Charter of the United Nations, G.A. res. 2625, Annex, 25 UN GAOR, Supp. (No. 28), UN Doc. A/5217 at 121 (1970).

27. *Religion within the Boundaries of Mere Reason*, part III, division I, paragraph 4, 132 (6:96).

28. "Idea for a Universal History from a Cosmopolitan Point of View," Thesis 5; in *On History*, trans. L. W. Beck (Indianapolis: Bobbs-Merrill, 1963), 17.

29. *Religion within the Boundaries of Mere Reason*, part II, paragraph 3, 102 (6:58).

30. *Toward Perpetual Peace*, Appendix I; in *Practical Philosophy*, ed. M. J. Gregor (Cambridge: Cambridge University Press, 1996), 359–360 (8:371).

31. Ibid., First Section; 319–320 (8:346).

32. Ibid., Article II; 327 (8:356).

33. Ibid., 324 (8:352).

34. *The Metaphysical Elements of Justice*, trans. L. W. Beck (Indianapolis: Bobbs-Merrill, 1967), 347.

35. "An Old Question," in *The Contest of the Faculties*, trans. M. J. Gregor (New York: Abaris Books, 1979), 165–167.

36. The "Fourteen Points" Speech, 8 January 1918.

37. *Political Liberalism* (New York: Columbia University Press, 1993), 15.

38. "The International Community as Moral Agent," *Journal of Military Ethics* 2:2 (2003): 103.

39. "Mending Wall," lines 27 and 45.

CHAPTER 12

Violent Civil Disobedience: Defending Human Rights, Rethinking Just War

Robert W. Hoag

In 1994, in a small, isolated country in east Africa, the world watched and did nothing as nearly one million people were brutally butchered in Rwanda, their basic human rights violated while not one state employed military force to intervene on humanitarian grounds and end the horror. In the late 1990s, many died unnecessarily in East Timor while the United Nations awaited permission from Indonesia to intervene and stop the government's savagery against its own citizens. In the Balkans, finally, in 1999 NATO bombed Serbia "to head off a potential genocide," even though the NATO action lacked UN authorization and is widely regarded as illegal. Unfortunately, situations such as these are not unusual around the globe. Such situations of gross human rights violations have prompted much discussion and many questions about humanitarian interventions, international law, and reforming international structures. In this essay I take such supreme humanitarian emergencies as central and explore states' use of military

This essay emerges from participation in a Jesse DuPont Seminar at the National Humanities Center in June, 2003, and a National Endowment for the Humanities Summer Institute at the United States Naval Academy in 2004. My thanks go to the Foundation and the Endowment for these quality opportunities. An earlier version of my essay was presented at one of Berea's Friday Faculty Colloquia. I thank my colleagues and the editors of this volume for their helpful comments.

force and violence as justifiable humanitarian interventions and as international civil disobedience aimed at reforming the restrictive international law of force. What might such violent civil disobedience suggest in thinking about traditional *ad bellum* principles for justifying recourse to war?

Some initial challenges lie in the apparent oxymorons running through this chapter's title and topic. The following domestic example illustrates how humanitarian intervention can involve deadly force and how civil disobedience can also be violent.[1] Consider America's antebellum fugitive slave laws, the statutory enforcers of the U.S. Constitution's Fugitive Slave Clause (Article IV, Sec. 3, Clause 3).[2] Given that enslavement violates basic human rights, such federal fugitive slave laws themselves violate human rights by protecting uses of force against persons to continue their enslavement. Now suppose that slaves having escaped into Civil War–era Ohio, for example, are about to be captured and returned to their owners, that there are third-party witnesses to the final stages of recapture, and that the only effective, available, and timely way to stop the recapture and return to slavery is for those third parties to intervene with violent or deadly force on behalf of the slave's human rights. If the third-party witnesses do act with violent, even deadly force against the abductors, then they thereby disobey the law against assault even though they interfere with others' violation of basic human rights. Absent some powerful pacifism, taking others' human rights seriously pulls toward moral plausibility for such illegal uses of force or violence. Furthermore, seeing the gap between morality and the legal proscriptions on force, suppose the interveners act illegally not only to protect others' human rights, but also in order to reform laws that enshrine slavery or proscribe assaults in defense of others' basic human rights. Such a violent intervention, then, respects law by becoming also an act of civil disobedience, an "illegal legal reform" strategy aimed at changing the restrictive law of force that proscribes "interposing to protect the defenseless."[3] It is conceptually and morally plausible that such a domestic humanitarian intervention is also an act of violent civil disobedience, a violent intervention in order to defend human rights and to reform the law of force that proscribes necessary interventions in such humanitarian emergencies.

In this essay I suggest an international analogue to domestic violent civil disobedience. Consider that a state's violation of human rights is legally protected under international law, like the capture of a fugitive slave once was legal under U.S. law. Consider that, like the domestic case, another state's violent, humanitarian intervention in defense of human rights is illegal under the current international law of force. Thus, another state's violent, illegal intervention in defense of human rights may be justifiable as an act of violent civil disobedience aimed at reforming the international law of force that proscribes humanitarian interventions by states. Such armed and violent state interventions raise questions of justification about the recourse to war by a state. I will proceed by describing humanitarian intervention and the related international law of force, by arguing for the necessity of illegal acts for timely, effective reform of the international law of force to allow states' intervening violently in defense of human rights, and by sketching how humanitarian interventions seen as violent civil disobedience lead to rethinking traditional *ad bellum* principles for justifying recourse to war.

The idea and practice of humanitarian intervention have received considerable attention in recent years. There are various kinds of interventions, from peaceful assistance programs aimed at refugee or famine relief to arming insurgency groups across state borders, and from the use of armed forces to rescue nationals abroad to invading territory and toppling regimes. Though the Rwanda case recently brought to the fore moral questions about justifying humanitarian interventions, and though many similar situations this past century involved genocide or ethnic cleansing, oft discussed are other, nongenocidal situations where armed interventions occurred: India's 1971 incursion into Bangladesh; Vietnam's crossing into Cambodia, toppling Pol Pot's murderous Khmer Rouge regime in 1979; Tanzania's ouster of Uganda's Idi Amin in the same year; the response to the plight of the Iraqi Kurds in the early nineties; America's brief military venture into Somalia in the early years of the Clinton administration; NATO's 1995 air war against the Bosnian Serbs in Kosovo. The relatively recent Australian intervention to stop political persecutions in East Timor, of course, can also be added to this list.

Amid such conceptual and situational diversity this essay takes as central many features of the Rwandan debacle. This argument here focuses on armed interventions in supreme humanitarian emergencies and understands a humanitarian intervention as: "the threat or use of force across state borders by a state (or group of states) aimed at preventing or ending widespread and grave violations of the fundamental human rights of individuals other than its own citizens, without the permission of the state within whose territory force is applied."[4] So,

humanitarian interventions are transnational border crossings that
employ force, threats of force, or violence by the interveners; excluded
are coercive, nonmilitary interventions such as economic sanctions,
negotiations, or provision of humanitarian aid. Thus, interventions
involve interstate military conflict. Also, interventions are not primarily a means to preserving international peace, but rather are aimed at
stopping gross violations of basic human rights, such as the right to
life, the right not to be tortured or to be enslaved.[5] In addition, the
rights violations are the responsibility of the viable state in which the
victims live, and other states are the interveners and protectors of individuals' rights.[6] Excluded are situations of failed states and the role of
non-state interveners. And insofar as humanitarian interventions as
civil disobedience might be warranted, the focus is supreme emergency
situations in which "the only hope of saving lives depends on outsiders
coming to the rescue."[7]

Humanitarian interventions involve using military force to defend
human rights and thereby raise questions about their legality under
international law, especially the UN Charter. The Charter lists a number of purposes regarding relations among states, emphasizing the aim
of "international peace and security" (Article 1). Human rights are also
a theme of the Charter (A. 1, 55, 62, 68). But the Charter itself
includes no list or articulation of what those human rights are (except
perhaps the collective right of self-determination in A. 1.2); and subsequent declarations on human rights require only that signatories
must protect human rights. There is no explicit acknowledgment in the
Charter of the use of force aimed at defending human rights; there is
no explicit provision for the legality of humanitarian interventions.

Humanitarian interventions directly challenge international law
and specific UN Charter provisions about states' use of force. States are
recognized as holding "the inherent right of individual or collective
self-defense if an armed attack occurs" (A. 51), the Charter precludes
"the United Nations to intervene in matters that are essentially within
the domestic jurisdiction of any state" (A. 2.7), and the use of force is
very narrowly limited in Article 2.4: "All members shall refrain in their
international relations from the threat or use of force against the territorial integrity or political independence of any state, or in any other
manner inconsistent with the Purposes of the United Nations."
Chapter VII of the Charter ensconces the Security Council as sole
arbiter of whether the use of armed force is warranted as a necessary
last resort "to maintain or restore international peace and security" and

in response to what the Council itself decides is "the existence of any threat to the peace, breach of the peace, or act of aggression" (A. 39; also, A. 41, 42). The body of international law builds on and confirms this charter system of restricting the use of force by states. Even in a supreme humanitarian emergency, then, defending human rights by force either is an authorized means to the end of peace between states or is illegal under the Charter and the international law of force.[8]

Given the moral pull to intervene in response to supreme humanitarian emergencies of the sort endured in Rwanda or Kosovo, for example, scholars have explored ways to interpret international law so as to close the gap between law and morality so starkly evident in such cases.[9] There are several strategies for accommodating legalities to the moral pull of humanitarian interventions. Regarding the specific UN Charter itself, there are the legal classicists' careful parsing of the specific texts themselves. For example, the crucial Charter provision A. 2.4 does not prohibit force *simpliciter*, but only force against territorial integrity or political independence, neither of which is the aim of a humanitarian intervention. But such ingenious exegeses soon seem Orwellian and confront Article 31(1) of the 1969 Vienna Convention on the Law of Treaties: "a treaty shall be interpreted in good faith in accordance with the ordinary meaning to be given to the terms of the treaty." Legal Realists' more expansive hermeneutical strategies invoke contexts, state practices, and other considerations external to the literal letter of the law. But such strategies both lack requisite evidence at crucial points and eschew the international rules about interpreting international rules of law.[10]

Another strategy of legal accommodation to moral pull is openly to acknowledge the exceptional character of humanitarian interventions, proposing that they be accepted as lawful illegalities.[11] Thomas Franck, for example, argues that there is now a customary international law of unauthorized humanitarian interventions and that strict readings of normative texts like the UN Charter must be tempered by a "pragmatic approach," a "rule of reasonableness": as with the domestic doctrine of exculpatory necessity, gross rights violations are exceptional circumstances that can exculpate or mitigate "what would otherwise be an illegal act."[12] The United Nations, Franck notes, has responded to unauthorized humanitarian interventions either by acquiescence or *via* some kind of retroactive endorsement. In the former case, the illegality of the armed intervention is mitigated or excused because of the necessity of the circumstances: unauthorized interventions are illegal, but UN acquiescence acknowledges the moral necessity and mitigation of an illegal act. The argument, then, takes illegal acts to be legally acceptable because of the United Nations' practice of acquiescence in responding to unauthorized humanitarian interventions.

This proposed lawful illegality strategy of accommodation faces overwhelming challenges. First, Franck's discussion sometimes confusingly conflates the distinct domestic analogues of excuse, justification, and mitigation. If an act is legally justified, then it is not illegal: killing in self-defense, for example, is not homicide at all. A legal excuse removes responsibility and thus punishment, while mitigation reduces the penalty: both acknowledge the illegality of the act, and neither make legal "what would otherwise be an illegal act." Franck's precise presentation of his position wanders among these importantly different conceptions. Second, the customary rule of exculpation or mitigation is said to be evidenced by the United Nations' practice in responding to interventions. Yet UN acquiescence often reflects gridlock, parochial reasons for exercising Security Council vetoes, or other factors that completely undermine acquiescence as acknowledging the necessity argument Franck so forcefully puts forward. In the case of Rwanda, for example, given the deliberate actions of the United States and others, Security Council and UN inaction cannot be taken as signifying approval of inaction by the international community.[13] Third, the strategy seems to be arguing that a customary international rule overrides treaty law, and in particular, the supreme treaty among them all, the UN Charter. This strategy ignores well-established understandings about the ordinal importance of the four sources of international law articulated in Article 38 of the Statute of the International Court of Justice, which is annexed to Article 92 of the UN Charter. Thus, the proposed lawful legality strategy is, at best, perhaps a tolerable solution to a current "practical conundrum"; however, this accommodation strategy implicitly asserts both the moral necessity and illegality of unauthorized humanitarian interventions. Given the problems with such accommodation strategies, taking seriously the gap between morality and legality indicates need for another strategy— reform the international law of force to accommodate the powerful moral pull of supreme humanitarian emergencies.

An obvious reform strategy is to change the written law of force and humanitarian interventions. Given the absence of any genuine legislative power, though, the legal change must be to the UN Charter provisions about use of force and its authorization. Thus, the aim might be to codify a discretionary right of humanitarian intervention under certain conditions, perhaps by amending the Charter to include not only a right of self-defense (Article 51), but also an individual or collective right to defend others' basic human rights.[14] But given practical reasons of politics, individual states protecting their own sovereignty, and the current "state consent super norm" built into international law, this approach is unlikely to be successful any time soon.[15] And in the interim the moral pull of human rights violations remains powerful and repetitious. Some other reform strategy is needed to address the moral pull of supreme humanitarian emergencies today.

Another approach to legal reform is gradual, incremental change *via* states repeatedly intervening to address gross violations of human rights and thereby eventually constituting a general practice constitutive of a customary rule of international law. Building on Franck's lawful illegality strategy, Jane Stromseth, for example, argues against now codifying a right of intervention and favors the gradual emergence of customary law recognizing "legal exception and justification."[16] But this approach cannot succeed in making humanitarian interventions legal so long as the supremacy of treaty law and the Charter provisions about force remain features of the international law system: even if such a customary rule were established, the hierarchical structure of international law would still leave humanitarian interventions illegal. Second, this legal reform strategy for the law of force not only faces difficulties, uncertainties, and moral risks associated with any change in customary law,[17] the process is entirely too slow to address now the moral pull of supreme humanitarian emergencies. Third, this reform strategy is initially an illegal legal reform strategy. According to Article 38 of the International Court of Justice Statute, customary international law exists only if there is an "international custom, as evidence of a general practice accepted as law": intervening must not only evidence a general practice, but the additional *opinio juris* requirement means interventions must be done because they are taken to be lawful, "accepted as law." But in the context of legal reform, an aim of the interventions is to change the extant law, to reform the proscription of armed humanitarian interventions. And that requires states see their interventions as illegal, as contrary to the law the reform aims to change. And so, at least in the early stages of customary law reform, states' humanitarian interventions violate international law.[18] This reform strategy requires states deliberately disobey the current international law of force.

The international law system itself provides very limited resources for timely change and improvement. The absence of a legislative power, the state consent required to constitute customary or treaty law, the practicalities of geopolitics operating through the Charter system, and other features all explain this systemic inertia. Given such features of the international law system, the moral pull of supreme humanitarian emergencies, and the gap between morality and legality, the only timely, effective strategy for change is some illegal legal reform strategy aimed at the restrictive international law of force. That changing customary law initially requires illegal state action does suggest such a strategy, one analogous to the domestic reform strategies with which this essay began. Given the moral pull of supreme humanitarian interventions, suppose that a state intervenes militarily to defend basic human rights, thereby committing an illegal act in violation of the current international law of force. Given the gap between morality and legality, suppose further that the illegal state action also aims at legal reform so that such humanitarian interventions are no longer proscribed under the international law of force. Analogous to the domestic example of seeking to abolish fugitive slave laws, then, such state interventions are acts of violent civil disobedience at the international level: the use of military force by a state in order to address gross violations of basic human rights by and in another state and in order to reform the extant and restrictive international law of force.

To see humanitarian interventions as acts of violent civil disobedience implies at least that a state's use of military force is more than violating the law, more than mere disobedience of the international law of force. Even in the domestic arena, there is great diversity regarding what constitutes an act of civil disobedience. But at a minimum, an act of civil disobedience is to be understood as a deliberate violation of the law, justified on moral grounds, and for the sake of civil reform that improves the law.[19] Direct civil disobedience is an act that violates the very law the actor aims to reform and improve; indirect civil disobedience violates laws other than those to be reformed, but as a means to and for the sake of bringing about other specific legal reforms.[20] Applied to humanitarian interventions in the international arena, then, the illegal legal reform proposal here is that states' interventions in defense of basic human rights be understood as acts of direct civil disobedience aimed at reforming the restrictive international law of force. As is the case for domestic civil disobedience, international civil disobedience respects the law: such violations of the law are a form of respect for and fidelity to the rule of law, and they need not be grounded in moral subjectivism.[21] As is the case for the domestic analogue of seeking to abolish fugitive slave laws, the proposed international civil disobedience is violent because it is direct: the humanitarian intervention aims to change the international law of force while also using force to defend basic human rights being violated by another state.

The idea of violent civil disobedience to defend basic human rights not only requires much more than interveners' violating the law, the proposed approach to legal reform also importantly limits interveners' use of violence and force. First, contrary to many theorists, the proposal here presumes that civil disobedience is not always or inherently nonviolent. But as with the aforementioned fugitive slave case, it is important to see that the violence involved follows from the civil disobedience being direct, aimed at reforming the law of force by disobeying that law, and from the moral pull of defending basic human rights. So, for example, killing a doctor outside an abortion clinic or domestic terrorism to protest U.S. policies are not here countenanced, for they are indirect civil disobedience acts that involve violence only as tactics to effect changes other than reforming the law of force that the acts violate. Second, there are implications for states' militaries being the actors: abuse of the reform strategy is possible, the force employed is great, the stakes are high when states violate the international law of force, and states are unlikely to endure legal penalties for their illegal acts.[22] Such warranted reservations can be balanced with other considerations. Acting on the moral pull of supreme humanitarian emergencies requires military force be used, and states are most likely to have the requisite command and control structures needed for effective defenses of basic human rights. Accepting the jurisdiction of the International Court of Justice, for example, could be a condition for states to intervene illegally, which may work against states' tendencies to abuse the reform strategy and which also provides a legal accountability important to acts of civil disobedience, whether domestic or international, whether the disobedient are corporate or private individuals. Furthermore, to the extent that risks run greater with states as agents of violent civil disobedience, changes in the international law of force may more likely occur sooner than through other reform strategies. An effect of states' violent civil disobedience, then, very well may be a quickly improved and more effective legal protection for basic human rights.

International civil disobedience as here suggested does raise the general question, "Under what conditions, if any, is it morally justified to engage in acts that violate existing international law in order to bring about supposed moral improvements in . . . international law?"[23] But there is not readily available a moral theory for violent civil disobedience in international situations of supreme humanitarian emergency. In the domestic arena there has been very little serious theoretical work in the past quarter century, and much past work understandably reflects contexts and presumptions about nonviolence and features of the American political and legal system.[24] John Rawls's discussion, for example, offers a "constitutional theory of civil disobedience" that presupposes "a nearly just society" requiring a "democratic regime," and, like many others, defines civil disobedience as nonviolent.[25] The American example set by Martin Luther King's morally rich appeal to objective and transcendent natural law principles insists on nonviolence, at least as a tactic, and presumes the U.S. system's strong legislative power to remedy the injustices of segregation laws.[26] And Henry David Thoreau's famous essay and actions also are not helpful: based on individual conscience, his stated purpose is not to change the laws, but to wash his hands of slavery in America, to, as he says, "sever his allegiance" to the institution and the state that supports it.[27]

Another approach may more immediately bear theoretical fruit for violent civil disobedience in defense of human rights in the international arena. Given that the proposed direct civil disobedience is violent and given that humanitarian interventions are interstate engagements of military force, it is worth considering relationships between the needed illegal legal reform strategy proposed here and some traditional *ad bellum* principles for justifying the recourse to war.

Others have acknowledged links between humanitarian interventions and traditional thinking about justifying the recourse to war. In his latest writing about just and unjust wars, for example, Michael Walzer explicitly acknowledges that humanitarian interventions challenge thinking about military force and violence, arguing that "we need a campaign for a strong international system . . . to stop massacres."[28] More specifically, Nicholas Wheeler requires that four *ad bellum* principles be satisfied as threshold conditions for justifying humanitarian interventions: just cause, last resort, proportionality, and likelihood of positive humanitarian outcome. Additional criteria are then not necessary conditions, "but if met correspondingly increase the legitimacy of a particular action."[29] How might seeing humanitarian interventions as violent civil disobedience lead to rethinking traditional *ad bellum* principles for justifying the recourse to war?

The use of military force to defend human rights is not a just cause new to the tradition of just war thinking, but a just cause that needs resurrection to address the moral pull of frequent supreme humanitarian emergencies today. The UN Charter essentially restricts states' use of force to self-defense, which "represents the most restrictive analysis of 'just cause' in the history of the subject"[30] and which contributes much to contemporary discussions proceeding as if self-defense expends the array of just war thinking about acceptable causes for the recourse to war. But the just war tradition contains a much richer vein of just causes. For example, St. Thomas Aquinas's classic trio of *ad bellum* requirements includes just causes much broader than self-defense, perhaps even allowing for humanitarian interventions. Quoting St. Augustine, Aquinas writes: "Secondly, a just cause is required—so that those against whom the war is waged deserve such a response because of some offense on their part. Augustine says, 'Just wars are usually defined as those that avenge injuries, when a nation or a city should be punished for failing to right a wrong done by its citizens, or to return what has been taken away unjustly.'"[31] Note how Aquinas's formulation allows that the offense, injury, wrong, or unjust taking justifies war even if the victim is not the state going to war for any of these causes. Thus, a state can have just cause for war as a third-party responder to an offense, injury, wrong, or taking committed against some other party. As another example, consider the modern secular thinker, Hugo Grotius, who even more clearly includes "interposing to protect the defenseless" among the just causes for war. In his classic work, *The Law of War and Peace*, Grotius characterizes "just cause" in terms of violating rights: "In speaking of belligerent powers, it was shown that the law of nature authorizes the assertion not only of our own rights, but of those also belonging to others. The causes therefore, which justify the principals engaged in war, will justify those also, who afford assistance to others."[32] And another just cause arises when any ruler, even one in another state, "inflicts upon his subjects such treatment as no one is warranted in inflicting."[33] Grotius says, in effect, that humanitarian interventions are a just cause for war.

These and many similar historical characterizations of just cause have led scholars to interpret the just war tradition in ways that can justify humanitarian interventions. For example, James Turner Johnson argues that just war theory is centrally about justice, not primarily about restricting uses of force: "the concept of just war does not begin with a 'presumption against war' focused on the harm which war may do, but with a presumption against *injustice* focused on the need for responsible use of force in response to wrongdoing."[34] Specifically with respect to just cause, Johnson maintains that the tradition is much broader than current international law's restrictions: it includes "the right to use force if necessary for such purposes as combating . . . systematic and sustained violations of universally recognized human rights."[35] From the perspective of just war theory, then, current international law discounts the moral pull of humanitarian emergencies, just as American domestic law has with respect to slavery and lynching, for example.

Seeing humanitarian interventions as violent civil disobedience also suggests building on a just war tradition aimed at injustice and "focused on the need for responsible use of force in response to wrongdoing." A just cause for violent civil disobedience may not be only in response to current human rights violations, but also in order to close the gap between morality and legality so that future forceful defenses of basic human rights can be accomplished legally and more often effectively. In short, the proposed illegal legal reform strategy of violent civil disobedience may itself provide a just cause for the recourse to using military force: a just cause is military intervention both to rescue now and reform soon, to defend human rights now and in the long-term. Furthermore, given the concern only with supreme humanitarian emergencies and given the embedded systemic inertia of the international law system today, an illegal legal reform strategy of violent civil disobedience as suggested here is necessary now as an effective response to states' wrongdoing. Violent civil disobedience, then, plausibly satisfies an *ad bellum* requirement of last resort,[36] both as the only hope of rescue in a supreme humanitarian emergency today and, as argued previously, the only timely, effective way to change soon the restrictive international law of force.

Considerations of last resort rely partially on the efficacy of alternatives for reasonable success as rescue and legal reform, which leads to rethinking the *ad bellum* principles of proportionality and the related requirement of reasonable success in achieving the aims in any recourse to war.[37] The plausible, basic idea of *ad bellum* proportionality is that the benefits and costs of recourse to war must be proportionate: the costs of recourse to war must be worthwhile compared to benefits and alternative ways of achieving the ends of using military force. Thus, balancing the effects of the recourse to war is counterfactual and comparative with respect to alternative means to given ends, and the balancing includes

effects other than quantifiable damages like deaths and property damages.[38] Applied to humanitarian interventions, proportionality considerations involve balancing the effects of such a use of military force: successful defense of basic human rights, lives saved and lost, horrors ended
and created. But seen as violent civil disobedience, interventions also
unleash powerful state military forces, and the balance must consider
the likelihood of states' success in effecting reform of the international
law of force, and, among other concerns, impacts on the international
system's stability, commitment to state sovereignty, and so forth. How
does the proposed illegal legal reform strategy involve the *ad bellum*
principle of proportionality for states' recourse to war?

The complex and various effects of violent civil disobedience high-
light some familiar challenges to the justificatory efficacy of *ad bellum*
proportionality. Consider, for example, that in a supreme humanitarian
emergency like Rwanda in 1994, lives saved would likely far exceed lives
lost had a state intervened illegally to end the genocide. But proportionality requires considering all the effects of an illegal intervention.
And seen as an act of violent civil disobedience, among those effects are
likely success in reforming the law of force, the erosion of state sovereignty, and unsettling of the current world order through such vigilante
violence. In such situations it is especially apparent that the proportionality requirement demands balancing incommensurable values, while
lacking anything close to a sufficiently clear, precise, measurable criterion for establishing what is or is not disproportionate among diverse
kinds of effects. Considering this just war requirement for acts of violent civil disobedience rightly forces seeing *ad bellum* proportionality as
an imprecise, blunt principle that can function only to rule out some
clear cases of disproportionate costs for the recourse to war.[39]

Given this understanding of the justificatory efficacy of *ad bellum*
proportionality, the violent civil disobedience proposed here does not
obviously violate this traditional requirement for justifying the recourse
to war. Concerns about humanitarian interventions destabilizing the
international order and its restrictions on states' use of force against
one another are surely warranted. But the focus of the concern is
diminished by the illegal legal reform strategy proposed, because to the
extent that destabilizing risks become greater it becomes more likely
the international law of force will be reformed to stabilize a new relationship among states and to protect basic human rights. That such
legal reform effectively draws anew the boundaries of state sovereignty rights is a cost not obviously disproportionate to the moral pull of

defending people's basic rights not to be killed, tortured, or enslaved by states acting with immunity under current international law. Furthermore, to the extent that states' violent civil disobedience effectively accomplishes rescues now, the merits of legalizing interventions will be more apparent, the reform strategy more likely to be successful. In short, done rightly, interventions are likely to defend human rights effectively now and into the future through reform. That an intervention can be done well and thereby help effect legal reform can very well sometimes tip the balance in favor of intervention, which will increase the numbers of lives saved both now and in the future.

Seeing humanitarian interventions as violent civil disobedience brings to the fore how important are the qualities of the state authorities engaged in defending human rights—the traditional *ad bellum* requirements of right intention and right authority. The "right intention" requirement for justifying war calls attention to the quality of states' purposes or aims in using military force, including humanitarian interventions. Modern just war theory since Grotius often ignores "right intention" as an *ad bellum* requirement, or at least as a requirement independent of just cause.[40] Classic just war thinking, though, explicitly excludes purposes such as vengeance, power, fame, glory, greed, or cruelty, while, according to Aquinas, requiring only the aim "to achieve some good or avoid some evil."[41] Violent civil disobedience involves multiple state purposes and thereby occasions resurrecting and rethinking the classic *ad bellum* requirement of "right intention" for justifying the recourse to war, even for the cause of defending basic human rights.

Humanitarian interventions as violent civil disobedience require states' purposes encompass both rescue now and legal reform soon. Classic just war thinking invokes the principle of "right intention" to exclude some state aims. But the principle's function in just war thinking also allows multiple purposes: justifying war or humanitarian interventions does not require singleness or purity of purpose.[42] Thus, states' multiple moral aims in acts of violent civil disobedience need not violate this *ad bellum* requirement. Second, states' complex aims may even include a modicum of other purposes, perhaps even amoral self-interest, so long as the other purposes are not incompatible with nor dominating the major moral goals of defending human rights and reforming international law.[43] The issue is the role of states' interests in their humanitarian interventions and civil disobedience, not whether those interests are factors at all.

The *ad bellum* requirement of right intention suggests taking seriously that states are corporate agents and that their interventions are deliberate, purposeful endeavors. And then there are applicable distinctions analogous to those made for individuals' purposeful and beneficent acts. Following Mill's analysis of the beneficent act of rescuing another, for example,[44] that a state benefits from its humanitarian intervention need not tarnish its moral purposes in using military force to defend human rights; and neither do states' aims to be seen as world powers or leaders of international legal reform thereby infect the moral merit of their intervention as violent civil disobedience. Just as one can rightly distinguish an individual person's moral goals in a course of action from accompanying beneficial effects of pursuing those goals, so can one distinguish states' goals from accompanying beneficial effects when states use military force to defend human rights and reform international law. Furthermore, and again following Mill, when judging either individuals' and states' actions one can distinguish intentions as purposes from mental states such as motives or desires of states or state leaders. Seeing humanitarian interventions as violent civil disobedience, then, brings to the fore again the role of states' purposes in justifying the recourse to war, and it occasions properly rethinking the *ad bellum* principle of "right intention" with a care and precision analogous to justifying and evaluating acts by individuals "interposing to protect the defenseless."

That states are the agents of rescue and legal reform not only emphasizes the importance of the traditional *ad bellum* requirement of right intention, it also makes important rethinking carefully the principle of "right authority" for the recourse to war. The illegal legal reform strategy proposed here requires states act responsibly and with legitimate moral purpose in addressing rights violations now and in effectively reforming the international law of force for the future. Scholars of the just war tradition observe that resurrecting humanitarian principles of just cause bring to the fore rethinking the just war concept of right authority: if justified wars are seen as addressing injustice and violations of human rights, then "responsible use of force in response to wrongdoing" becomes central.[45] And the centrality of responsible state behavior is only increased by states' violent civil disobedience for purposes of defending human rights.

Rethinking right authority raises a number of issues at the intersection of traditional political philosophy, just war theory, and international human rights. The contemporary presumption that any state is a right authority has not always been the case—not all legally recognized states are normatively equal, and questions of domestic legitimacy and citizens' vigilance are perhaps crucial to satisfying plausible criteria of right authority to pursue humanitarian interventions as violent civil disobedience in the international arena.[46] For the illegal legal reform strategy proposed here, rethinking right authority suggests that states may qualify to commit acts of violent civil disobedience only if, for example, they accept their own accountability to the International Court of Justice and possess command and control structures and a trained military adequate for exemplary interventions. In supreme humanitarian interventions success is a matter of life and death for many; as violent civil disobedience, interventions done well are best both for defending rights now and for effecting needed legal reform soon.

We live in a world in which too frequently states violate the basic human rights of those who live within their borders. The line of thought proposed here develops a domestic analogy: just as violent civil disobedience in defense of fugitive slaves' basic human rights is sometimes warranted, so states' humanitarian interventions can be seen as an illegal act grounded in moral principle and for the purpose of reforming the restrictive international law of force. After carefully characterizing what constitutes a supreme humanitarian emergency, and given the powerful moral pull of defending basic human rights, the urgent need for timely, effective reform of the international law of force supports states' acts of violent civil disobedience in order to rescue now and effect legal reform soon. Such direct civil disobedience on the international level leads to considering anew traditional *ad bellum* principles for justifying the recourse to war. Such rethinking of *ad bellum* principles challenges principles of just cause, right authority, right intention, and the complex consequential thinking embodied in the notions of proportionality, last resort, and reasonable success. As has been an aspect of the long just war tradition, changing circumstances occasion rethinking requirements for the recourse to war. Today, amid states' frequent gross misbehavior toward their own people, with a restrictive international law of force, and in a global legal system unsuited for rapid changes that are needed to defend basic human rights, an illegal legal reform strategy that countenances rethinking the just war tradition both responds to these circumstances and can improve a world too oft enduring supreme humanitarian emergencies and other states' morally troubling failures to stop events such as the brief, brutal horror that was Rwanda in 1994.

NOTES

1. The first of these oxymorons is noted by Nicholas Wheeler, *Saving Strangers: Humanitarian Intervention in International Society* (Oxford: Oxford University Press, 2000); the latter is implicit amid much of the literature on domestic civil disobedience. For definitional issues related to the latter, see Paul Harris, "Introduction: The Nature and Moral Justification of Civil Disobedience," in *Civil Disobedience*, ed. Paul Harris (Lanham: University Press of America, 1989), 1–55. The domestic example is adapted from John Morreall, "The Justifiability of Violent Civil Disobedience," in *Civil Disobedience in Focus*, ed. Hugo Adam Bedau (London: Routledge, 1991), 137–138.

2. "No person held to service or labor in one State, under the laws thereof, escaping into another, shall, in consequence of any law or regulation therein, be discharged from such service or labor, but shall be delivered up on claim of the party to whom such service or labor may be due." Another domestic example of similarly justifiable acts of violent civil disobedience arises in the context of about a century ago, amid the horrible practice of lynching in America and the refusal of state and federal legislators to proscribe this abomination.

3. The latter phrase is from John Stuart Mill, On Liberty (1859), chapter I, paragraph 11. The term *illegal legal reform* is from Allen Buchanan, *Justice, Legitimacy, and Self-Determination: Moral Foundations for International Law* (Oxford: Oxford University Press, 2004), 456–461. My discussion in this chapter is much informed by his work on the morality of international legal reform.

4. Jeff Holzgrefe, "The Humanitarian Intervention Debate," in *Humanitarian Intervention: Ethical, Legal, and Political Dilemmas*, ed. J. L. Holzgrefe and Robert O. Keohane (Cambridge: Cambridge University Press, 2003), 18. The term *supreme humanitarian emergency* is from Wheeler, *Saving Strangers*, 34.

5. The idea of fundamental or basic human rights perhaps approximates those rights from which no derogation is permitted under Article 4 of the 1966 UN Covenant on Civil and Political Rights. A somewhat broader notion of basic human rights is proposed and used by Buchanan, *Justice, Legitimacy, and Self-Determination*, 129 and *passim*.

6. There are different views about the threshold conditions for humanitarian emergencies or armed interventions: Michael Walzer's famous "acts that shock the conscience of mankind" (see *Just and Unjust War: A Moral Argument with Historical Illustrations*, third ed. [New York: Basic Books, 2000], chapter 6); genocide, perhaps as broadly defined by the UN Convention on Genocide; crimes against humanity, now defined by the Statute of the International Criminal Court; quantitative or qualitative

human rights violations. Some openly despair of there being a precise or objective definition of what is to count (e.g., Wheeler, *Saving Strangers*, 34). The characterization does not specify precise right violation boundaries as threshold for interventions, though it does exclude considering violations of collective rights, for example, of self-determination.

7. Wheeler, *Saving Strangers*, 34–35.

8. Thomas Franck, "Interpretation and Change in the Law of Humanitarian Intervention," in *Humanitarian Intervention*, ed. Holzgrefe and Keohane, 216.

9. The phrase "moral pull" is adapted from Robert Nozick, *Philosophical Explanations* (Cambridge: Harvard University Press, 1981), 399–402, 451ff. Thorough, theoretical grounds for the moral pull of humanitarian emergencies must be taken as intuitive and undeveloped in this brief essay.

10. Tom Farer, "Humanitarian Interventions Before and After 9/11: Legality and Legitimacy," in *Humanitarian Intervention*, ed. Holzgrefe and Keohane, 61–69.

11. The term "lawful illegality" is from Allen Buchanan, "Reforming the International Law of Humanitarian Intervention," in *Humanitarian Intervention*, ed. Holzgrefe and Keohane, 132.

12. See Thomas Franck, *Fairness in International Law and Institutions* (Oxford: Oxford University Press, 1995), 267–274. My comments are based on his essay, "Interpretation and Change in the Law of Humanitarian Intervention," in *Humanitarian Intervention*, ed. Holzgrefe and Keohane, 204–231.

13. Samantha Power, *"A Problem from Hell": America and the Age of Genocide* (New York: Harper Collins, 2002), 329–390.

14. The UN Charter has been amended but twice, and both were procedural changes. Though this essay focuses on directly reforming the international law of force, procedural changes in the UN Charter might also involve, for example, modifying the grounds for Security Council authorizations of armed force, or the council membership and veto powers.

15. Allen Buchanan, "From Nuremberg to Kosovo: The Morality of Illegal International Legal Reform," in *Humanitarian Intervention: Moral and Philosophical Issues*, ed. Aleksandar Jokic (Toronto: Broadview, 2003), 126–128; *Justice, Legitimacy, and Self-Determination*, 301–310.

16. "Rethinking Humanitarian Intervention: The Case for Incremental Change," in *Humanitarian Intervention*, ed. Holzgrefe and Keohane, 232–272.

17. Michael Byers and Simon Chesterman, "Changing the Rules About Rules? Unilateral Humanitarian Intervention and the Future of International Law," in *Humanitarian Intervention*, ed. Holzgrefe and Keohane, 177–203.

18. Wheeler, *Saving Strangers*, 47–48; Buchanan, *Justice, Legitimacy, and Self-Determination*, 447–448.

19. Harris, "Introduction," in *Civil Disobedience*, 1–55.

20. The distinction is from Hugo Adam Bedau, "Civil Disobedience and Personal Responsibility for Injustice," *Civil Disobedience in Focus*, ed. Bedau, 49–67.

21. The opposition suggested here comes from international lawyers and others who subscribe to forms of Legal Absolutism. See Buchanan, *Justice, Legitimacy, and Self-Determination*, 456–472.

22. Buchanan, "From Nuremberg to Kosovo," 126. Some of these concerns are also discussed as "exceptional legality" by Byers and Chesterman, "Changing the Rules About Rules?" 177–203.

23. Buchanan, "From Nuremberg to Kosovo," 124.

24. David Lyons, "Moral Judgment, Historical Reality, and Civil Disobedience," *Philosophy and Public Affairs* 27 (1998): 31–33. Many define civil disobedience as nonviolent. See references in note 1.

25. *A Theory of Justice: Revised Edition* (Cambridge: Harvard University Press, 1999), 319–323.

26. "Letter from Birmingham Jail," in *Civil Disobedience in Focus*, ed. Bedau, 68–84.

27. "Civil Disobedience," in *Civil Disobedience in Focus*, ed. Bedau, 28–48.

28. Preface to the Third Edition, *Just and Unjust Wars*, xi–xvi; *Arguing About War* (New Haven: Yale University Press, 2004), 155.

29. *Saving Strangers*, 33–49.

30. Douglas Lackey, *The Ethics of War and Peace* (Englewood Cliffs: Prentice-Hall, 1989), 34.

31. *Summa Theologiae*, II-II, 40, a.1, in *St. Thomas Aquinas on Politics and Ethics*, translated and edited by Paul E. Sigmund (New York: Norton, 1988), 64–65.

32. *The Law and War of Peace*, trans. Francis W. Kelsey (Indianapolis: Bobbs-Merrill, 1962), book II, chapter 25.

33. Ibid.

34. *Morality and Contemporary Warfare* (Princeton: Princeton University Press, 1996), 35.

35. Ibid., 31–32; see also 28–29. For a related historical discussion of just cause and justice, see my essay, "The Recourse to War: A Historical Theme in Just War Theory," *Studies in the History of Ethics* (February 2006), http://www.historyofethics.org. Issue on the Ethics of War and Peace in Historical Perspective, guest edited by Larry May.

36. I follow A. J. Coates's helpful characterization and discussions of the last resort requirement for recourse to war, in *The Ethics of War* (Manchester: Manchester University Press, 1997), 189–207.

37. There is considerable diversity among contemporary and historical discussions of the three related *ad bellum* requirements of last resort, reasonable success, and proportionality. All involve balancing the consequences of

the recourse to war among the alternatives open to achieving certain ends. But not only do formulations of the requirements vary considerably, individuations of the principles are often different, as well. For example, compare: Johnson, *Morality and Contemporary Warfare*, Lackey, *The Ethics of War and Peace*, A. J. Coates, *The Ethics of War*, Henry Shue, "War," in *The Oxford Handbook of Practical Ethics*, ed. Hugh LaFollette (Oxford: Oxford University Press, 2003).

38. Shue, "War," 748–752. Considerations here are restricted to *ad bellum* proportionality, a distinctly different principle from its *in bello* cousin that requires proportional conducting of a war. Rethinking *in bello* principles in light of proposed violent civil disobedience is warranted, too, but on another occasion.

39. Ibid. See also Walzer, *Arguing About War*, 89–91.

40. Some simply do not discuss the idea: for example, Coates, *The Ethics of War*, and Shue, "War." In *Morality and Contemporary Warfare*, Johnson, for example, sometimes says the positive content of the principle directly depends on the just cause for war. Also, the idea is often discussed in terms of leaders' or states' mental states, such as motives, beliefs, desires, and not in less private and perhaps more discernable notions such as goals or purposes.

41. In describing the classic requirement of right intention in terms of authorities' goals or purposes, I follow John Finnis, *Aquinas* (Oxford: Oxford University Press, 1998), 284–287.

42. Lackey, *The Ethics of War and Peace*, 31–33; Gregory S. Kavka, "Was the Gulf War a Just War?" *Journal of Social Philosophy* 22 (1991): 20–29.

43. Wheeler, *Saving Strangers*, 37–40, 48; Kavka, "Was the Gulf War a Just War?" 21–22.

44. John Stuart Mill, *Utilitarianism* (1861), chapter II, paragraph 19, note 2.

45. Johnson, *Morality and Contemporary Warfare*, 35.

46. Buchanan, *Justice, Legitimacy, and Self-Determination*, 233–327.

APPENDIX

Just War Principles:
An Introduction with Further Reading

The just war tradition is based on two highly contested ideas: that there are norms on the basis of which one can conclude that in some situations the resort to war is just, and that there are norms that enable war to be conducted in a just manner. What makes the first idea controversial, and especially disconcerting to pacifists, is the claim that the massive and systematic killing and maiming of human beings can sometimes be just. What makes the second idea controversial—and naive or unacceptable to the realist who holds that only self-preservation, national interest, and seeking power motivate conduct between states— is the belief that wars with all their horrors and unanticipated consequences can be fought in a morally constrained manner. Traditionally, the first set of norms, the *jus ad bellum* (justice in the resort to war) principles, is thought to be the responsibility mainly of the political leadership of a country, while the second set of norms, the *jus in bello* (justice in the conduct of war) principles, is viewed as the primary responsibility of military commanders and soldiers. This traditional understanding is not without controversy. It may be questioned, for example, whether soldiers in a war of aggression can be honored for killing in accordance with *jus in bello* principles. And, it may be argued that, since citizens in a democratic society are to some degree responsible for the wars fought in their name, just war thinking is their civic duty.

Not all contemporary just war theorists offer the same list of just war principles, and instead of the term *principles* some authors use other terms, such as *criteria* or *norms*. More importantly, there is disagreement about how the various principles are to be articulated or comprehended. And there are other disagreements—for example, concerning how (and even whether) *jus ad bellum* principles are to be weighed in the resort to war decision. Our view is that much philosophical work remains to be done in terms of clarifying the individual principles and elucidating their rationale, their relative weight, and their connection to international law. This task—which is central to the project of rethinking the just war tradition—is an ongoing one, since (among other reasons) just war thinking should evolve with the changing nature of warfare caused by broader economic, cultural, technological, and political developments.

The list of just war principles stated here is widely accepted. The accounts of the different principles include some controversies about their interpretation and significance, which illustrate the need to rethink the principles. It should be noted that some recent just war theorists have argued that the conclusion of war must be guided by a third set of just war norms, *jus post bellum* principles. These principles are not included here, but they are addressed in chapter 2.

We have added an annotated list of writings pertinent to the theme of this book. It is not a comprehensive bibliography but rather a list of suggestions for further reading, especially for readers less familiar with the just war tradition. For lack of space, we had to leave out equally valuable writings. We have not included writings by our contributors. Joan T. Philips of Air University Library, Maxwell Air Force Base, Alabama, maintains a detailed online bibliography of current publications on just war theory at http://www.au.af.mil/au/aul/bibs/just/justwar.htm.

JUS AD BELLUM PRINCIPLES

1. Just cause. A war is justified only if waged for one or more just causes. Just war theorists generally agree that defense against an unjust attack is a just cause. Similarly, although this might be contested, assisting an ally against an unjust attack is a just cause. More controversial just causes include protecting civilians from massive basic human rights violations committed by their own government or by other parties in a civil war (humanitarian intervention), the imminent threat of aggression (preemptive war), and, especially, future threats—notably, as posed by the possible use of weapons of mass destruction by terrorists or "rogue" states (preventive war).

2. Legitimate authority. The use of military force is permissible only if it is authorized by a political body that is widely recognized as having this power. This principle is also referred to as the *proper, right*, or *competent authority principle*. It is matter of some controversy whether governments irrespective of their moral status or credibility have legitimate authority. There is also disagreement about whether non-state actors, such as guerrilla, insurgent groups, or terrorist groups, can have legitimate authority. And there is dispute about whether an international body—in particular, the United Nations, but also regional organizations, such as NATO or the African Union—can have legitimate authority and what the scope of this authority might be vis-à-vis states.

3. Right intention. A war must be waged with the pursuit of its just cause as its sole (or primary) motive. For instance, if the just cause is stopping genocide, then the sole (or primary) motive guiding the armed humanitarian intervention must be to stop the genocide. As signaled by the parenthetical word *primary*, it is controversial whether there may be other motives. Thus it is controversial whether armed intervention with a primary humanitarian motive may also be secondarily motivated by national self-interest. Clearly, some secondary motives, such as access to resources, economic gain, territorial expansion, increased international influence and power, or ethnic hatred, may weaken or undermine the moral legitimacy of a war.

4. Last resort. Nonmilitary alternatives, including diplomacy, negotiations, sanctions, and legal adjudication, must be pursued—within reasonable limits—prior to resorting to military force. Delaying the use of military force, or threat thereof, too long may be morally objectionable in that it may stimulate aggression or allow for the escalation of a humanitarian disaster. Crucial to a correct explication of this principle is determining what is meant by *within reasonable limits*.

5. Reasonable chance (hope) of success. A war should be fought only if there is a reasonable hope that the goals embedded in its just cause will be realized. It is objectionable to demand great sacrifices of combatants—or inflict serious harms on noncombatants—if military victory seems a very remote possibility. On a broader and more controversial account, a just war entails a possibility of creating an enduring peace.

6. Proportionality. The anticipated goods of waging a war must be proportionate or commensurate to its expected evils. On the common interpretation, this means that the anticipated benefits of war must outweigh its harms, but on a less demanding account it requires only that the expected harms do not greatly exceed the benefits. The principle of proportionality is also referred to as the *principle of macro-proportionality*, so as to distinguish it from the *jus in bello* proportionality principle, which is then referred to as the principle of micro-proportionality. The benefits and costs for one's own people of resorting to war should definitely be counted, but how much weight should be given to the goods and evils that the war imposes upon the enemy or non-warring countries is a matter of debate. Whether goods should be counted resulting from war but not related to its just cause is also a matter of dispute. In light of the history of controversies about how to measure utility, it is not surprising that some just war theorists have contested whether the proportionality principle provides significant moral guidance.

JUS IN BELLO PRINCIPLES

7. Discrimination. Soldiers should discriminate between combatants and noncombatants and target only the former. This principle is also called the *principle of noncombatant immunity*. Just war theorists offer differing accounts of who is to be counted as noncombatants and why. Harm to noncombatants is typically seen as an acceptable result of a military action if it is not intentionally inflicted and is proportionate to the importance of the goals of the military action. A more stringent—and contested—view of how much "collateral damage" is morally acceptable is to demand of soldiers that they seek to minimize noncombatant casualties even at the risk of greater costs to themselves. It is morally impermissible to destroy targets that have primarily civilian purposes. It is a matter of controversy whether structures with both weighty military and civilian significance may be directly targeted. Some weapons, such as nuclear weapons, biological weapons, and (more controversially) landmines, are morally objectionable due to their indiscriminate impact.

8. Proportionality. Force should be used in proportion to the end pursued, and destruction beyond what is necessary to reach a military objective is morally suspect. It might be claimed that the laws of war allow the killing of enemy soldiers without limit, but such a claim is objectionable in terms of the principle of proportionality. Weapons that cause injuries to people long after they have ceased to be combatants, such as nuclear and biological weapons, are disproportionate.

Additionally, as with the *jus ad bellum* proportionality principle, there are disputes about which benefits and costs are to be counted, and how they are to be weighted.

FURTHER READING

Chatterjee, Deen K., and Scheid, Don E., eds. *Ethics and Foreign Intervention.* Cambridge: Cambridge University Press, 2003.
   A collection of essays exploring the ethics and legality of secession and humanitarian intervention. A few essays offer qualified support for humanitarian intervention on the basis of the just war tradition. Several contributions articulate a normative and pragmatic "critique of interventionism," concluding that "altruistic wars" are seldom, if ever, justified.

Childress, James F. "Just War Theories: The Bases, Interrelations, Priorities, and Functions of Their Criteria." *Theological Studies* 39 (1978). Revised as chapter 3 in his *Moral Responsibility in Conflicts: Essays on Nonviolence, War, and Conscience.* Baton Rouge: Louisiana State University Press, 1982.
   Instead of simply presupposing just war principles, the author attempts to ground them in W. D. Ross's conception of prima facie duties, especially the duty of nonmaleficence. In terms of such a grounding, he discusses the order, strength, and function of the principles.

Coates, A. J. *The Ethics of War.* Manchester: Manchester University Press, 1997.
   The book offers chapter-length discussions of just war principles, paying attention to their historical roots but focusing on their contemporary significance and interpretative controversies. Many historical illustrations are provided.

Coppieters, Bruno, and Fotion, Nick, eds. *Moral Constraints on War: Principles and Cases.* Lanham, MD: Lexington Books, 2002.
   Scholars from Belgium, China, Russia, and the United States analyze each of the just war principles in a separate chapter with a wide range of historical examples. The book also offers five case studies, all involving American resort to war except for a study of the First Chechen War.

Evans, Mark, ed. *Just War Theory: A Reappraisal.* Edinburgh: Edinburgh University Press, 2005.

>A collection of essays, mainly by political scientists, that are distributed among parts entitled "Just Cause," "Justice in the Conduct of War," and "Justice and the End of War." The essays are on such topics as preventive war, proportionality, supreme emergency, and *jus post bellum.*

Held, Virginia. "Legitimate Authority in Non-State Groups Using Violence." *Journal of Social Philosophy* 36 (2005): 175–193.

>The author argues that non-state groups using violence and even terrorism may represent their people and meet the requirement of legitimate authority.

Hurka, Thomas. "Proportionality in the Morality of War." *Philosophy and Public Affairs* 33 (2005): 34–66.

>With respect to both the *jus ad bellum* and *jus in bello* principles of proportionality, this article discusses which goods and evils fall within their scope and how they should be weighted against one another. Hurka argues that only goods included in the sufficient and contributing just causes of a war should be counted in macro-proportionality.

Johnson, James Turner. *Morality and Contemporary Warfare.* New Haven: Yale University Press, 1999.

>This book offers an introduction to the just war tradition and covers such topics as humanitarian intervention, noncombatant immunity and modern war, and reconciliation after war. Johnson draws from his influential historical studies of the just war tradition.

Luban, David. "Just War and Human Rights." *Philosophy and Public Affairs* 9 (1980): 160–181.

>The author argues that only wars in defense of "socially basic human rights" are just, so that self-defensive wars by corrupt regimes may be unjust and an attack on such regimes may be just.

Lucas, George R., Jr., *Perspectives on Humanitarian Military Intervention.* Berkeley: Berkeley Public Policy Press, 2001.

>On analogy with just war theory's *jus ad bellum* and *jus in bello* principles, the author advocates principles for just humanitarian military intervention, which are termed *jus ad interventionem* and *jus in interventione* criteria.

————. "The Role of the 'International Community' in Just War Tradition—Confronting the Challenges of Humanitarian Intervention and Preemptive War." *Journal of Military Ethics* 2 (2003): 122–144.

> The author describes important similarities between preemptive war and humanitarian intervention, including that both in their justification appeal to a poorly defined notion of the "international community." Criteria for just resort to force in both cases are proposed with special attention to the issue of international authorization.

McMahan, Jeff. "The Ethics of Killing in War." *Ethics* 114 (2004): 693–733.

> The author challenges the principle of noncombatant immunity and the common view that soldiers in an unjust war do not act wrongly as long as they uphold the *jus in bello* principles.

Orend, Brian. *War and International Justice: A Kantian Perspective.* Waterloo: Wilfrid Laurier University Press, 2000.

> Orend makes the controversial claim that Kant had a just war theory and was the first thinker to maintain that just war theory should be completed by a category of *jus post bellum*. The book articulates a list of Kantian principles of justice after war. See also Orend, "Justice after War," *Ethics and International Affairs* 16 (2002): 43–56.

Rodin, David. *War and Self-Defense.* Oxford: Oxford University Press, 2002.

> This book contests the commonly accepted idea that war is justified in case of national self-defense and carefully argues that the domestic analogy of individual self-defense fails. Rodin proposes that the use of armed force may be justified as a police action against enemy soldiers involved in an aggressive war. His view is commented upon in "Symposium: War and Self-Defense," *Ethics and International Affairs* 18 (Winter 2004).

Sterba, James P., ed. *Terrorism and International Justice.* Oxford: Oxford University Press, 2003.

> A collection of essays focused on 9/11 and its aftermath. Several contributors argue that 9/11 was a criminal act, requiring a legal response. The U.S. war against the Taliban is also assessed on the basis of "just war pacifism" and more traditional just war criteria. Attention is also paid to whether weaker parties in asymmetric conflict may rightfully loosen *jus in bello* criteria.

Walzer, Michael. *Just and Unjust Wars: A Moral Argument with Historical Illustrations*, third edition with a new preface by the author. New York: Basic Books, 2000. First edition appeared in 1977.

Even almost three decades after its publication it remains a reference point for much current just war thinking. At the occasion of its twentieth year of publication, *Ethics and International Affairs* 11 (1997) published a handful of critical essays with a response by Walzer.

————. *Arguing About War*. New Haven: Yale University Press, 2004.

A collection of Walzer's essays written after his classic *Just and Unjust War* (1977). Topics include military responsibility, humanitarian intervention, and terrorism. The very recent essays are all applications of just war criteria, covering Kosovo, the Israel-Palestine conflict, 9/11, and the Iraq war, with the exception of an essay that proclaims the triumph of just war theory and poses the question of what is still left to be done for just war theorists.

Zupan, Daniel S. *War, Morality, and Autonomy: An Investigation in Just War Theory*. Burlington, VT: Ashgate, 2003.

The author argues that autonomy, based on a Kantian notion of humanity, provides a better theoretical underpinning for the war convention or *jus in bello* principles than consequentialist or rights-based theories. The analysis is applied to the supreme emergency doctrine and the war on terrorism.

CONTRIBUTORS

Reuben E. Brigety II is Assistant Professor of Government and Politics at George Mason University. He has previously served as a U.S. naval officer and as a field researcher with the Arms Division of Human Rights Watch, where he conducted research missions to Afghanistan and Iraq.

Michael W. Brough is a previous Assistant Professor of Philosophy at the U.S. Military Academy at West Point. A major in the U.S. Army, he has held a variety of positions in combat engineer units and was deployed to Iraq during the final stages of editing of this volume. He has written on issues in political philosophy and ethics, and is especially interested in the ethics of armed conflict.

Robert W. Hoag is the Henry Mixter Penniman Professor of Philosophy and Department Chair at Berea College in Kentucky. His scholarly and teaching emphases include ethics, political philosophy, philosophy of law, especially contemporary topics in social ethics and law, and John Stuart Mill's consequentialist political morality. His current research interests include just war theory, humanitarian intervention, and Mill's international ethics.

Frederik Kaufman is Professor of Philosophy in the Department of Philosophy and Religion at Ithaca College, Ithaca, NY. He is currently department chair. His published works include *Foundations of Environmental Philosophy* (McGraw-Hill, 2003) and articles in *The American Philosophical Quarterly*, *Australasian Journal of Philosophy*, *Midwest Studies in Philosophy*, *International Journal of Applied Philosophy*, and *Environmental Ethics*. He teaches primarily in moral philosophy and applied ethics.

Whitley R. P. Kaufman is Associate Professor of Philosophy at the University of Massachusetts Lowell. He specializes in both ethics and philosophy of law, with a particular focus on the ethics of intention and the doctrine of double effect. His current area of research is the ethical basis for the use of force, for example, in self-defense, in war, and as punishment.

Pauline Kaurin is Visiting Assistant Professor of Philosophy at Pacific Lutheran University in Tacoma, Washington, where she teaches classes on war and morality, philosophy of law, social and political philosophy, and applied ethics. Her areas of interest and research are religious toleration, military ethics, and the role of the passions and identity in moral life (specifically in the philosophies of Hume and Nietzsche).

John W. Lango is Professor of Philosophy at Hunter College of the City University of New York. Concerning the subject of war and morality, he has written articles on nuclear deterrence, armed humanitarian intervention, and preventive war. He has also written articles on other ethical subjects. In the field of metaphysics, he has written articles on the philosophy of time, the theory of tropes, and the metaphysics of Alfred North Whitehead. He is author of *Whitehead's Ontology*.

Eric Patterson is Assistant Professor of Political Science at Vanguard University in Costa Mesa, California, where he teaches courses such as U.S. Foreign Policy and War, Peace, and Security. During the 2005–2006 academic year he was a William C. Foster Fellow in the Bureau of Political and Military Affairs, U.S. Department of State. He is the author of *Latin America's Neo-Reformation* as well as a manuscript on just war and the War on Terror, and the editor of *The Christian Realists*.

Jordy Rocheleau is Assistant Professor of Philosophy at Austin Peay State University in Clarksville, Tennessee. He has published articles on the politics of Habermas's discourse ethic, the nature of democratic environmentalism, the ethics and politics of recognition, and the appropriateness of advocacy in college teaching. His current research is in democratic theory, human rights, and international justice.

Hartley S. Spatt is Distinguished Teaching Professor at the State University of New York Maritime College. He has published essays on writers including Mary Shelley, William Morris, Dante Gabriel

Rossetti, Alfred Lord Tennyson, Joseph Conrad, and Kurt Vonnegut. He has also published essays on significant figures in the history of technology, aviation, and twentieth-century architecture.

Rachel Stohl is Senior Analyst at the Center for Defense Information (CDI) at the World Security Institute in Washington, DC, and Adjunct Professor at Georgetown University. She is the coauthor of *A Beginner's Guide to the Small Arms Trade* (November 2006), and writes frequently on small arms and child soldier issues.

Harry van der Linden is Professor of Philosophy at Butler University and the author of *Kantian Ethics and Socialism* (Hackett) and other writings on Kant, Marx, and Marburg neo-Kantianism. His most recent articles are on global poverty, economic migration, humanitarian intervention, and preventive war. He is coeditor of *Philosophy Against Empire*, volume 4 of *Radical Philosophy Today* (Philosophy Documentation Center). He serves on the executive committees of Concerned Philosophers for Peace and the Radical Philosophy Association.

Mark Woods is Associate Professor of Philosophy at the University of San Diego, where he teaches a variety of courses in practical ethics. He is completing a book about wilderness philosophy. His interest in matters of war and peace began with an enlistment in the United States Marine Corps as a child soldier at the age of 17. He is now a member of Veterans for Peace, a group dedicated to abolishing war as an instrument of state policy.

INDEX

Israel, 187, 189, 192, 201, 219, 250
Israelites (ancient), 17, 22

Jamaa Islamiyah, 216
Japan, 60, 81, 84–85
Jefferson, Thomas, 213
Jesus, 159–160, 162
Johnson, James Turner, 22, 36,
    56–57, 113 n. 7, 233–234, 248
jus ad bellum principles (or criteria),
    25–26, 28, 56, 67, 68, 69,
    75–77, 83, 89, 90–92, 232–238
  distinguished from *jus in bello*
    principles, 26, 28, 76–77,
    89–90, 243
  distinguished from *jus potentia ad
    bellum* principles, 69
jus in bello principles (or criteria),
    23–24, 25–26, 75–77, 89–90,
    131–132, 137, 141
  distinguished from *jus ad bellum*
    principles, 26, 28, 76–77,
    89–90, 243
  distinguished from *jus potentia ad
    bellum* principles, 29
jus post bellum principles (or criteria),
    30, 244, 248, 249
  distinguished from *jus ad bellum*
    principles, 39–40
  distinguished from *jus in bello*
    principles, 39–40
jus potentia ad bellum principles (or
    criteria), 29–30, 69, 74 n. 40
just cause(s), 56, 75, 233–234, 244,
    246, 248, 249
  and just goals, 63, 83, 242 n. 40
just cause principle (or criterion), 3,
    27, 34 n. 34, 75, 82, 83–88,
    162, 183, 187, 244
  and armed humanitarian inter-
    vention, 28, 85–86, 88, 186,
    233–234
  generalized, 85–86

and goal specificity, 77–78, 83–88
  temporalized, 86–88, 94 n. 23
justice, 233–234
  procedural, 119
  subjective, 63, 68
just war principles (or criteria), 6,
    30–31, 75–79, 83, 88–92, 175,
    232–238, 247
  analogues of, 78
  and five basic criteria of legitima-
    cy, 2–5, 93 n. 11
  generalized as just armed-conflict
    principles, 75–79, 85–86,
    88–92
  specifying, 77–78
  temporalizing, 75–77, 82, 86–87,
    89–91, 94 n. 23
just war theory, 1–7, 26, 75–76,
    232–238
  and coherentism, 77
  and consequentialism, 105,
    162–163, 172, 174–175, 185,
    187, 250
  credibility of, 53–54, 56, 66, 67,
    69, 188
  and democracy, 63, 200
  and deontology, 56, 184, 187, 250
  and foundationalism, 77
  generalized as just armed-conflict
    theory, 75–76
  and moral theory, 77
  and non-Western countries,
    54–56, 58, 61–69, 71 n. 10
  and U.S. military hegemony,
    53–56, 67–69
just war tradition, 1–6, 17–18, 22,
    23, 28–31, 83, 84, 89, 90, 91,
    233–234, 236, 243
  history of, 1, 76, 233–234,
    241 n. 35
  revisions of, 1–6, 17, 23–24,
    25–27, 28–31, 66–69, 75–76,
    83, 233–234, 236–238

262   INDEX

Nuclear Non-Proliferation Treaty
(NPT), 190, 197
Nuremberg Trials, 45

O'Brien, William V., 26
Old Testament, 211
Operation Enduring Freedom, 144
Optional Protocol to the
Convention on the Rights of the
Child on the Involvement of
Children in Armed Conflict,
135–136, 145 n. 15
Orend, Brian, 30, 39–40, 42,
51 n. 19, 114 n. 19, 249
Osirak, Israeli bombing of nuclear
facility at, 199–201

pacifism, 162, 243, 249
Pape, Robert A., 60
Patterson, Eric, 30
peace, 30, 69, 245
and the UN Charter, 69, 226–227
peacekeeping, 78, 127–128
by the United Nations, 75, 76,
78, 82, 86, 90–91, 217
Pearl Harbor, 186
perception management, 66
Peron, Juan, 214
Philippines, 136
Philips, Joan T., 244
Philo Judaeus, 17, 22
Pol Pot, 225
Post Traumatic Stress Disorder
(PTSD), 155
precautionary principle, 26–27
preemptive war, 6, 186–187
and just cause principle (or criterion), 186, 244
distinguished from preventive
war, 186–187
preventive war, 4, 6, 87, 186–193
distinguished from preemptive
war, 186–187

legitimacy of, 188–193
and rogue states, 189–191, 244
and weapons of mass destruction,
183, 184, 188–193
See also military actions, preventive
propaganda, 149–150, 200
proper authority principle. *See* legitimate authority principle
proportionality, 235, 242 n. 38
of consequences, 24, 26–27, 175,
234–235
of ends, 162–163
macro. *See* proportionality, *jus ad
bellum* principle of
micro. *See* proportionality, *jus in
bello* principle of
proportionality, *jus ad bellum* principle (or criterion) of, 26–27, 55,
56, 67, 70 n. 5, 89,
166–167 n. 39, 192, 199,
234–235, 245–246, 248
proportionality, *jus in bello* principle
(or criterion) of, 23–24, 89, 120,
141, 143–144, 147 n. 29, 166–167
n. 39, 246, 246–247, 248
punishment, 44
and just war, 30, 172–176, 191,
233–234

Qaddafi, Muammar, 171

racism, 151, 153–157
Ramsey, Paul, 76, 103, 132
Rawls, John, 72 n. 20, 92–93 n. 7,
105, 106, 185, 218, 232
Reagan administration, 54
realism, in international relations,
198
and just war theory, 243
reasonable chance (hope, likelihood,
or probability) of success,
principle of, 3, 55, 56–58, 69,
245